Academic Language in Second Language Learning

A Volume in
Research In Second Language Learning

Series Editors:
JoAnn Hammadou Sullivan, *University of Rhode Island*

Research In Second Language Learning

JoAnn Hammadou Sullivan, Series Editor

Academic Language in Second Language Learning

edited by

M. Beatriz Arias
University of California

and

Christian J. Faltis
Arizona State University

Information Age Publishing, Inc.
Charlotte, North Carolina • www.infoagepub.com

Library of Congress Cataloging-in-Publication Data

Academic Language in Second Language Learning / edited by M. Beatriz Arias, University of California and Christian J. Faltis, Arizona State University
pages cm.
ISBN 978-1-62396-114-5 (paperback.) -- ISBN 978-1-62396-115-2 (hardcover) --
ISBN 978-1-62396-116-9 (ebook) 1. English language--Study and
teaching (Higher)--Foreign speakers. 2. Academic language--Study and
teaching. 3. English teachers--Training of. I. Faltis, Christian, 1950-
II. Arias, M. Beatriz.
PE1128.A2A323 2012
428.0071'1--dc23

2012042432

Printed in the United States of America

CONTENTS

SECTION III: ACADEMIC LANGUAGE IN SUBJECT-AREA CONTENT

FOREWORD

M. Beatriz Arias

As second language acquisition (SLA) theory takes a social turn, new understandings of the language demands of English learners (ELs) in schools point to the complexities of the types of oral and written language students need to be successful in school. From a sociocultural perspective, SLA requires learners to create and develop new identities as members of academic communities and to share affinities for using language in multiple ways to demonstrate membership. This volume examines the issues and complexities of academic language as a developing construct in the field of second language learning.

As a construct, academic language has a number of possible interpretations, due mainly to its historical antecedents—elaborated code and CALP, both of which are problematic and contested in the research literature, but nonetheless maintain currency in within and across teacher communities.

Accordingly, there is a need to expand the research on academic language, to shed new light on the complexities involved in learning subject-matter content where academic language is inextricably coupled with social language. The need is also acute considering that a majority of teachers of ELs and other second language learners (Spanish for bilingual speakers, heritage language learners, among others), are grossly underprepared in both the teaching of ELs and understanding role of academic language in successful learning in school and society.

ELs are now attending schools in all 50 states; they comprise nearly half the student populations in at least 5 states, and in many states (e.g., Georgia and North Carolina) they are the fastest growing student population. In

Academic Language in Second Language Learning, pp. vii–xi
Copyright © 2013 by Information Age Publishing

states like California and Arizona, ELs represent a quarter of the student population, and in many school districts, they comprise the majority of the student population. EL enrollment is also increasingly at the secondary level, where success depends heavily on participating in school-based experiences involving academic language.

Teachers who work in these settings are now being challenged to meet the academic language needs of ELs while responding to the increasing demand for rigor in the common core curriculum. Academic language in its coupling with language learning has been largely ignored in school settings, where academic language predominates as an indicator of membership in school-based learning experiences. Typically, teachers learn about strategies for engaging students in learning, but little, if any, attention is paid to intersection between academic and social language and the challenges involved in learning academic language while learning a second language.

This volume aims to examine academic language learning from a research perspective, with an eye toward demystifying the construct, and exploring the various ways that researchers and educators have worked to ensure that ELs and other linguistic minority students gain access to, participate in and benefit from experiences involving the use of academic language. The chapters are organized into three sections. Section I provides readers with an overview of the academic learning (AL) construct and introduces readers to the sociocultural and functional language approaches to studying academic language. Section II moves the discussion of academic language to the preparation of teachers of ELs and Section III examines recent research on academic language in the content areas and elaborates on the importance of structural functional linguistics (SFL) in understanding the registers of subject matter disciplines. The contributors represent leading scholars in the field who have begun to elucidate the complexities of academic language for second language learners.

In Chapter 1, Faltis lays the groundwork for deconstructing, demystifying and critiquing the concept of academic language and its implications for teacher preparation. Relevant to an understanding of one aspect of AL, Professor Faltis asks whose language variety counts, and why? Starting with a historical review of the genesis of academic language he presents the grand narrative of academic language by tracing its roots to the deficit arguments of Bernstein, Bereiter, and Engelmann. He uses the concept of Spanish heritage language study as an example of an approach which marks the community language as inferior and less cognitively challenging than the standard Spanish variety, suggesting that one definition of academic language reifies social order. In this vein, the author notes the importance of informing teachers of the deficit orientation given to social language and the implications for ELs. Dr. Faltis suggests that we turn to a view of academic language as social practices, a practice that students can benefit from learning.

Chapters 2 and 3 continue the focus on the overall understanding of AL. Fitts and Bowers focus on the teaching of Academic English Language (AEL) and stress the importance of learners acquiring communicative competence as well as a body of knowledge of vocabulary and grammar. They look for themes in the teaching of AEL and find four useful approaches: building background, providing comprehensible input, explicit teaching and opportunities to practice academic content. This review is instrumental to understanding how teachers scaffold understanding of AEL for ELs.

The chapter by Lucero extends our understanding of how teachers make AEL comprehensible to students in the early elementary grades. She looks for evidence of instructional moves that teachers use to make AEL explicit finding that the most prevalent approaches included a simultaneous focus of language and content, instructional scaffolding and varying amounts of content. Interestingly, the author note that in her research she rarely found teachers who explained AL to students. Professor Lucero's recommendations for teacher education include helping teaching understand the components of AEL, help teachers recognize the linguistic demands of the content and help teacher integrated AEL in content.

The second section of this volume includes chapters which review how AL is presented in preparation of teachers. Merino et al look at the preparation of effective beginning teachers to investigate the embodied understanding of practice within their professional development. Embodied understanding theory allowed the researchers to see teaching performance addressing AL as an integrated whole. Teachers who participated in the preservice preparation were attentive to scaffolding, accessing multiple modalities for presentation and response, coconstructed discussion with examples and most notably presented AL as discourse and not just as decontextualized vocabulary. They note that discipline knowledge shapes teachers' understanding of the nature of the linguistic demands of the task.

In the following chapter, Professor Galaguera provides a self-study of teacher preparation asking what counts as critical language awareness within a digital context. Professor Galaguera shares his students' experiences in synchronous and asynchronous online discussions. He makes the case that information and communication technologies (ICTs) are new literacies which provide teacher educators to transform their pedagogy. This initial research points to the power of electronic media and Web 2.0 tools to foster critical language awareness and pedagogical skill development for preservice teachers.

The final chapter in this section by Professor Athanases and Juliet Wahleithner presents the findings of an annual academic literacy summit focusing on educator's conception of academic literacy. In their goal to develop a professional knowledge base for effective AL teaching, they engaged P-16 educators to make public their AL conceptions, learning and practices. They found educators to have widely varying conceptions of AL. An interesting finding from this work is that most educators focus on constructing and deconstructing text and far less attention to subject-specific ways of knowing and literacy practices tied explicitly to particular content areas.

Section III of this volume explores the concept of AL within content area instruction. It is interesting to note that the authors unanimously stress the importance of a systemic functional linguistics (SFL) approach in assisting students to understand AL. Dr Oliveira begins with the recognition that AL is a "second language" for all students. She reviews how a functional analysis of texts helps ELs learn within the context of history. She reminds us that AL in history involves much more than lexical vocabulary. Professor Oliveira analyzes the linguistic knowledge that history teachers need in order to teach AL to ELs. This knowledge includes knowledge of how abstractions function in different kinds of text, how cohesive devices work and how causality is expressed.

An appreciation for SFL is echoed by Professors Ramirez-Marin and Clark within the context of science instruction. They recommend SFL as an approach to help teachers identify the linguistic features common to school language. These authors review two popular science instruction frameworks: instructional congruence (IC), and effective science teaching for English language learners (ESTELL). They look for evidence of authentic science literacy in these models and stress the need for teachers to conceptualize AL as a discourse type. They conclude that the SFL approach provides significant assistance to content-area teachers and ELs to identify the linguistic features common to school language and their relationship to specialized knowledge within the discipline.

In the last chapter in this section on content area instruction, Professor Middlefield and his colleagues stress the need to look at the mathematics curriculum as a register. They emphasize the need to develop mathematical discourse with ELs which entails not only "doing" mathematics, but also "talking" mathematics. In order for ELs to interpret, make sense, and be able to articulate the relationships between abstract mathematical ideas, ELs must have ample opportunities to use and practice the language of mathematics.

In the Afterword, Professor Lillie underscores the importance of preparing teachers to understand AL particularly in view of the implementation of the common core standards and its impact on English language learners.

At a time when educators are being challenged to align instruction to the common core curriculum, these readings provide an important insight to the challenges that AL is presenting to the field. Not only is it critical that teachers become proficient in the registers of their content area, they must also be able to convey this language awareness to their students. This volume provides an important foundation toward promoting sound practices for addressing and teaching AL to ELs.

SECTION 1

LANGUAGE IN ACADEMIC CONTENTS

CHAPTER 1

DEMYSTIFYING AND QUESTIONING THE POWER OF ACADEMIC LANGUAGE

Christian J. Faltis

One of most imperfectly understood and yet widely popular concepts in language education as well as teacher education is the notion of *academic language*. Since 2000, the number of articles, books, and book chapters dedicated to understanding academic language and how to teach it in classroom where there are English learners has burgeoned (e.g., Bailey, 2007; Bunch, 2006; Bunch, 2010; Bunch, Abram, Lotan, & Valdés, 2001; Cummins, 2008; Enright, 2011; Freeman & Freeman, 2009; Hyland, 2009; Scarcella, 2003; Schleppegrell, 2004; Schleppegrell, 2006; Swales, 2004; Valdés, 2004a, 2004b; and Zwiers, 2009). Moreover, teachers of English learners and bilingual students across the nation are instructed by their State Departments of Education to teach their students academic language in addition to other socially-oriented language needed to participate in school and classroom experiences. Despite it being a hot topic in educational linguistics, there is little agreement on what academic language is (Francis & Rivera, 2007; Valdés, 2004a; Wiley, 2005) or whether it is another means of stratifying students based on spurious distinctions between the language styles of poor children and those of mainstream middle class children (Edelsky, 2007).

Academic Language in Second Language Learning, pp. 3–26
Copyright © 2013 by Information Age Publishing
All rights of reproduction in any form reserved.

The goal of this chapter is ambitious and threefold: first, we will deconstruct the meanings of academic language across time, by showing its development as distinct from social language over the past 50 years; second, we will attempt to demystify its power and scope in educational and broader social contexts, using Spanish as a heritage language as an current example; and third, we present and critique more recent approaches to academic language, ones that endeavor to promote understanding of language associated with academic disciplines and how to make it more accessible to emergent bilinguals and struggling students generally in ways that ignore the broader social contexts. Of the three areas of interest, the last two are the most challenging, because the belief that academic language is cognitively and inherently superior to social language has become deeply woven into the social fabric of contemporary educational thought. Indeed, efforts are already in motion to develop new standards for academic language and measures to reflect how well students demonstrate it (see, e.g., Abedi, 2007; Bailey & Butler, 2003; Sato & Worth, 2010). And in California, teacher certification requires a passing score on the Performance Assessment for California Teachers (PACT), which includes academic language of one of the five areas of competency that new teachers must demonstrate (see Merino, this volume). In other words, the train has left the station. The direction it takes depends a great deal the way that language in academic settings is understood in school contexts and more broadly by those who study it.

We begin with an important declaration made by James Gee (2001), who asserts that that academic language does not exist as a single construct, but rather as one of many styles of language used in academic contexts:

> There is, of course, no such thing as "school language" or "academic language" as single things. There are, rather, many different school languages, different styles of language used in different academic practices. There are, too, many different sorts of public-sphere language, different styles of language used for a variety of civic, economic, and political purposes. None of these many styles of language is "decontextualized." They are all—just like "everyday" face-to-face language—contextualized." (p. 63)

If there is no such thing as academic language as a single event, then why has it been elevated to such a powerful force in education? A significant clue to the reason for its rise to power among some teachers is precisely because as Gee (2001) also points out correctly, language is always used for "civic, economic, and political purposes." Chief among these purposes in school settings is to socially stratify children and adolescents based on which language styles or varieties they learn prior to school.

Many teachers of English learners and bilingual youth are taught in workshops and college courses that immigrant children from nonmainstream backgrounds tend to come to school speaking a style of language referred to as Basic Interpersonal Communication Skills (BICS), and as they become bilingual learners, they continue to speak and understand via their proficiency in BICS, which is often characterized as less abstract and cognitively demanding than the language needed to succeed in academic contexts (Cummins, 1981, 1983, 1984, 2003). Accordingly, bilingual learners from poor socioeconomic backgrounds rely on a language proficiency that is not considered useful for learning in school contexts, where ideas and concepts needed for academic success are more abstract and more cognitively demanding than ideas and concepts expressed through BICS. From this view, to be successful in school, bilingual learners need to acquire *Cognitive Academic Language Proficiency* (CALP; Cummins, 1981, 1983, 1984, 2003), which of late has been shorted to *academic language* (see Bailey, 2007; Schleppegrell, 2006; Solomon & Rhodes, 1995; Valdés, 2004a). To quote Solomon and Rhodes (1995):

> There is general agreement among educators and researchers that the distinct type of English used in classrooms, referred to as *academic language, is* a variable that often hinders the academic achievement of some language minority students, even though such students might be proficient in varieties of English used in non-academic contexts. (p. 1)

There are two issues associated with this claim. First, there is not general agreement among educators and researchers that mastering or not mastering academic language alone leads to academic success (Aukerman, 2007; Bartolomé, 1998; Edelsky, 2007; MacSwan & Rolstad, 2003; Valdés, 2004a, 2004b; Valdés, MacSwan, & Alvarez, 2009; Wiley, 1996). There are too many other factors—civic, economic, and political positions about whose language style or variety counts as worthwhile for learning—that have much more bearing on achieving academic success, as we will attempt to show below. Second, that certain varieties of English used in academic contexts hinder learning in academic contexts places the blame squarely on language, rather than on the larger social contexts of classroom learning, where many students have been alienated from participating in a system which maligns their language varieties and fails to teach them (Gándara & Contreras, 2009; Olsen, 2010).

We will attempt to explain below how academic language has come to be part of a grand narrative about language varieties and about the people who raise their children using these varieties to express love, dissatisfaction, understanding, well-being, and their knowledge of the world. In this grand narrative, language use is considered a sign of intelligence and the ability to learn. Accordingly, when children enter school already having acquired

CALP, they are considered to be intelligent and teachable. Children who begin school with BICS in either their non-English home language or English as a second language, are considered to be less intelligent and at risk of not learning.

We begin by asking the following questions: (1) What is the origin of the idea that social language differs from academic language? and (2) How are these differences portrayed in the literature?

Origins of the Distinctions Between Social and Academic Language

It may come as a surprise to some readers that Jim Cummins was not the first nor is it likely that he will be the last to posit a distinction between social and academic language. In the early 1980s, Cummins christened the difference between social and academic language as BICS and CALP. Cummins posited the distinction in response to theoretical work by Oller and Perkins (1980) who argued for a single factor of global language proficiency, which he claimed accounted for most of the variance in educational tests. Cummins (1981) disagreed, arguing instead that language proficiency needed to be divided into two main dimensions: conversational language and academic language. His argument, ostensibly based on language proficiency test data, was that "conversational" aspects of proficiency (e.g., phonology and fluency)" were highly contextualized, and had little to do with the language proficiency students required to be successful with academic tasks. In particular, he argued that academic tasks are inherently less contextualized (context-reduced), rely on abstract concepts, and are more cognitively demanding; ergo, he argued, the language needed to engage with decontextualized, abstract concepts, necessarily requires a cognitively more challenging language proficiency than was available to speakers who could only rely on conversational language proficiency. Cummins' analysis led to the development of a number of theoretical ideas that were embraced early on by many in bilingual education. For Cummins and many of his phalanxes of followers, CALP became a primary goal of bilingual schooling. He argued that CALP facilitated the transfer of knowledge learned through the first language to the second language. He developed the *common underlying proficiency* (CUP) model (Cummins, 1981), positing that academic knowledge developed in the first language would positively transfer to the second language, if and only if it were developed to a sufficient threshold (the "threshold" hypothesis) and only through CALP (see MacSwan, 2000 for a thorough critique of the threshold hypothesis).

These ideas, invariably attributed to Cummins, have a long history in the literature about the relationship between language and learning. Mac-Swan (2000) mentions that Schatzmann and Strauss (1955) were among the first psychologists to assert based on their research that there was a distinct difference in the way members of the lower class and the middle class exchanged meaningful information. They concluded on the basis of speech data gathered from members of the two social classes concerning a disaster that had recently occurred, and they had witnessed, that lower class people relied on emotion-laden language and elliptic structures, while middle class members used explicit, verbally rich language to describe their postdisaster experiences.

The age of the "culture of poverty" began to take hold in the United States in the 1960s (parenthetically, the culture of poverty rhetoric has resurfaced with former Texas educator, Ruby Payne (2008). Payne has self-published a number of deficit-model writings about poverty and schooling, and these have been generally well received in high-poverty school districts.) In the 1960s, it was not uncommon to read in print that "systematic differences in cognitive ability" between children of different classes and ethnic groups existed, differences that resulted from "the way symbols were used in the homes of the very poor and the middle class [which] are so great as to be perhaps ineradicable (Friedenberg, 1969, p. 57). Vernon (1969) claimed that the kind of English Black children spoke hindered them from acquiring cognitively deep language proficiency, "advanced education, communication, and thinking (p. 231).

The racist message during this time period was crystal clear: poor children of color spoke a kind of language that indicated they were cognitively and linguistically inferior. Conversely, White middle class members of Western culture were portrayed as abstract, rational, and logical in the way they used language to organize thought (Leacock, 1972). Werner (1961) distinguished Western thought from primitive thought by alluding to differences in the ability to decontextualize language and thought. Primitive people were concrete, and limited to personal reference, while "typical European reflection is universal in nature, abstract; it functions more or less independently of the immediate concrete reality and it is governed by an awareness of general laws" (p. 299).

Bernstein's Restricted and Elaborated Codes

About the time that American academics were propounding about the differences between concrete and abstract thought that could be evinced by comparing and contrasting language use among poor children of color and White European-origin children of mainstream educated families,

across the ocean in England, sociologist Basil Bernstein (2010) was formulating his verbal deficit hypothesis by postulating a distinction between
public and formal language, which later become known as "restricted"
and "elaborated" codes. (Note, however, that Bernstein (2010) has rein-
troduced public language.) At the core of the distinction is the extent to
which users of the two code types rely on rational, abstract thought. As
Bernstein (1973) writes,

> I shall go on to suggest that restricted codes have their basis in condensed
> symbols, whereas elaborated codes have their basis in articulated symbols;
> that restricted codes draw on metaphor, whereas elaborated codes draw
> upon rationality; that these codes constrain the contextual use of language
> in critical socialising contexts and in this way they regulate the orders of rel-
> evance and relation which the socialized take over. (p. 200)

Bernstein (1973) contended that restricted code was used primarily
among unskilled working class families; middle class educated families
used both restricted and elaborated codes, leaning toward elaborated
codes for schooling and business. According to Bernstein, the main function of restricted code was to express emotions and group solidarity;
exchanging ideas and expressing more cognitive functions was secondary
and difficult to obtain because, he maintained, restricted code does not
rely on logical connectors. For Bernstein, restricted codes lack sharpness
and scope. *Sharpness* relates to the individual and group ability to use
principals of rationality; namely, theoretical and practical reasoning
when using language (Winch, 1985). *Scope* is the extent to which language structures are used in the formation of reasoned thought. In
restricted code, meanings are limited to the immediate context, and syntactic structures are highly predictable because they are likely to be "simple." Likewise, speech in restricted code is marked by frequent use of
pronouns, where it is assumed that interlocutors share knowledge of who
is being discussed. In contrast, Bernstein argues, elaborated code users,
wishing to give direction to the rational organization of thinking, generate "accurate grammatical order and syntax" to regulate their thoughts;
"rely heavily on "logical modification" and "grammatically complex sentence construction, especially through the use of a range of conjunctions
and subordinate clauses"; incorporate prepositions to "indicate logical
relationships as well as to indicate temporal and spatial contiguity"; and
select from a wide range of descriptive adjectives and modifying adverbs.
Figure 1.1 shows a graphic representation of Bernstein's analysis. Bernstein argued that the primary difference between the speech of working
class and middle class children was that the scope of their language structure available to and used by the two groups. Because working class children drew from a restricted code base, they were in a sense imprisoned

Narrow Scope

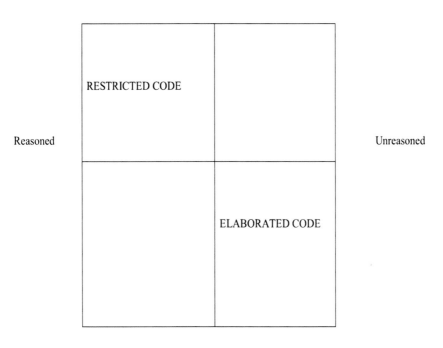

Reasoned

RESTRICTED CODE

ELABORATED CODE

Unreasoned

Wide Scope

Figure 1.1.   Bernstein's analysis.

by simple language structure and limited vocabulary, which ultimately meant that they would do poorly in school unless they were taught how to use a more elaborated code. Middle class children, capable of drawing on both restricted and elaborated codes, and especially able to access elaborated code in school settings, were deemed more likely to succeed in school.

Bernstein's work resembles that of the American academics of the time, such as Bereiter and Engelmann (1966) who argued that certain children (poor, Black children) rely on such concrete, personalized language, with a proclivity for simple structures. Bereiter and Engelmann questioned whether these students were actually capable of producing rational thought in language.

There are a number of educational scholars who argue that Bernstein's dichotomy between restricted and elaborated code has been largely misunderstood. For example, Danzig (1995) refutes the claim that Bernstein's work supports a deficit view of minority children rhetorically. He argues that "code focuses attention not on deficits in the children or families but on the ways in which performances are judged and evaluated (p. 155). For Danzig, it is the way people assess the language performance of children that leads to deficit thinking, not that the codes they draw on are any more or less capable of reasoned thought. That may well be the case, but a thorough reading of Bernstein (1973), reveals a different narrative on whose code counts as better language for dealing with abstract (decontextualized) ideas and using what he considers to be eloquent, grammatically complex language.

Cummins' BICS and CALP Distinction

Nearly 2 decades after Bernstein's restricted and elaborated code entered the sociological discourse, Canadian educational psychologist Jim Cummins came on to the educational scene touting a "new" way of understanding language dimensions as these relate to successful schooling. While Bernstein developed his work from a sociological framework, Cummins was interested in learning as it pertained to school settings. At the outset of his work, Cummins was concerned with refuting the idea that children with special learning needs were failing on standardized tests because the tests were biased toward a certain kind of language style. He came to the conclusion that indeed the tests required a language ability that special education children had not yet mastered. They were relying what he eventually referred to as Basic Interpersonal Communication Skills, which enabled them to participate in many school contexts, but not in those contexts where more cognitively demanding language was required. For these contexts, he coined the phrase *Cognitive Academic Language Proficiency*, arguing that children acquire BICS for face-to-face, here and now personal interactions relatively quickly with little need for instruction. To gain CALP, children require a longer period of time and need to be supported by teachers or instructional-like interactions where children are socialized to use language that is highly decontextualized and cognitively more demanding than would normally be the case with experiences where BICS is used.

Cummins' dimensions of BICS and CALP became the impetus for several other theoretical ideas about how and why bilingual children did well or failed in school. One of the early uses of the dimensions can be seen in the concept of "semilingualism," little or no ability to communicate in any language (Skutnabb-Kangas & Toukomaa, 1976), which Cummins brought into his idea of the threshold hypothesis. In this hypothesis, bilingual children who were considered semilingual (low in both the first and second language; the lower threshold of language attainment) according to their performance on a language proficiency test were highly likely to fail in school. Conversely, he predicted that gaining high proficiency in two languages (the highest threshold) augured well for bilingual children's academic success. BICS and CALP figured into this hypothesis as follows: Semilingualism always involved the mere acquisition of BICS; children who acquired CALP in one of more of their languages, preferably their first, stood a much better chance of succeeding in school.

Cummins' theoretical ideas spread like wild fire among the bilingual education community in the United States. He was invited as a keynote speaker to almost every major conference on bilingual education throughout the late 1980s and early 1990s. He readings were required in nearly every course on the theoretical foundations of bilingual education, and it would be rare not to find the influence of his work in district workshops for teachers of English learners and dual language learners even today.

However, by early 1980, Cummins appears to have abandoned the BICS and CALP distinction in favor of two continua: one along the continuum of context-embedded and context reduced tasks; the other along the continuum of cognitively undemanding and cognitively demanding tasks (Cummins, 1981). BICS became language used in highly context embedded settings, for cognitively undemanding (interpersonal) communicative purposes; CALP became language use in highly context-reduced settings, for cognitively demanding (academic) communicative purposes. Gibbons (1991) refers to BICS as "playground" language, and CALP as "classroom language." She goes on to claim, with no empirical research to back up her claim that, "The playground situation does not normally ... require the language associated with the higher order thinking skills, such as hypothesizing, evaluating, inferring, generalizing, predicting or classifying" (p. 3).

Early on, the implications for bilingual education were as follows: children who enter U.S. schools speaking BICS in their primary language, need to develop CALP in that language to be successful once they move into an all English mainstream classroom setting; BICS in a second language is unrelated to academic success because there is no higher thinking going on in BICS. As MacSwan (2000) points out, the idea that higher order thinking only happens in CALP can be traced to Cummins' threshold hypothesis, which places BICS in two languages in the bottom threshold, and CALP in the top threshold. Out of the implicit ranking came a slough of research on how long it takes to develop BICS and CALP in a second language. It is not uncommon to hear from teacher educators and teachers who work in dual language settings assert that it takes from 4-7 years to develop CALP in a second language (see Hakuta, Butler, & Witt, 2000), while it only takes between 6 months to 2 years to develop BICS. While it may be the case that many children and adolescents pick up social language for face-to-face interactions relatively quickly, social language is no less cognitively demanding or abstract than language used in learning any of the academic disciplines. Anyone who spent time with children and adolescents or who has taught in school and talked extensively with children about their work and play surely knows this to be the case. Bilingual children and adolescents are also acquiring new ways of using their two languages, switching from one to the other for any number of communicative and stylistic reasons, in addition to learning ways to navigate language in academic contexts with new sets of cues, ways of expressing ideas that are connected to content-oriented discourses, and ways of extending to growing vocabularies to include specialized meanings of words and expressions (see Zentella, 1997).

What we find particularly troublesome about the discussions about how much time it takes children and adolescents to acquire BICS and CALP is the implication that as a group of people, bilingual learners take longer to acquire CALP than BICS, presumably because it is too cognitively difficult for them. This may not have been the original intention of the distinction, and it is certainly was not the intention of researchers who point out the difference in time needs to acquire CALP, but given the long history of scholars who make it a point of their work to show that certain children are incapable of higher levels of thinking because of the "restricted code" or language they are born into, we believe caution is warranted.

A Current Example of Reification of Academic Language as Cognitively Superior

One of more recent examples of how academic language is presented as more cognitively advanced than social language involves the heritage language education movement, which began in the mid-1990s and into the 2000s (see Kreeft Peyton, Ranard, & McGinnis, 2001). A relatively new field within bilingual education, heritage language education promotes the development of immigrant languages, indigenous language, and colonial languages (Fishman, 2001). Interestingly, for many in the field of heritage language education, Spanish is considered a heritage language; in some instances, however, it is labeled a colonial language (Fishman, 2001) and in others, as an immigrant language (Carreira, 2004, footnote 1, p. 24).

In the literature, heritage language speakers of Spanish vary according to oral and written proficiency in Spanish and English as these are in circumstantial contact and used separately or in a blended manner for communicative purposes (Carreira, 2004; Stavens, 2003; Valdés, 2001; Villa, 1996). If bilingual Spanish speakers intend to expand their heritage language, it is possible to do so by enrolling in Spanish for bilingual speakers (aka, Spanish for native speakers (Valdés, 1997, 2001, usually offered alongside Spanish as-a-foreign language curricula. In the case of Spanish for bilingual speakers, we are newly confronted with the distinction between social and academic language, with social language [Spanish spoken by heritage language speakers] being the problem, and academic language [Spanish taught to heritage language speakers] being the solution. Why is this problematic? Is it not the case that Spanish speakers in the United States, many of whom have not experienced formal education in Spanish, might wish to improve their Spanish, to extend the range of their oral and written Spanish? Surely, these Spanish speakers, most of whom are bilingually proficient in various ways—aurally and orally (Carreira, 2004), were they to study Spanish, need a pedagogical approach that differs from what is offered in Spanish as a foreign language, where the goals and linguistic profiles of students are entirely distinct. Bilingual speakers of Spanish, it is argued, are heritage language speakers, who are connected in multiple ways to bilingual communities, and to a Spanish language past, to generations who once spoke only or mainly Spanish.

Framed in this manner, Spanish as a heritage language is riddled with issues. For one, the term *heritage language* points to the past, something that is inherited, ignoring contemporary uses of Spanish in bilingual communities. Accordingly, the Spanish used in contemporary communities becomes invisible, while the Spanish of the past is elevated to the ideal, as a model of what students could regain if they were to study Spanish as a heritage language. The second and more troubling issue is the way Spanish is positioned in Spanish for heritage speakers: Spanish is a language, the language that students must learn to move from heritage language speakers of Spanish to contemporary Spanish speakers, with educated, monolingual Spanish as its model. Bilingual Spanish, Spanglish bilingualism, or any other forms of circumstantial bilingualism, where the learner is proficient in the local varieties of Spanish and English (which are grammatically sophisticated) are not considered to be worthy of development; instead the goal for Spanish development is to move students away from the local through a process of nonstandard extirpation and into standard, academic forms of Spanish. In this manner, standard oral and written academic Spanish becomes the implicit and often, explicit goal of Spanish as a heritage language.

The Culture of the Standard and Academic Language

Silverstein (1996) makes the argument that there is a "culture of the standard" operating in many, if not all language education programs. For Silverstein, this cultural orientation toward reification of the standard language represents "A semiotic ensemble in which referential clarity is next to godliness, social divisions are natural, if not blessed, and a neoliberal scramble for a market-competitive language-and-literacy is humanity's last, best hope for equality" (paraphrased in Collins, 1999, p. 221).

A point of commonality between Silverstein's characterization of the culture of the standard and the previous discussion on BICS and CALP and restricted and elaborated codes is the centrality of three semiotic processes: referential displacement, naturalization, and commodification.

Referential Displacement. In referential displacement, the standard variety of language used in academic settings is placed above the local vernaculars because of it clarity and precision, coupled with the richness of the referential information and distinctions its speakers/writers are able to convey. In contrast, speakers of local vernaculars, including bilingual varieties, use language that is considered to be impoverished lexically, grammatically, and phonologically, and lacking in precision and clarity. As a result, these local varieties of language may confuse audiences who are expecting and accustomed to more standard language varieties.

It is not difficult to detect the similarities between referential displacement and Bernstein's position on the distinctions between restricted and elaborated codes. Likewise, Cummins contends that CALP is more cognitively advanced than BICS because it relies on higher order thinking and more precise language, arguing that BICS limits access not only to the cognitive benefits of bilingualism, but also to a greater web of interlocutors. Through the perspective of the culture of the standard, circumstantial bilinguals who disregard the conventions of the standard language risk communication breakdown. In other words, if Spanish heritage language speakers do not obey the rules of the standard language, they are not able to communicate with referential meaning and intelligibility with those who do use language precisely and clearly. For example, Montes (2003), an author of children's books on the topic Spanglish communicated the message that bilingual Spanish used in the United States represented the following cultural model:

> There are good varieties of Spanish and there are poor varieties of Spanish. People who are well educated and bilingual speak "pure" Spanish; uneducated people who are bilingual speak Spanglish, a lesser variety of Spanish that has been corrupted by English. These people are either in a confused state, or they are negligent in their responsibility to speak "pure" Spanish. (as cited in Chappell & Faltis, 2007, p. 257)

Similarly, scholars interested in bilingual hip-hop have had to deal with the idea that standard language is more sophisticated than the language varieties used in hip-hop communities (Pennycook, 2007; Sarker, 2009). For members of the hip-hop community, however, standard language limits creativity and expression because it is so tied to prescriptive grammar; speakers who use hip-hop language varieties, on the contrary, view them as "limitless" and transformative (Alim, 2010, p. 121).

Naturalization. For Silverstein (1996), the second central process that contributes to the culture of standardization is naturalization. The inherent hybridization of circumstantial bilingualism characteristic of heritage Spanish speakers conceals the social hierarchical relations between those who use language how it ought to be used, and those who do not. In this hierarchy, the assumption is that there is a natural connection between deviant language use and social position, essentializing "the relationship between social position and nonstandard and between standard and nonstandard" (Kramer-Dahl, 2003, p. 178).

In this manner, naturalization works hand in hand with referential displacement to diminish the value and complexity of local varieties spoken by hoi polloi, and at the same time, to assert the natural order of the standard as the highest form of language. Accordingly, heritage Spanish, which incorporates English words and expressions accompanied by rapid switches between Spanish and English is referred to as *español pocho*, *casteyanqui*, *argot sajón*, and *español bastardo*. All of these designations are meant to portray local bilingual Spanish and English as something impure, illegitimate, and uncouth, naturally less complex and intelligible than standard Spanish and standard English used by educated speakers. Again, this complete mockery of the local varieties can also be seen in the how some scholars portray bilingual hip-hop as illiterate and more conventional poetry as elaborate (Sarkar, 2009).

Commodification. In postcapitalist times, language can be viewed as a commodity with market value attached to it. In this case, Silverstein (1996) points out that language has value in terms of its shared inheritance and as a means of communication for establishing identity and relations. The standard form of language comes to have the highest market value, while other varieties of language carry much lower values. The message to speakers of nonstandard language varieties, in this case, bilingual Spanish, is because they do not speak standard Spanish, which is a learnable commodity, they will not be able to complete in the market. However, if they have the will and means to learn the standard variety, and give up their "improper" ways of speaking, they can improve to social position. This perspective ignores the social realities of classism and racism as gatekeepers of social position.

Silverstein's (1996) analysis reminds us of Bourdieu's (1986) concept of cultural capital, which focuses attention on the role of the educational system in fixing and reinforcing the cultural and linguistic value of standard language and those who speak it. Both Bourdieu and Silverstein highlight the objectification and hierarchy of culture and language, which then serve as capital; there are people with "good' language capital and "bad" language capital. Those who speak the "bad' version of language are also least likely to gain entrance to the natural hierarchy reserved for those who already possess the "good" version of the language because in order to do so, they would need to actively collaborate in the destruction of their own means of local communication.

For Spanish speakers who live and grow up in communities and contexts where local varieties of Spanish are able to meet their communicative, emotional, and expressive needs, it is clear that adding academic language may be helpful only if it enables them to add to their personal identities as Spanish speakers. Nonetheless, it is also clear that within education, where the culture of the standard dominates, without a counter-narrative that rejects the position that local languages are inherently flawed, the message remains intact that their social language will always be "bad."

The example of Spanish for bilingual speakers illustrates how in a non-core academic field (Spanish education), models of language that degrade social language as imprecise and lacking the capacity to express reasonable thoughts can persist. However, not all approaches to making academic language available to bilingual children and youth cast explicit aspersions on social language or view it as dispensable for learning. In the following section, we provide brief summaries of the ways that educational scholars have discussed language in academic settings without making the binary distinction between social and academic language the main reason for learning academic language. Rather, the rationale for learning language is academic contexts stems from the assertion that children lacking experience with academic language need to be taught it explicitly.

We begin with some of the early work where the focus was on providing bilingual learners access to features of language in formal classroom settings. We then move to more current work that endeavors to cut the Gordian knot of academic language by looking deeply into how language is used within the various academic disciplines. Each of the approaches to understanding academic language suggests that language in academic contexts requires special attention by both the teacher and students, working together on social practices that enable students to acquire and be acquired by the language of classrooms. None of them overtly deny the value of students' social language for learning in academic contexts; instead they puzzle over ways to help students move into discipline-specific uses of language in ways that are recognized as appropriate for the discipline, with little or no attention to broader sociopolitical contexts.

Focusing on Language in Academic Contexts

Classrooms are locally situated contexts in which language used by the teacher and students throughout the day includes the use of informational and procedural sequences organized through oral interactions with often accompanied by written texts and text types. Many of the interactions occur within the ubiquitous initiation-response-feedback pattern (Cazden, 2001), familiar to most mainstream, middle class families and teachers. Beyond this ordinary routine, however, language uses in academic contexts involve increasingly discipline-specific social practices around oral and written language used to create, share, and evaluate knowledge within the disciplines.

Classroom Language. In the early 1980s, Lily Wong Fillmore began theorizing about the kinds of language emergent bilingual children needed to comprehend and participate in classroom discussions about academic content in general. Wong Fillmore (1982) proposed that in order for children to fully participate in classroom discussions about academic topics, they needed to be aware of the kinds of informative and interactional sequences teacher use, as well as the kinds of language teachers used for regulating behavior, especially during whole class teaching events. For example, she posited that students need to know when the teacher is calling their attention a particular feature; asking for examples of a concept or event; wanting a definition of a word or concept; requesting a summary of an activity or story; requesting intertextual connections or how some new topic related to something students have studied previously. Likewise, participation in academic-oriented lessons required students to detect when the teacher is asking for specific information in the text, with examples, or for their opinions about something that have read or discussed. Students also need to comprehend classroom language used for regulating student behavior, especially procedures for getting into and how turns at talk are allocated during small group work organized around learning academic content and academic text. For Wong Fillmore, it is important for teachers to be conscious of these particular aspects of classroom language because students do not typically notice these ways of organizing talk when they are outside of school settings.

In a subsequent paper, Wong Fillmore (1985) also recommended that teachers learn about academic lesson markers, signals to students about where they are in the lesson at all times. For example, teachers often mark the beginning and ending of any lesson with explicit cues, such as "Okay, let's begin by…" and "that's all for now; let's put your books away." Teachers also signal movement through the phases of a lesson by telling students what they are doing, how it relates to what has already been discussed, and what is coming up next. To the extent that teachers can recognize informational and interactional features of language and include lesson markers, Wong Fillmore argued that teachers are better prepared to scaffold their students' comprehension of academic content, which allows students to be engaged with the teacher and classmates, hearing a range of language varieties others and communicating meaning in academic contexts.

Language and Content as Knowledge Structures. Bernard Mohan was one of the first educators to move the discussion beyond issues of access to classroom learning for bilingual youth to the kinds of language needed to support the development spoken and written academic content. Mohan (1986) theorized that the key to language development in academic settings rested mainly in understanding the knowledge structures that organize the academic disciplines. He argued that if teachers taught their students about the knowledge structures, and then helped them acquire the language that supported the knowledge structures, students would be more likely to succeed in formal classroom settings, especially as academic content became increasing text-based and relied on students' abilities to discuss topics they were learning through text.

Mohan (1986) proposed that academic content children are exposed to in school used language in ways that teachers and other educated members of society recognize and reinforce as important for social and academic success within the communities where the academic content was being discussed. His approach to academic language focused on the nature of knowledge structures and the language needed to show membership within the academic disciplines where these knowledge structures prevail. Mohan proposed two groups of knowledge structures important for academic language: (1) structures that deal with specific aspects of knowledge and (2) structures that deal with more general features of knowledge valued in formal school settings. He then went on to argue that for bilingual children to be successful in using language in academic settings, they needed to be taught how to use the language functions relevant to the two main groups of knowledge structures. For specific knowledge structures, Mohan cited the ability to describe people, objects and events; to narrate the sequence of events in the correct temporal and/or logical order; and to compare and contrast alternatives, choices and decisions about objects and events. For Mohan, each of these abilities requires modeling and other kinds of scaffolding support, to draw on what children have already acquired with respect to these structures, and to help children use them within the appropriate academic contexts. At the more general level of knowledge structures, Mohan listed the ability to classify, especially the definition of words and their meaning networks; to explain ideas to others through analysis and interpretation of data in order to develop generalizations and draw conclusions; and to evaluate objects, actions, and events by judging, appreciating, and critiquing. Each of these knowledge structures involves the use of certain kinds of language that, according to Mohan, must be taught.

Academic Language as a Social Practice. In the 1990s, a new strand of language theory emerged about the essence of academic language. This movement was based largely on the work of Jay Lemke (1990), who contented that "learning science means learning to talk science" and "talking science means observing, describing, comparing, classifying, analyzing, discussing, hypothesizing, theorizing, questioning, challenging, designing experiments, following procedures, judging, evaluation, deciding, concluding, generalizing and reporting (p. 1). For Lemke, learning the language of science in classroom contexts is fundamentally a social practice, a way of using language by actually doing science, and being identified by oneself and others as a scientist. That is, students learn science by showing membership in science through talking, expressing, acting, and thinking in ways that scientists recognize and value. In the manner, language is a set of socially constructed rules encompassing knowledge about what is said (or written) in particularly contexts, how it is said (or written), and to what intended effect (Lemke, 1990).

Drawing on Lemke's ideas as language as social practice and Mohan's work on knowledge structures, researchers interested in language in academic settings began to focus their attention on the language demands of important academic content areas taught in school. Deborah Short (1994, 1996) was among the first educators to examine the intersection between language and academic content from a discipline-based perspective. Short's work focused on the features of oral and written language within the social studies she contended were especially challenging for bilingual youth, who are learning English as a second language. Her analysis of classroom interactions between history teachers and students indicated that certain language functions, similar to Mohan's (1986) knowledge structures, occurred regularly across all lessons, while others, were particular to teachers: asking recall questions, giving directions, clarifying, extending, previewing and reviewing (Short, 1994, p. 597). Short argued that the text structures of cause and effect, chronological order, and problem-solution, and the particular syntactical structures embedded in the text structures were difficult for bilingual students based on the assumption that students were unfamiliar with these structures. Short's work emphasized helping teachers understand the language of social studies, how it was organized in text, and how to help students begin to converse and write in ways that are recognized within the larger social studies communities of history in particular.

Systemic Functional Linguistics. By the late 1990s, a number of educational researchers began to rely on systemic functional linguistics (Halliday, 1985), as a means to better understand the particular text-based demands of language in academic settings. Lead by Mary Schleppegrell (2001, 2004, 2006, 2010), this new group of researchers began to pay attention to language and the relationship between language (form) and content (meaning), within the main genres of schooling—recounts, narratives, procedures, reports, accounts, explanations, and expositions, particularly in written text (Schleppegrell, 2044, p. 85; see de Oliveira, this volume), arguing that students' academic success depends on the extent to which teachers are able to help students master the language of a variety of academic communities represented in school contexts. The goal was to uncover, using systemic functional linguistic principles, how language was organized traditionally for spoken and written text-types and language genres within the various academic disciplines. If teachers could learn about language formations within different academic disciplines and teach students to recognize and use these patterns, students would have more access to the academic content because the features of language in academic contexts would become transparent.

Schleppegrall (2004) argued that in the particular situational context of schooling, successful learners are expected to display knowledge of some kind, to do so with authority, and to show evidence of mastery of the organization and presentation various text-types represented in each of the disciplines. To accomplish these meaningful uses of language, learners need to engage with language features that condense information and rely on abstract and technical terms, and be able to present knowledge that is formal and largely disconnected from their everyday life. So, for example, the following sentence (from Gee, 2005, p. 22) displays some knowledge about an unusual topic:

Hornworms sure vary a lot in how well they grow.

However, the sentence relies on several features of language that also occur in typical informational interaction about everything things. The use of "sure" and "a lot" mark the sentence as informal and too close to everyday language, essentially disqualifying it as academic language.

Recast in the academic language of schooling, the sentence (Gee, 2005, p. 22) might be constructed as follows:

Hornworm growth exhibits a significant amount of variation.

This sentence, which conveys essentially the same meaning as the one above, differs in several key linguistic features and social conventions associated with the language of science. The sentence begins with an interesting noun phrase, where what was once a plural noun (hornworms) is now an adjective modifying the new nominalized subject (hornworm growth). The verb phrase (vary) has also been nominalized to become "variation" in the object position. And lastly, a new, more scientifically-oriented (Latinate) and abstract verb, "exhibits" (rather than "*shows*") is used to convey an authoritative stance of evidence.

Refocusing on Broader Contexts

A critical question for any approach to teaching students to focus on the language of the classroom, and the languages of disciplines is how are teachers prepared to understand the language of bilingual children and youth bring to the classroom? This question connects language to the broader social contexts in which schools are embedded. It is not far-fetched to consider why bilingual children and youth may not want to affiliate with the academic communities schools value, when in the broader social contexts, they and their families are afforded limited access to power based on pervasive views about their language abilities, social class, and ethnic backgrounds.

It is simply naïve to assume that all bilingual students need to do to become successful in school and life is to learn academic varieties of language (all in standard language; namely, English). There are too many social and racial barriers in play, one the most pernicious being that elaborated code, CALP, or standard forms of language are more intelligible, more complex, more precise, and more intelligent than social language varieties and especially non-English and bilingual social language varieties. This belief positions bilingual and poor children from uneducated families as inherently inferior and perpetuates a social order than keeps the poor and less educated in their "natural" order of society.

One could argue that providing the poor and less educated with access to academic language is a good start at upsetting this social order, and is thus, morally justified. Furthermore, it could be argued that helping students from nonacademic backgrounds attend to the language of schooling is necessary for their eventual academic success. We would argue that unless we also seriously address the cultural baggage of standard language, prescriptivism, market value references, and deficit-oriented conceptualizations of social language and bilingualism, efforts to prepare teachers and students to understand and become proficient in academic language are unlikely to yield significant changes in the educational and social achievement of bilingual children and youth. Finally, helping some students understand and become proficient may be necessary, but it is not sufficient. Teachers and students must also address the larger issue of whose language and language varieties count and why.

REFERENCES

Abedi, J. (2007). *English language proficiency assessment in the nation: Current status and future practice*. Davis, CA: University of California.

Alim, H. S. (2010). Global ill-literacies: Hip hop cultures, youth identities and the politics of literacy. *Review of Research in Education, 35*, 120-146.

Aukerman, M. (2007). A culpable CALP: Rethinking the conversational/academic language proficiency distinction in early literacy instruction. *The Reading Teacher, 60*(7), 626-635.

Bailey, A. (Ed.). (2007). The language demands of school: Putting academic English to the test. New Haven, CT: Yale University Press.

Bailey, A., & Butler, F. (2003). *An evidentiary framework for operationalizing academic language for broad application to K-12 education: A design document*. Los Angeles, CA: CRESST.

Bartolomé, L. (1998). *The misteaching of academic discourses: The politics of language in the classroom*. Oxford, England: Westview Press.

Bereiter, C., & Engelmann, S. (1966). Teaching disadvantaged children in the preschool. Englewood Cliffs, NJ: Prentice-Hall.

Bernstein, B. (1973). *Class, codes, and control*. London, England: Routledge & Kegan Paul.

Bernstein, B. (2010). A public language: Some sociological implications of linguistic form. *The British Journal of Sociology, 61*(Issue Supplement 1), 53-69.

Bourdieu, P. (1986). The forms of capital. In J. Richardson (Ed.), *Handbook of theory and research for the sociology of education* (pp. 241-258). New York, NY: Greenwood.

Bunch, G. (2006). "Academic English" in the 7th grade: Broadening the lens, expanding access. *Journal of English for Academic Purposes, 5*, 284-301.

Bunch, G. (2010). Preparing mainstream secondary content-area teachers to facilitate English learners' development of academic language. In C. Faltis & G. Valdés (Eds.), *Education, immigrant students, refugee students, and English learners* (pp. 351-383). New York, NY: Teachers College Press.

Bunch, G., Abram, P., Lotan, R., & Valdés, G. (2001). Beyond sheltered instruction: Rethinking conditions for academic language development. *TESOL Journal, 10* (2/3), 28-33.

Cazden, C. (2001). *Classroom discourse: The language of teaching and learning* (2nd ed.). Portsmouth, NH: Heinemann.

Carreira, M. (2004). Seeking explanatory adequacy: A dual approach to understanding the term "heritage language learner". *Heritage Language Journal, 2*(1). Retrieved from http://www.heritagelanguages.org

Chappell, S., & Faltis, C. (2007). Bilingualism, Spanglish, culture and identity in Latino children's literature. *Children's Literature in Education, 38*(4), 253-262.

Collins, J. (1999). The Ebonic controversy in context: Literacies, subjectivities and language ideologies in the United States. In J. Blommaert (Ed.), *Language ideological debates* (pp. 201-233). Berlin, Germany: Mouton de Gruyter.

Cummins, J. (1981). The role of primary language development in promoting educational success for language minority students. *In schooling and language minority students: A theoretical framework* (1st ed.). Developed by the. Sacramento, CA: California State Department of Education, Office of Bilingual Bicultural Education.

Cummins, J. (1983). *Language proficiency and academic achievement.* In J. W. Oller (Ed.), Issues in language testing research (pp. 108-130). Rowley, MA: Newbury House.

Cummins, J. (1984) *Bilingualism and special education: Issues in assessment and pedagogy.* Clevedon, England: Multilingual Matters.

Cummins, J. (2003). BICS and CALP: Origins and rationale for the distinction. In C. B. Paulston & G. R. Tucker (Eds.), *Sociolinguistics: The essential readings* (pp. 322-328). London, England: Blackwell.

Cummins, J. (2008). BICS and CALP: Empirical and theoretical status of the distinction. In B. Street & N. H. Hornberger (Eds.), *Encyclopedia of language and education: Vol. 2 Literacy* (2nd ed., pp. 71-83). New York, NY: Springer.

Danzig, A. (1995). Applications and distortions of Basil Bernstein's code theory. In A. Sadovnik (Ed.), *Knowledge and pedagogy: The sociology of Basil Bernstein* (pp. 145-170). Norwood, NJ: Ablex.

Edelsky, C. (2007). *With literacy and justice for all: Rethinking the social in language and education* (3 ed.). London, England: Falmer Press.

Enright, K. (2011). Language and literacy for a new mainstream. *American Educational Research Journal, 48*(1), 80-119.

Fishman, J. A. (2001). 300-plus years of heritage language education in the United States. In J. K. Peyton, D. A. Ranard, & S. McGinnis (Eds.), *Heritage languages in America: Preserving a national resource* (pp. 81-97). Washington DC: Center for Applied Linguistics/Delta Systems.

Francis, D., & Rivera, C. (2007). Principles underlying English language proficiency tests and academic accountability for ELLs. In J. Abebi (Ed.), *English language proficiency assessment in the nation: Current status and future practice* (pp. 13-32). Davis, CA: University of California.

Freeman, Y. S., & Freeman, D. E. (2009). *Academic language for English language learners and struggling readers: How to help students succeed across content areas.* Portsmouth, NH: Heinemann.

Friedenberg, E. (1969, September 4). "What are our schools trying to do? *The New York Times Book Review*(Special Education Supplement).

Gándara, P., & Contreras, F. (2009). *The Latino education crisis.* Cambridge, MA: Harvard University Press.

Gee, J. P. (2001). Forward. In T.M. Kalmar, *Illegal Alphabets: Latino Migrants Crossing the Linguistic Border* (pp. i-iv). Mahwah, NJ: Lawrence Erlbaum Associates.

Gee, J. P. (2005). Language in the science classroom: Academic social languages as the heart of school-based literacy. In R. Yerrick & W.-.M Roth, *Establishing sci-*

entific classroom discourse communities: Multiple voices of teaching and learning research (pp. 19-39). Mahwah, NJ: Lawrence Erlbaum Associates.

Gibbons, P. (1991) *Learning to learn in a second language.* Newton, Australia: Primary English Teaching Association.

Hakuta, K., Butler, Y. G., & Witt, D. (2000). *How long does it take English learners to attain proficiency.* Oakland, CA: University of California Linguistic Minority Research Institute Report.

Halliday, M. A. K. (1985). *An introduction to functional grammar.* London, England: Edward Arnold.

Hyland, K. (2009). *Academic discourse: English as a global context.* New York, NY: Continuum.

Kramer-Dahl, A. (2003). Reading the "Singlish Debate": Construction of a crisis of language standards and language teaching in Singapore. *Journal of Language, Identity & Education, 2*(3), 159-190.

Kreeft Peyton, J., Ranard, D. A., & McGinnis, S. (Eds.). (2001). *Heritage languages in America. Preserving a natural resource.* Washington, DC: Center for Applied Linguistics/Delta Systems.

Leacock, E. (1972). Abstract versus concrete speech: A false dichotomy. In C. Cazden, V. John, & D. Hymes (Eds.), *Functions of language in the classroom* (pp. 111-134). New York, NY: Teachers College Press.

Lemke, J. (1990). *Talking science: Language, learning, and values.* Norwood, NJ: Ablex.

MacSwan, J. (2000). The threshold hypothesis, semilingualism, and other contributions to a deficit view of linguistic minorities. *Hispanic Journal of Behavioral Sciences, 20*(1), 3-45.

MacSwan, J., & Rolstad, K. (2003). Linguistic diversity, schooling, and social class: Rethinking our conception of language proficiency in language minority education. In C. B. Paulston & R. Tucker (Eds.), *Sociolinguistics: The Essential Readings* (pp. 329-340). Oxford, England: Blackwell.

Mohan, B. (1986). *Language and content.* Reading, MA: Addison-Wesley.

Montes, M. (2003). *Get ready for Gabi: A crazy, mixed-up Spanglish day.* New York, NY: Scholastic.

Oller, J., & Perkins, K. (Eds.). (1980). *Research in language testing.* Rowley, MA: Newbury House.

Olsen, L. (2010). *Reparable harm: Fulfilling the upkept promise of educational opportunity for California's long term English learners.* Long Beach, CA: Californians Together.

Payne, R. (2008). *A framework for understanding proverty* (3rd ed.). Highlands, Texas: Aha! Process.

Pennycook, A. (2007). Global Englishes: Rip slime and performativity. *Journal of Sociolinguistics, 7,* 513-533.

Sarkar, M. (2009). "Still reppin *por mi gente*": The transformative power of language mixing in Quebec hip hop. In H. S. Alim, A. Ibrahim, & A. Pennycook (Eds.), *Global linguistic flows: Hip hop cultures, youth identities, and the politics of language* (pp. 139-158). New York, NY: Routledge.

Sato, E., & Worth, P. (2010). *Academic language demands and complexity: A taxonomy for supporting English language development in the academic context.* Oakland, CA: WestEd Report.

Scarcella, R. (2003). *Academic English: A conceptual framework* (Technical report). Santa Barbara, CA: Linguistic Minority Research Institute.

Schatzmann, L., & Strauss, A. (1955). Social class and modes of communication. *American Journal of Sociology, 60*(4), 329-338.

Schleppegrell, M (2001). Linguistic features of the language of school. *Linguistics and Education, 12*(4), 431-459.

Schleppegrell, M. (2004). *The language of schooling: A functional linguistics perspective.* Mahwah, NJ: Lawrence Erlbaum Associates.

Schleppegrell, M. (2006). The challenges of academic language in school subjects. In I. Lindberg & K. Sandwall (Eds.), *Språket och kunskapen: att lära på sitt andraspråk i skola och högskola* (pp. 47-69). Göteborg, Sweden: Göteborgs universitet institutet för svenska som andraspråk.

Schleppegrell, M. (2010). Functional grammar in the classroom. In M. Olofsson, (Ed.), *Symposium 2009. Genrer och funktionellt språk i teori och praktik* (pp. 79-95). Stockholm: Stockholms universitets förlag.

Short, D. (1994). Expanding middle school horizons: Integrating language, culture, and social studies. *TESOL Quarterly, 28*(3), 581-608.

Short, D. (1996). *Integrating language and culture in the social studies: Final report to the U. S. Department of Education, Office of Educational Research and Improvement.* Santa Cruz, CA: National Center for Research on Cultural Diversity and Second Language Learning; U S. Department of Education; Educational Resources Information Center.

Silverstein, M. (1996). Monoglot "standard" in America. In D. Brenneis & R. Macaulay (Eds.), *The matrix of language: Contemporary linguistic anthropology* (pp. 284-306). Boulder, CO: Westview.

Skutnabb-Kangas, T., & Toukomaa, P. (1976). *Teaching migrant children's mother tongue and learning the language of the host country in the context of the socio-cultural situation of the migrant family.* Helsinki: The Finnish National Commission for UNESCO.

Solomon, J., & Rhodes, N. (1995). *Conceptualizing academic language* (Research Report No. 15). Santa Cruz, CA: National Center for Research on Cultural Diversity and Second Language Learning.

Stavens, I. (2003). *Spanglish: The making of a new American language.* New York, NY: HarperCollins.

Swales, J. (2004). *Research genres.* Cambridge, England: Cambridge University Press.

Valdés, G. (1997). The teaching of Spanish to bilingual Spanish-speaking students: Outstanding issues and unanswered questions. In M. C. Colombi & F. X. Alarcón (Eds.), *La enseñanza del español a hispanohablantes* (pp. 8-44). Boston, MA: Houghton Mifflin.

Valdés, G. (2001). Heritage language students: profiles and possibilities. In J. Kreef, D. Ranard, & S. McGinnis (Eds.), *Heritage languages in America: Preserving a national resource* (pp. 37-77). Washington, DC: Delta Center for Applied Linguistics/Delta Systems.

Valdés, G. (2004a). The teaching of academic language to minority second language learners. In A. Ball & S. W. Freedman (Eds.), *Bakhtinian perspectives on language, literacy, and learning* (pp. 66-98). Cambridge, England: Cambridge University Press.

Valdés, G. (2004b). Between support and marginalization: The development of academic language in linguistic minority children. *Bilingual Education and Bilingualism, 7*(2&3), 102-132.

Valdés, G., MacSwan, J., and Alvarez, L. (2009). *Deficits and Differences: Perspectives on Language and Education.* Paper prepared for the Workshop on the Role of Language in School Learning: Implications for Closing the Achievement Gap, October 15-16, Hewlett Foundation, Menlo Park, CA. Retrieved from http://www7.nationalacademies.org/cfe/Paper_Valdes_MacSwan_and_Alvarez.pdf

Vernon, P. (1969). *Intelligence and cultural environment.* London, England: Methuen.

Villa, D. (1996). Choosing a "standard" variety of Spanish for the instruction of native Spanish speakers in the U.S. *Foreign Language Annals, 29*(2), 191-200.

Werner, H. (1961). *Comparative psychology of mental development.* New York, NY: Science Editions.

Wiley, T. G. (1996). *Literacy and language diversity in the United States.* Washington, DC & McHenry, IL: Center for Applied Linguistics & Delta Systems.

Wiley, T. G. (2005). *Literacy and language diversity in the United States* (2nd ed.). Washington, DC & McHenry, IL: Center for Applied Linguistics & Delta Systems.

Winch, C. (1985). Verbal deficit and educational success. *Journal of Applied Philosophy, 2*(1), 109-120.

Wong Fillmore, L. (1982). Language minority students and school participation: What kind of English is needed? *Journal of Education, 164,* 143-156.

Wong Fillmore, L.(1985). When does teacher talk work as input? In S. Gass & C. Madden (Eds.), *Input in second language acquisition* (pp. 17-50). Rowley, MA: Newbury House.

Zentella, C. (1997). *Growing up bilingual: Puerto Rican children in New York.* Malden, MA: Blackwell.

Zwiers, J. (2009). *Building academic language: Essential practices for content classrooms.* San Francisco, CA: Jossey-Bass.

CHAPTER 2

DEVELOPING ACADEMIC ENGLISH WITH ENGLISH LANGUAGE LEARNERS

A Study of Mainstream Classroom Practices

Shanan Fitts and Erica Bowers

Academic English is defined in terms of language forms, specific lexical and syntactical forms associated with a particular task or content area, language functions, specific contexts or tasks for which specialized language is needed (Schleppegrell, 2004). Unfortunately, many English language learners (ELLs) continue to struggle academically even after years in U.S. public schools possibly due to lack of appropriate instruction in academic English (Zwiers, 2007). Early research on academic language use in the classroom suggested that while teachers expected students to be able to navigate Academic English Language (AEL), they did not typically instruct students with regards to the various forms and functions of language used in academic texts and tasks (Solomon & Rhodes, 1995). More recently, with the advent of sheltered instruction and world class instructional design (WIDA) (Gottlieb, Cranley, & Oliver, 2007), teachers are receiving more professional development related to the explicit instruction of AEL even in the elementary grades.

Academic Language in Second Language Learning, pp. 27–56
Copyright © 2013 by Information Age Publishing
All rights of reproduction in any form reserved.

In the present study, we conducted observations in classrooms that enrolled high percentages of children who had been identified as ELLs, or who had been recently reclassified as fluent English speakers, to investigate the teaching strategies used to support students' understanding and use of academic English. The broad research question guiding this study was: what classroom practices are upper elementary teachers using to help English language learners develop academic English literacy? We examined how teachers explicitly instructed students in language form and function, and how teachers supported students' participation in contexts that require AEL. Finally, we were also interested in learning about how teachers understood and explained their instructional approaches to teaching academic language.

DEFINING ACADEMIC ENGLISH LANGUAGE AND LITERACY

Our understanding of AEL has been influenced by the fields of systemic functional linguistics (Schleppegrell, 2004) and sociolinguistics (Gee, 2002). These linguists emphasize that forms and functions of language are interdependent, and stress the importance of the social context of communication. In any communicative exchange, individuals have to interpret the social context, their goals within that context, and their status in relation to the other people present. Taken together, these three considerations determine the *register* of a text or speech event. People make linguistic choices based upon their understandings of these registers. No one register is *inherently* better than any other, but rather registers have different values depending upon context and the audience. In schools, the constellation of related registers referred to as "academic English language" is valued because speakers who use AEL adeptly are able to communicate a lot of information in a small space and position themselves as knowledgeable within a particular discipline.

Cummins (1979, 1981) developed an early definition of academic literacy that established a division between social language, Basic Interpersonal Communication Skills (BICS) and academic language, Cognitive Academic Language Proficiency (CALP). Cummins asserted that while most immigrant children acquire the requisite English language skills needed for interpersonal communication within 2 or 3 years, it can take between 4 and 7 years to develop the skills needed for successfully understanding and completing academic tasks. The BICS/CALP distinction has come under heavy criticism for implying that academic language requires greater cognitive skills, an assumption that has clearly been dismantled (McSwan, 2000). Learning to navigate the social language needed to interact successfully with native English-speaking peer groups and teachers is both cognitively challenging and imperative for English learners (Aukerman, 2007; Duff, 2003; Hawkins, 2004). Additionally, idiomatic expressions or references to popular culture that teachers insert into their instruction in order to provide illustrations that they believe are comprehensible or relatable for students may be unfamiliar to ELLs (Duff, 2003; Zwiers, 2007). Thus all forms of discourse are essentially hybrid, and limitations in social English may inhibit a student's access to academic discourse communities. It is also important to acknowledge that the current focus on helping students acquire AEL may distract researchers and educators from advocating a more productive view of academic literacy which should include an emphasis on developing multilingualism and multiliteracies, as well as cross-cultural competence (Commins & Miramontes, 2005; Valdés, 2004).

However, even if multilingualism is the ultimate goal for an academically literate person, this does not negate the existence of an academic English register. Studies of language corpora that compare conversational language to the language found in texts have affirmed that there are significant differences between spoken and written English, particularly in relation to vocabulary. Written academic texts use significantly more technical Greek and Latin-based vocabulary, while conversational English uses more words that are Germanic, specifically Anglo-Saxon, in origin (Corson, 1997; Nation, 2005). In addition to major differences in vocabulary, expository texts use particular forms of syntax and grammar in order to pack a lot of information into a small space and connote a tone of authority (Schleppegrell, 2004). Researchers have found that teachers can instruct students in the vocabulary, grammar, and discourse structures used to create and produce academic texts (Schleppegrell, 2004; Schleppegrell & Go, 2007; Townsend & Lapp, 2010). In the present study, we document some of the ways that teachers endeavor to instruct their students in AEL.

Developing proficiency in academic English language is not just a matter of acquiring a specific body of declarative knowledge of vocabulary and grammar rules. Such knowledge will not be useful if we lack communicative competence and are not sure how or when to apply the rules we have learned (Hymes, 1974). People develop specific forms of discourse, language, and literacy through active participation in specific discourse communities (Schleppegrell & Colombi, 2002). Most students, regardless of linguistic background, must be actively apprenticed into these communities by their teachers (Gee, 2002; Townsend & Lapp, 2010). We designed this study to observe not only how teachers taught students the language, grammar, syntax and vocabulary associated with AEL, but also how they scaffolded students' participation in discourse communities that required AEL.

Teaching AEL in Elementary Classrooms

Teachers are increasingly urged by standards and professional development sessions to include a focus on language structures, grammar, and vocabulary in their instruction for English learners (Dutro & Moran, 2003; Schleppegrell & Go, 2007). In reviewing research that explores how teachers instruct students in AEL, several important trends emerged that influenced the development of the observation protocol used in this study. We grouped these trends into the following categories: building background knowledge, explicit teaching, comprehensible input, and opportunities for practice. The following brief explanation of each category is not intended to be exhaustive and is provided to contextualize the development and purpose of our observational protocol. For a thorough review of relevant literature on teaching AEL please consult Anstrom et al. (2010).

Building background knowledge and schema. The first theme in teaching AEL relates to developing or building on students' vocabulary knowledge, content-area knowledge, and cultural schema. Multiple studies emphasize the importance of vocabulary instruction for developing academic English and text-level comprehension skills with ELLs (August, Carlo, Dressler, & Snow, 2005; Carlo et al., 2004; Kieffer & Lesaux, 2007). Research has found that directly teaching key vocabulary, relevant cognates, and word analysis skills can all be effective approaches to enhancing students' knowledge and use of academic language and comprehension of texts. In particular, ELLs who are Spanish-speakers profit from learning how to use their knowledge of their first language and how to recognize cognates as tools for figuring out the meanings of new words (Carlo et al. 2004; Jiménez, Garcia, & Pearson, 1996).

Clearly developing both a wider and deeper reservoir of vocabulary knowledge is crucial for students as they encounter more complex academic texts and tasks. But, building background knowledge should comprise more than teaching vocabulary words. Considering how to connect to students' schema is important because schemata, or our mental organization of knowledge, mediate our comprehension and interpretation of texts (Abu-Rabia, 1998; Droop & Verhooven, 1998; Gibbons, 2002). Our schemata assist us in making contextually accurate predictions, interpretations, and analysis of new information. Research has demonstrated that the cultural familiarity of texts influences student interest and comprehension (Abu-Rabia, 1998; Droop & Verhooven, 1998); although it should be acknowledged that the complexity of the language in texts appears to contribute more to comprehension than cultural familiarity. In addition, the concept of "culturally relevant" should not be interpreted statically as simplistic connections between home and school practices or texts.

Instead, the concept may also include associations with popular culture or with day-to-day lived experiences that are not necessarily directly related to aspects of a child's ethnic or cultural group (Goldenberg, Rueda, & August, 2006).

Comprehensible input. The second theme in teaching AEL relates to comprehensible input. In order for teachers to effectively build background knowledge and make connections to students' prior knowledge, they must utilize texts, strategies, and resources that are engaging, age-appropriate, and comprehensible (Allington, 2002). Teachers of beginning ELLs usually recognize the importance of providing realia and visuals, modeling procedures, and modifying spoken language in order to clarify instruction and content. However, teachers may forget that advanced language learners also can benefit from appropriate scaffolding to clarify concepts and vocabulary (Echevarría, Vogt, & Short, 2008). Echevarria et al. (2008) operationalized comprehensible input as speech and communication that is "appropriate to students' proficiency levels" (p. 79). Rate of speech, enunciation, complexity of vocabulary, and the use of idiomatic expressions all contribute to the comprehensibility of the teacher's input (Echevarria et al., 2008; Zwiers, 2007).

Effective teachers of ELLs employ a variety of techniques aimed at clarifying the objective of the task, the language being used in instruction, as well as the content concepts that are the focus of the lesson (Tikunoff, 1983). It is important to emphasize that while comprehensible input is a foundational aspect of effective instruction for English language learners; it is not sufficient on its own to ensure the acquisition of AEL. In fact, most research examines the ways that student interaction with the textual or linguistic input, with one another, and with the teacher, influences learning and language acquisition (Swain & Lapkin, 1995, 1998; Swain, 2005). In order for language learners to acquire high levels of academic proficiency in their first and second languages, they must be provided with ample opportunities to use the language they are learning.

Explicit teaching. The third theme that arose out of the literature on teaching AEL is the concept of explicit teaching. Explicit teaching refers to increasing student awareness of AEL as a particular language register with specific forms and functions (Dutro & Moran, 2003; Scheppegrell, 2004). Explicit teaching is critical for making challenging academic concepts and language accessible to English language learners without oversimplifying content. This approach calls for teachers to instruct students regarding the ways that specific sentence structures and vocabulary are used to achieve particular discursive ends. Thereby increasing students' ability to comprehend academic content and employ AEL orally and in written formats.

Explicit teaching might include teaching students how to recognize different genres typically used in academic writing (Schleppegrell, 2004); for example, teaching students what kinds of words or grammatical structures signal that a text is meant to be persuasive versus informative. In Townsend and Lapp's (2010) research, the authors worked to make teachers and students more aware of the academic demands of different content areas, and also taught students about the concept of register, and the ways in which context influences the language varieties people choose to use. At the elementary level, teachers can use scaffolding devices such as thinking aloud, questioning or prompts, and sentence stems to help students begin to use academic language to write or speak in different genres successfully (Chamot, 2009).

As we observed teachers use of explicit instruction, we looked for not just the explicit instruction of vocabulary or grammar, but also strategy instruction. Research suggests that ELLs who are successful readers apply a wide variety of cognitive and metacognitive strategies (Jiménez et al., 1996). These thinking skills and strategies can and should be explicitly taught to students (Chamot, 2009; Echevarría et al., 2008; Klingner, Vaughn, & Schumm, 1998). For example, Klingner et al. (1998) found that teaching students how to use collaborative strategic reading (CSR), a combination of learning strategies and text comprehension skills including previewing text, identifying tricky vocabulary, identifying main ideas, and summarizing, was effective in increasing fourth-grade students' comprehension of social studies texts.

Opportunities to Practice Academic Language and Content. The fourth theme in our review of the literature was providing students with varied opportunities to practice AEL through speaking and writing. Students need to be able to rehearse and hone academic grammar and vocabulary in order to communicate effectively, both orally and in writing, in different genres (Gibbons, 2002; Schleppegrell & Go, 2007). Advanced ELLs benefit from opportunities to interact with native English speakers and adults in academic contexts in order to be encouraged to express abstract ideas or events clearly (Chamot, 2009; Gibbons, 2002). Providing students with ample opportunities to talk and write also gives teachers valuable insight into students' background knowledge, conceptual development, language development, and analytical abilities.

Second language acquisition research has emphasized the importance of peer-to-peer interaction and student-to-teacher interaction for scaffolding language development, as learners' efforts to communicate push them to modify or restate their output or utterances (Gibbons, 2002; Mohan & Beckett, 2003; Swain, 2005). As students produce language in academic contexts that include proficient or native speakers of the target language, they must convey their ideas in ways that are precise, coherent, and appropriate (Swain, 2005, p. 473). As one produces language, one is more apt to notice or analyze language as an object, and reflect on the accuracy of utterances (Swain, 2005). The learner is also provided with chances to test hypotheses about how language works and solve problems related to how best to express ideas (Martin-Beltran, 2010; Swain & Lapkin, 1995). Research on cooperative learning and instructional conversations has demonstrated that providing students with opportunities to discuss the central concepts, themes, and language of a text or instructional unit not only helps students acquire language, but also allows students to understand the material more deeply (Carlo et al., 2004; Saunders & Goldenberg, 1999). During our observations, we noted the opportunities students had to interact with one another, elaborate on their thinking, and use academic language and vocabulary. We also noted the kinds of grouping configurations and classroom discourse structures utilized.

METHODS OF DATA COLLECTION AND ANALYSIS

Participants and Research Context

The current study is the qualitative aspect of an investigation into teachers' efforts to instruct academic English language. The quantitative study (Bowers, Fitts, Quirk, & Jung, 2010) surveyed 108 fourth and fifth grade teachers from twelve schools in Southern California with high populations of ELLs to ascertain what types of strategies teachers were using to build students' AEL. Of the 108 teachers who responded to the initial survey, 28 teachers volunteered to participate in the observational phase of the study. Ultimately, eight teachers agreed to be observed. All observations were conducted in May of 2008. Table 2.1 summarizes some key characteristics of the teachers and classrooms observed. All teachers, with the exception of Ms. Burnett, reported that they had participated in the district run professional development (PD). In lieu of the district training, Ms. Burnett had completed coursework and a summer institute focused on serving gifted and talented students.

Classrooms observed included students who were identified as monolingual English speakers (EO), English language learners (ELL), and as ELL students who had been *redesignated* as fluent English proficient (RFEP). RFEP students were monitored for 2 years before being officially exited from the English language development program. As detailed in Table 2.1, the "regular" and literacy classes had larger percentages of students who were at earlier stages of English language acquisition. Although the reader will note that some of the classrooms we observed

Table 2.1. Participating Teachers, Preparation, Experience and Numbers of ELLs

Teacher Name	# Yrs Tch	Degree & Cert.	Grade, Class Type, (#)	% NNES	% ELL	Beg	Early Int	Int	Early Adv	Adv	FEP	EO
Lee**	16	MA Regular CLAD	4th Excel (30)	n/a	77%	1a	0	10	9	3	n/a	7
Knight	7	BA Regular CLAD	5th Regular (25)	72%	44%	3	4	4	0	0	7	4
Dooley	2	BA Prelim CLAD	4th Regular (25)	40%	32%	0	3	5	0	0	2	15
Amechi	7	MA Regular CLAD	4th Enriched (28)	86%	4%	0	0	0	0	1	23	4
George	3	BA Regular CLAD	4th Excel (30)	70%	0%	0	0	0	0	0	21	9
Burnett**	4	MA Regular CLAD	4th Excel (28)	n/a	75%	0	0	14	6	1	n/a	7
Apple	8	MA Regular CLAD	4th Regular (31)	87%	13%	0	0	4	0	0	23	4
Martinez	9	BA Regular BCLAD	4th Literacy (25)	88%	88%	2	14	6	0	0	0	3

Notes: CLAD: Cross-Cultural Language and Academic Development. At the time of this study, the state of California required that all teachers be CLAD certified. This was either completed through a licensure program, or through a certificate program.

BCLAD: Bilingual Cross-Cultural Language and Academic Development. This was the name of the bilingual teacher certification program used in California at the time of this study.

% ELL = Percent of students who were identified as English language learners according to the California English Language Development Test.

% NNES = Nonnative English speakers. Percent of students in class who were not classified as monolingual English speakers (EO). Includes students who had been redesignated as Fluent English Proficient (FEP).

a. Numbers of students in each category were reported by the teachers as of May 2008 with the exception of Ms. Lee and Ms. Burnett. Lee and Burnett did not report the numbers and levels of ELL students in their classes; and therefore, district data from Spring 2007 were used.

*Numbers of EO students for Burnett and Lee may include students who were redesignated as FEP. District data did not distinguish RFEP students from EO.

**Numbers of EO students from EO.

34

enrolled mostly RFEP students, we feel that it is important to examine the types of instructional scaffolds and supports that general education teachers provide to students who have been exited from English language development (ELD) or English as a second language (ESL) programs. Students designated as fluent in English can still benefit from extra support related to developing the academic English needed for success in mainstream classrooms (Chamot, 2009).

In this school district, it was common practice to form classes based on students' test scores. Of the eight classrooms that were observed, three were termed *Excel*, one was called *Enriched*, one was designated as a *Literacy* classroom, and three had no special designation. In this district, literacy classes included students who were deemed to be reading at least 2 years below grade level according to the district reading benchmarks and the CST. Excel and enriched classrooms were for students determined to be performing above grade level. According to district documentation, one of the primary goals of the Excel program was to increase identification of gifted or intellectually advanced children among underrepresented populations. The presence of Excel classrooms in more schools throughout the district was meant to make differentiated and cognitively complex instruction available to more children. Each school site established the qualifications for enrolling students in these classes, but criteria typically included teacher recommendations, district reading benchmark scores, and California State Test (CST) scores. Excel or Enriched classrooms might also enroll students who had been identified as gifted and talented. All of the teachers who taught in the Excel classrooms were invited to participate in professional development related to differentiation, and were provided with opportunities to pursue certification in Gifted and Talented Education (GATE). However, none of the Excel teachers in this study indicated that they were GATE certified.

Professional Development

In the summer of 2006, prior to the administration of the survey used in the first phase of this study, the school district began their fourth year of implementation of *The Mathematics and Reading Professional Development Program* as authorized by California Assembly Bill 466 (AB 466) (2001). AB 466 reimbursed districts for providing training in reading and math on State Board of Education approved materials for their teachers through a 40-hour institute and 80 hours of follow-up practicum (California Department of Education, 2005). Teachers were given a stipend for their participation. The school district's focus for the fourth year of professional development was the enhancement of reading instruction for

ELLs. To accomplish this, the district chose to train teachers in the use of *A Focused Approach* (Adams & Dutro, 2005). As a district employee, the second author provided the weeklong professional development on *A Focused Approach* to the fourth and fifth grade teachers.

A Focused Approach is a method of teaching ELLs about the forms (vocabulary and grammatical structures) and functions (purposes) of the English language. Dutro and Moran (2003) advocate that implicit language learning must be balanced with the explicit instruction of language. Furthermore, all teachers must learn to attend to the language demands of the texts and tasks that they would like English learners to comprehend or produce. Their work is informed by systemic functional linguistics that conceptualizes language forms and functions as mutually constitutive. *A Focused Approach* requires the explicit instruction of topic specific words (*brick* words), and grammatical forms and general vocabulary needed for connecting and relating topic-specific words within a sentence (*mortar*) (see Dutro & Moran, 2003, p. 239). For example, in a unit on metamorphosis, a teacher would instruct students on topic specific vocabulary (bricks) such as *pupa*, *chrysalis*, and *caterpillar*. Since metamorphosis requires an understanding of sequencing, students would also learn grammatical structures and vocabulary such as *first*, *initially*, *then*, and *after* (mortar). A focused approach training also emphasized the need to "front-load" (p. 230) or preteach vocabulary and grammatical structures, and provide students with opportunities to practice academic language through the use of sentence frames for speaking or writing.

Classroom Observation Protocol and Exit Survey

In developing our observation protocol, we consulted other instruments designed to evaluate effective classroom practices for ELLs including the sheltered instruction observation protocol (SIOP) (Echevarría, Vogt, & Short, 2008), the standards performance continuum (Doherty, Hilberg, Epaloose, & Tharp, 2002), and the differentiating instruction for English learners observation protocol (Goldenberg, Coleman, & Amabisca, 2008). We reviewed related classroom observation studies and protocol including the English learners classroom observation instrument (ELCOI) (Graves, Gersten, & Haager, 2004), which was designed to observe the features of literacy instruction in first-grade classrooms. As noted above, we incorporated areas suggested by relevant literature and used the themes that came out of this review of the literature to organize the protocol into four broad categories—building background knowledge, providing comprehensible input, explicit teaching, and providing opportunities for practice. The protocol is located in the Appendix.

Data Collection and Analysis

A minimum of four distinct lessons, each approximately 30-60 minutes in duration, were observed for each participating teacher. Three researchers conducted the observations, both authors, as well as an additional research assistant. During each formal observation, two researchers were present; one took detailed field notes while the other used the protocol to record teaching practices. In this way, the researchers captured a thick description of what occurred during each observation. Observations were focused on collecting information about *teachers'* practices and utterances. The researcher who used the protocol during the observation assigned a rating to each category using a four-point rating scale with zero indicating that the component was not observed and a three indicating that the component was central to the lesson. Ratings were based on the observers' evaluation of the extent to which the approaches in each category were central to the lesson objectives and how often these approaches or strategies were used during the observation. We accounted for inter-rater reliability of our protocol and rating system by conducting two observation sessions with all three observers present. Notes and ratings were discussed immediately after the initial session and a second observation was conducted to recalibrate. This process ensured that all observers were using the protocol in the same manner.

The observation protocol assisted with both the collection and analysis of data. After all subsequent observations, each researcher typed and disseminated her notes or protocol. This necessitated the reduction of our initial data and comprised the first step in the analysis because field notes were clarified, expanded, and organized (Miles & Huberman, 1994). Next, both researchers discussed the protocol for the specific observation, the field notes, and generated a final rating. It is important to note that ratings of each teacher's level of implementation were based upon our qualitative observations and were not related to the performance of students. An overall average rating was calculated for each teacher for each category on the protocol. These are reported on Table 2.2.

Upon completion of the observations, the researchers conducted an exit survey through e-mail with each participating teacher. These semistructured surveys consisted of eight questions designed to verify the demographic make-up of the classroom and to allow the teacher to explain their instructional choices and their approaches to teaching AEL. For example, since we noticed that one teacher (George) used a lot of "thinking aloud" during her instruction, we asked her about her reasons for employing this approach.

After all observations and exit surveys were complete, the authors read through all of the qualitative data independently in order to gain a

Table 2.1.   Average Ratings for Each Instructional Area Observed

Teacher Name	Building Background	Comprehensible Input	Explicit Teaching	Opportunities for Practice
Lee	2.2*	2.1	1.8	2.7
Knight	1	1.4	1.5	1.25
Dooley	2	2	1.25	2
Amechi	1.7	1.5	1.7	1.3
George	2.3	2	2.7	3
Burnett	2	2.6	2	2.75
Apple	1.25	1	1.25	1
Martinez	1	1.7	1	1.3

*Rating Scale

0 = Not Observed

1= Shows ineffective implementation or use. Limited understanding of strategies. Done w/out necessarily considering sts. Needs or prior knowledge.

2= Partial implementation. Meeting some sts. needs & trying to take some sts. needs/ prior knowledge into consideration

3= Effective implementation of strategy. Meets the needs of the student.

thorough sense of the findings for each teacher and immerse herself in the data (Marshall & Rossman, 2006). Each author made notes for each participant, and recorded any further questions related to the findings. After the initial independent data analysis, the authors worked together to develop a profile of each teacher and her classroom practices. The researchers met frequently during the analysis of the data to discuss the findings and resolve discrepancies collaboratively.

FINDINGS: TEACHING PRACTICES FOR DEVELOPING AEL

In reporting our findings, we focus on instructional strategies that teachers are implementing effectively while pointing towards areas that may need further attention. In focusing on the positive, we are not attempting to portray an overly optimistic view of classrooms. However, we believe that educators need positive examples of what they *can* do to develop advanced literacy with English learners and we hope that some of these examples have the potential to be instructive. The findings shared below are categorized in alignment with our protocol: building background knowledge and schema, comprehensible input, opportunities for practice, and explicit teaching.

Building Background Knowledge and Schema

The first area of the protocol was focused on the extent to which teachers activated and built upon student content knowledge, personal experiences, and cultural schema. We also included previewing or preteaching vocabulary in this section of our observation protocol. Teachers who were strong in this area were able to identify potentially unfamiliar aspects of the curricula, and devise ways to connect with and build on students' prior knowledge or cultural schema as related to the topic explored in the lesson. Of the eight teachers observed, four were particularly effective: Lee, Dooley, George, and Burnett. These teachers provided extra resources and materials to help students develop knowledge on the topic or procedure being taught, consistently used graphic organizers both to organize previously learned material and to guide future learning, and emphasized academic vocabulary. These teachers were also flexible and responded to student needs or contributions as they were teaching.

Ms. Lee's introduction of her unit on the European colonists in the U.S. provides a cogent example of positive teacher practices in this area. Ms. Lee began her unit on "The Changing America" by displaying a map of the United States and asking students a focusing question, "When America started did it look like this U.S. map?" She used a read-aloud to develop students' knowledge of the European colonists of America. As she read, she asked the students to reflect on what they knew about how colonists lived, "Do you think people in the towns, colonies lived the same way we do?" Next, she provided students with excerpts from the same text on posters that were hung around the room. Students circulated in small groups, read the information on each poster, and recorded key facts and ideas on a simple graphic organizer in their journals. Thus students were able to hear the text read aloud and discuss several key concepts with the teacher before they had to read it independently and identify the important information. Since the independent reading was completed with a group, students could ask for clarification from peers if necessary.

In a subsequent observation, students discussed the key vocabulary they would be using during the unit. Ms. Lee asked students to make connections to the previous day's lesson, the reading, and the graphic organizer they had completed. Ms. Lee stated in her exit survey that she found thinking maps (Hyerle, 1995) useful and that she used them consistently to help students chunk and comprehend text. This assertion was borne out by our observational data. In her exit survey, Ms. Lee noted:

> It's important to build their background and/or schema before reading. I bring in other texts (articles, books, etc.) so we are "frontloaded" on the subject matter before we read. It really helps students to connect to what they

are reading. It also helps give the text more relevance. Also, breaking the text into smaller chunks, and talking about the reading and/or mapping the text (with appropriate thinking maps) as we go, helps comprehension.

Ms. Lee combined several strategies to build students' knowledge and vocabulary on this new content. This teaching method provided students with different ways to practice and use new concepts and vocabulary, and worked to make potentially challenging text more comprehensible for her students.

A second teacher, Ms. George, was also rated highly in this area of our protocol because she consistently reminded students how the current lesson built on what they had learned in the past and was purposeful about preteaching and emphasizing academic vocabulary. In this example, Ms. George had taught her students a three-step process for using their knowledge about morphemes (root words and affixes), and context clues to figure out the meanings for potentially unfamiliar words. First they had to circle the root word, which in this lesson was always *ped* or *pod*; next, students were to look at the rest of the word to see if there were other familiar affixes; and finally, they had to look for and underline relevant context clues in the sentence. With all of this information they were required to determine the definition for the word and come up with a new sentence. Ms. George clarified her expectations for the students' work:

> Now when you write the sentence, make sure you don't write: I saw a centipede. Because that doesn't show me that you know the word. You could have seen anything. Who remembers what we use to make a better sentence. [One or two students say "conjunctions."] We use conjunctions like 'but, so, because.' So, you have to make a sentence that will really *show* me you understand the word. You need to prove to me that you know how to use the word.

In addition to giving students opportunities to work with and discuss vocabulary, Ms. George was also asking them to apply a previously learned skill of using a conjunction to add details and evidence to a sentence. She also made an effort to connect the strategy that she was teaching to a situation that a child might face in his or her daily life:

> Let's say you see a word in a book you are reading or on a test and you only know the root part of the word ... if you follow these three steps on any state test or if you're reading an article in a science magazine and you're reading a difficult passage and you see a word you don't know, follow these three steps to find the meaning of a word when you know the root.

Although Ms. George did provide the students with a context or purpose for learning the strategy, it is difficult to ignore that the emphasis seemed to be developing the strategy for on state exams.

In addition to the importance of developing students' content knowledge, another important aspect of building background knowledge relates to cultural schema. Building on students' cultural schema and funds of knowledge is an essential feature of effective instruction for ELLs (González, Moll, & Amanti, 2005; Lucas & Grinberg, 2008). We observed few examples of teaching or curricula that built on students' cultural schema. One example we can provide occurred as a teachable moment during a lesson on nutrition in Ms. Amechi's fourth grade classroom. In this lesson, students were learning how to read and analyze food labels and were encouraged to bring in labels from home. This was a simple way for the teacher to involve students' home-based cultural practices, but a discussion of food choices, food preparation practices, or units of measure utilized in different students' families was not included in the lesson. However, as some of the labels were in Spanish, Ms. Amechi was able to draw students' attention to the cognates *información* and *information*. This occurred incidentally and the teacher seemed to be surprised: "I just saw información and brain just keyed in because the word is the same in English." This connection was not planned by the teacher and did not result in further investigation of cognates or any other differences in how food labels are written in different countries, but is an example of a teacher making at least a *limited* connection to students' personal lives and home languages.

Comprehensible Input

In our observations, we examined how teachers made their texts, lectures, and activities more comprehensible to their students. Specifically we observed the extent to which teachers emphasized distinctive features of new concepts, provided examples and nonexamples to illustrate new concepts; broke down skills or concepts into simpler components; clarified instructions; provided wait time; or used a variety of levels of questions or tasks. Again, half of the teachers we observed (Lee, Burnett, George, and Dooley), consistently employed these comprehensible input strategies. We found that Ms. Burnett clearly and explicitly employed each and every one of these strategies consistently, naturally, and energetically. She used all available tools to clarify vocabulary including thinking aloud, acting things out, and asking students to look for cognates. The following excerpts from our notes provide examples of these approaches. The first two examples come from a small-group instructional conversation that Ms. Burnett was conducting with her literature circle and the last one from an individual writing conference:

T: ok, deflated, that's the opposite of inflated. (Pantomimed inflate/deflate). So why would that be important that he has a deflated dinghy?

T is reading and comes to the word, "tranquility," stops and asks, those who speak Spanish- what does 'tranquilo' mean? (Student responds.) So what do you think "tranquility" means?

T (to student): Hmm, I think I've already read this. You already wrote that over here. That's repetitive. Do you know what repetitive means? (Student responds.) Yes, when you say something more than once. So do you know why I'm crossing this out? Because I was being repetitive.

Ms. Burnett's classroom illustrated the importance of differentiated instruction for scaffolding students' advanced literacy learning. In her exit survey, Ms. Burnett explained that she put a lot of effort into locating resources that would be appropriate and engaging for students. She also stated that she provided opportunities for student choice and independent study. She noted that "time, patience, knowledge about students' levels, and resources are the keys to differentiating. At this point in the year, I know my students' strengths and weaknesses very well…" Ms. Burnett's approach to instruction, which was strongly influenced by her training in gifted and talented education, reflects recommendations to provide ELLs with opportunities for inquiry and reflection (Téllez & Waxman, 2006). The gifted and talented teaching team at Ms. Burnett's school appeared to be a key source of support for her and her students. According to Ms. Burnett, other teachers on her team had "the same core values and similar learning structures, which I really think helps our kids succeed." Thus, students learned critical thinking and analytical literacy skills over the course of several years as they became members of a particular discourse community. The lessons Ms. Burnett had learned through her training in the field of gifted and talented education about differentiation and planning for student engagement, as well as the presence of supportive and engaged colleagues at her school had benefitted students' development of advanced literacy skills over time—including her students who were English language learners or who had been redesignated as fluent in English. Ms. Burnett's instructional practices exemplified ways that teachers of more advanced students can make instruction simultaneously comprehensible and challenging.

Explicit Teaching

Seven of the eight teachers in this sample attended *A Focused Approach* (Adams & Dutro, 2005) trainings, which are described above. A key focus of these professional development sessions was the explicit instruction of language forms and functions. In addition, the Open Court reading program adopted by this district promoted the instruction of cognitive strategies to enhance students' reading comprehension. Due to the extensive professional development that the teachers in our sample received, the researchers were expecting to observe these approaches and strategies in each of the classrooms visited. Our observational data revealed that each teacher did employ at least one instructional strategy related to explicit instruction in at least one of our observation sessions. However, only two of the teachers obtained high average ratings in this area based on our observations. We noted that oftentimes teachers' explicit instruction was narrowly focused on defining and using specific vocabulary, using specific sentence stems, or mastering processes or strategies such as using context clues to define vocabulary. However, there were several instances in which we observed teachers creating authentic purposes for learning language forms or cognitive strategies.

As an illustration, we share a description of the way that Ms. George helped her fourth-grade students write open-ended, thought-provoking questions to prepare for a Socratic seminar on the story they were reading. To help her students accomplish this, Ms. George used a graphic organizer to review and discuss the different kinds of questions that people can ask about texts. She had labeled these questions Level 1, Level 2, and Level 3 and explained: "Level 1 questions are factual questions. The answer is right there in the text and there is a right or wrong answer. Level 2 questions require you to make a connection. Level three questions require reflection and evidence to back-up a personal opinion." During this interactive review, students discussed and identified different types of questions before moving on to writing their own. In order to scaffold students in the process of writing effective questions, Ms. George provided the students with a handout of sentence stems, such as, "How did ____ feel about ____?" and "Why couldn't ____ do ____?" Ms. George demonstrated the process of creating a good seminar question by using a think-aloud with a section of a story about the Titanic, which was familiar to students, displayed on the overhead projector:

> I have these stems that are gonna help me. A good idea is to find a fact and go from there. Here's an interesting fact (highlighting and reading aloud): **The Titanic was thought to be the world's first unsinkable ship.** I'm gonna go with this first stem (referring to handout). **How did <u>the passengers</u> feel about <u>being on an unsinkable ship?</u>** (They discuss this question with tables and with the class.) Okay, so first I'm going to find an interesting fact, something that makes me think. Here's one (she underlines the fact on the overhead)—the fact that only 700 people got on life boats but the life boats were suppose to be for 1178 people—that makes me think … that makes me confused … so I'm gonna ask: "what caused the boat to carry only 700 people?"

This question resulted in a buzz of conversation and engaged the students' interest in the task at hand. The teacher gave the students a minute for discussion before she stopped them so they could write their own questions and noted aloud, "a good sign of a Level 3 question is that there is more talking." So motivated, the students used the story from their anthology and their question stems to develop questions for the next day's discussion, which we also observed. Students were successful in using AEL to write effective discussion questions due to the modeling and scaffolding that Ms. George provided.

Exit survey data demonstrated that participants were aware of the importance of the explicit instruction of AEL. Three teachers (George, Lee, and Martinez) explained that they use sentence stems to assist students in applying academic language to their oral and written discussion of content. For example, Ms. Lee explained:

> (I) start with a thinking map (to organize complex concept(s)) and give students a frame w/ appropriate academic language. For example: create a multi-flow map, and then use it to "sound like a scholar." If you were explaining why Wilbur (in Charlotte's Web) escaped from his pen, you might say, "Due to the fact that _____, Wilbur escaped from his pen." (insert cause into blank). Once students receive the proper academic language, they will start using it!

Overall five of the eight participating teachers, including Amechi, Burnett, George, Lee, and Martinez, specifically discussed ways that they explicitly instructed students in AEL on their exit surveys. Given that we did not always observe teachers utilizing the strategies they noted on their surveys, we conclude that the explicit teaching of AEL is challenging and teachers probably need further support. Recent research confirms this finding (Schleppegrell & Go, 2007; Townsend & Lapp, 2010).

Opportunities for Practice

As noted in our review of the literature, providing students with various opportunities to practice academic language and negotiate meaning with their teachers and with more competent peers is a crucial aspect of developing academic literacy. All of the teachers we visited provided students with some opportunities to apply academic concepts and vocabulary; however, there were significant differences in regards to the quality or intensity of these opportunities. Part of this seemed to be related to the participation structures favored by the teachers. For example, in four of the classrooms that we visited (Amechi, Apple, Knight, and Martinez), the teachers were engaged in whole class, direct instruction during all of the instructional sessions observed. This format lent itself to the more traditional, teacher-controlled, recitation style discourse pattern known as initiation-response-evaluation (I-R-E). I-R-E requires students to display knowledge regarding specific facts (Cazden, 2001). Most teachers modified this participation structure somewhat to allow for further student interaction and elaboration. In the following discussion, Ms. Amechi and her students were discussing ecosystems by describing pictures in their science text. They began their discussion by identifying abiotic and biotic features of an ecosystem. In parts of the lesson, students were encouraged by the teacher to elaborate on their ideas, as in the following example:

> Ms. A.: How do living and non-living things in this pond interact? What relationships can you find?
>
> ST: The water helps the fish live.
>
> Ms. A.: Okay good, the water helps the fish live. What else? What other relationships can you find?
>
> ST: Grass and water.
>
> Ms. A.: Grass and water what? Finish your idea.
>
> ST: The grass needs the water to grow.

Here Ms. Amechi's scaffolding was essential in prodding the student to elaborate her response and express the relationship she was thinking of more clearly, but the discourse pattern was still I-R-E.

Teacher scaffolding and modeling are central to maximizing student elaboration of academic concepts and academic vocabulary (Gibbons, 2002). The best example of this came from Ms. George's class where over the course of two of the class sessions that we observed, she prepared her students to run a Socratic seminar discussion based on the story they were reading. The students were well-prepared to be active participants because they had had the time to practice the skills needed for the discussion. First, as shown in the *Explicit Teaching* section above, Ms. George led students to construct effective discussion questions. The following day, students led the class discussion with some coaching from the teacher and support in the form of a handout that provided models of ways to enter a discussion, disagree with someone's point, or bring in a new idea. Prior to the discussion, Ms. George modeled how they might ask questions, comment, or respond to one another.

To emphasize her peripheral role during the discussion, Ms. George had a pair of sunglasses that she put on when she went from teacher to observer—she put them on and the students were in control, and when she took them off she would provide the students with some coaching. For example, the students began their discussion using an I-R-E structure whereby one person asked a question, another answered it, and then they moved to another question. Ms. George removed her sunglasses to remind the students to ask for more than one perspective: "Can I have one volunteer who will ask, 'Does anyone have anything that they would like to add?' after each question has been answered?" With support and modeling from the teacher, and from their handout, the students were able to run a rich and interesting discussion. Students utilized evidence from the story to argue their points, asked one another for clarification and agreed or disagreed with one another in appropriate ways. During this Socratic seminar, students were using academic language in purposive ways to participate in a discourse community.

DISCUSSION AND CONCLUSIONS

The findings of this observational study indicate that it is important for teachers to attend to all four areas delineated on our observation protocol in order to effectively scaffold students' understanding of and access to academic English literacy. Although practices on our protocol were categorized for ease of analysis, no one area would stand on its own. For example, in order for teachers to be successful in their attempts to build knowledge in a particular content area, the materials and texts used to build that knowledge must be both interesting and comprehensible to the students targeted. Teachers can use explicit teaching to instruct students in specific language forms or functions, but unless students have ample opportunities to practice, they may not be able to internalize these discursive forms. In addition, without authentic opportunities to practice AEL, students may not develop an understanding of the functions of AEL or how language choices relate to contexts.

With regards to building background and connecting to students' prior schema, we found that most teacher practices in this area were related to vocabulary development. All of the teachers observed for this study employed practices that were specifically aimed at building students' content and vocabulary knowledge, and teachers had clearly been trained in specific approaches for teaching vocabulary. Most teachers spent time previewing and discussing discipline specific words and morphemes. While the formula used for vocabulary instruction always included time for students to think about or discuss where they had heard the word before, or what they thought the word meant, in some classrooms these discussions were dominated by teacher-talk. Thus, in most cases, it did not appear that teachers were designing these background-building activities with the students' cultural and linguistic background experiences in mind. We did not observe many instances of the kinds of culturally responsive curricula or instruction that are recommended for increasing success with ELLs (Lucas & Grinberg, 2008). Providing students with texts that are culturally familiar may serve to increase the comprehensibility of texts, as well as student engagement and ability to demonstrate analytical skills (Abu-Rabia, 1998; Droop & Verhoeven, 1998; Martínez-Roldán & Newcomer, 2011). In future studies, it would be useful to examine teachers' perspectives relative to tapping students' cultural and linguistic backgrounds to develop AEL.

In a related vein, effective literacy instruction for ELLs in mainstream or monolingual-English environments should allow for the thoughtful inclusion of students' native languages. Researchers have explored some of the ways that bilingual children's home language literacy skills can transfer positively to second language literacy (see, e.g., Nagy, Garcia, Durgunoglu, & Hancin-Bhatt, 1993). For many bilingual children, learning about Latin root words and cognates can be a powerful tool in developing AEL (Carlo et al., 2004; Kieffer & Lesaux, 2007). We occasionally observed the use of Spanish used to clarify instructions or content for specific students on an individual basis, especially in Martinez's room where there were more beginning English language learners. But, we rarely saw teachers purposively providing explicit instruction in cognates or common affixes that might be able to assist comprehension and make connections between first and second languages. Research has shown that students' ability to recognize and use cognate knowledge improves as they get older (August et al., 2005) and also suggests that students benefit from direct instruction to increase their awareness of cognates. Therefore we would recommend that teachers be instructed with regards to common cognates and suffixes in Spanish and English.

In addition to helping students learn to use their first language to increase word-level reading skills, the inclusion of native language texts in the content areas to help build background knowledge can be effective (Carlo et al., 2004). Furthermore, allowing bilingual children to talk through their ideas in their native language prior to a discussion or writing assignment in English can improve students' comprehension and written expression (Jiménez, 2000; Moll & Diaz, 1985). But, teachers should not assume that this linguistic transfer occurs without instruction and scaffolding (Harper & DeJong, 2004). Mainstream classroom teachers need to be provided with more information and support with regards to incorporating native language resources and strategies into their classrooms. As ELLs are exited from special language development programs, it appears that teachers allow themselves to overlook these students' cultural and linguistic diversity. Developing a deeper understanding of students' linguistic and cultural resources will likely assist teachers in developing instructional approaches that are both academically challenging and culturally competent. In this way teachers may be encouraged to broaden their conceptualization of academic literacy to include bilingualism and biliteracy.

In reflecting upon possible reasons that we did not see more use of students' language resources in these classrooms, we were reminded of the extent to which teachers may continue to be wary of using languages other than English in instruction due to the stipulations of Proposition 227. Proposition 227, passed in 1998, mandates that instruction occur overwhelmingly in English. Even if teachers are instructed in professional development with regards to the utility of teaching bilingual children how to look for and use cognates, teacher educators need to continue to debunk the pervasive notion that including the native language in the mainstream classroom is not acceptable.

With regards to explicit instruction of AEL, our observations revealed that teachers were successfully implementing some of these instructional strategies. For example, all of the teachers we observed used sentence frames to scaffold students' oral and written expression thus providing a model of academic English language that students could emulate and use until they appropriated that language themselves. However, the teachers in our sample needed more practice with these approaches. Explicit teaching strategies require time and support for successful implementation. Teachers have to learn how to analyze the academic language found in texts, and identify the cognitive skills and communicative goals embedded in the task or genre (Schleppegrell, 2004; Townsend & Lapp, 2010). They then need to determine the best way to scaffold students' understandings of those language forms and their functions.

In order for the explicit instruction of AEL to be meaningful, students must be afforded with authentic and engaging contexts that require them to use AEL. Acquiring AEL comprises much more than simply learning more specialized vocabulary or knowing how to construct a grammatically correct sentence or paragraph. It requires invitation and apprenticeship into particular discourse communities and opportunities for all students to envision themselves as members of those communities (Schleppegrell, & Colombi, 2002). While we did observe teachers creating *some* authentic purposes for communication, it appeared that the main purpose emphasized was school or state mandated assessments. Teachers are under enormous pressure to prepare students to succeed on these exams, but does this constitute a sufficiently motivating context for applying AEL? In those instances in which teachers took the time to try to create rich contexts for communication, such as the Socratic seminar observed in George's class, students were able to apply the AEL learned for an authentic purpose—to have a conversation about a story that they had read. We suggest that teachers may need more assistance in terms of connecting their explicit teaching practices to communicative activities that are meaningful and engaging for students.

The results of our observations suggest that teachers may want to allow students more opportunities to practice oral or written academic language. Research on second language acquisition points to the importance of extending oral language development into the upper grades; however, there is little research on oral language development in older children (Geva, 2006). Most teachers noted the importance of allowing students the time and opportunity to discuss academic concepts on their exit surveys and we did see several excellent examples of this during our observations. However, as has been found in numerous other studies on classroom discourse (Cazden, 2001), many of the class discussions we observed were dominated by recitation of facts and an I-R-E participation structure. In his study of teachers' practices for scaffolding academic language in the classroom, Zwiers (2007) refers to a negative practice he observed termed "linguistic enabling." When teachers engaged in linguistic enabling they accepted nonacademic or limited responses from students perhaps because they felt rushed or to avoid making students feel uncomfortable. In these instances, teachers would expand on students' responses themselves rather than pushing the student to explain his or her idea or would accept the student's response without correction. In our example from Amechi's classroom discussion about ecosystems, the teacher did work to get students to expand their ideas to an extent, but this could have been improved. Thus our findings confirm Zwiers' observations and we agree with his assertion that teachers and researchers need to reflect on the balance between teacher modeling and student production of academic language. Teachers should probably attend to the prevalence and quality of both teacher and student talk, and would likely benefit from consciously attempting to encourage students to express their ideas in more fully formed and academic ways. In addition, we noted a lack of opportunities to practice written expression, especially in the content areas. While there has been an excessive amount of attention paid to the teaching of literacy, this has focused on reading and not writing. Future studies on the acquisition of AEL should include an investigation of students' oral and written language output in the content areas. A limitation of the present study was the lack of data pertaining to both student output and student achievement. In future studies, it would be beneficial to collect data on student output over time to track patterns in students' appropriation and use of academic language (Zwiers, 2007).

Students who are acquiring English as an additional language need to be afforded opportunities to practice their language skills and negotiate meaning with more proficient peers. This district's practice of assigning students to different classrooms based on their performance on standardized tests had the effect of separating fluent English speakers from ELLs. English language learners should have the chance to work with and communicate with their fluent English-speaking peers on a regular basis and engage in instructional conversations that require critical thinking and more elaborated forms of language production (Zwiers, 2007; Saunders & Goldenberg, 1999; Swain, 2005). The separation of children into "Excel" classrooms and "Literacy" classrooms is a policy that this district should reconsider.

Although it may appear to the reader that the rich contexts for student interaction that were present in George and Burnett's classroom were primarily a result of grouping all of the higher achieving students together in the same classroom, other factors should be considered. For example, Apple's classroom enrolled students who were primarily redesignated as fluent in English and all of her students were performing at or above grade level. Yet all of the class sessions we observed in that environment were dominated by an I-R-E discourse pattern with little opportunity students to practice language in any elaborated fashion. Conversely, Lee's classroom enrolled many students who were still acquiring English and this did not prevent her from providing her students with opportunities to engage with challenging content and explain their thinking. This leads us to believe that a combination of factors produced some of the qualitative differences observed. According to district documentation, Excel classroom teachers were offered opportunities for professional development that focused on making their instruction more cognitively complex. This may result in more emphasis on critical thinking and inquiry learning in Excel classrooms. If this is the case, then perhaps all teachers should be allowed to participate in such workshops. During both phases of this study, we inquired into the participating teachers PD related to teaching ELLs; however, our observational data suggest that the Excel teachers were more adept at using participation structures that might benefit ELLs, such as inquiry-based learning, cooperative learning, and dialogic instructional practices. Therefore, future research should include a closer examination of all of PD provided to teachers, not just PD specifically targeted towards teaching ELLs.

This district is to be commended for their acknowledgment that all students should have equal access to the language of school (AEL) and in its determination to provide professional development to their teachers specifically addressing this area. It is clear that instructing children to recognize and use academic language and genres is a challenging proposition. Professional development should go beyond the one-stop workshop (Nieto, 2009); teachers require ongoing support so that they can hone and refine their newly acquired strategies (Chappius, Chappius, & Stiggins, 2009).

Appendix: Observation Protocol

Teacher Name:	School:	District:	
Date of Observation:	Time In:	Time Out:	
Grade:	Total # Students Present:	# of ELLs:	Observer:

Summary of Lesson (list grouping strategies if observed):

Rating Scale

0 = Not Observed

1= Shows ineffective implementation or use. Limited understanding of strategies. Done w/out necessarily considering sts. Needs or prior knowledge.

2= Partial implementation. Meeting some sts. needs & trying to take some sts. needs/prior knowledge into consideration

3= Effective implementation of strategy. Meets the needs of the student.

Building Background		Specifically, I observed:
Links new concepts to students' background experiences and past learning • Activates prior knowledge (student's personal experiences) • Linking past content learning (links to past lessons) • Using graphic organizers or semantic webs • Previewing or teaching vocabulary	Rating	

Comprehensible Input		Specifically, I observed:
Making content accessible to students • Emphasizes distinctive features of new concepts • Provides examples and/or nonexamples to illustrate new skills/concepts/strategies • Breaks down skills /strategies/concepts into smaller/simpler components • Provides clear info/input about the new concept • Clarifies instructions • Wait time • Leveled questions or tasks	Rating	

(Appendix continues on next page)

Appendix: (Continued)

Explicit Teaching	Specifically, I observed:
Providing explicit input and modeling related to concept/academic language instruction. • T models processes and skills/strategies/ concepts • Strategy Instruction • Ss locate Information in Expository Text • Instruct Academic Language • Explicitly teaches vocabulary	Rating

Opportunities to Practice	Specifically, I observed:
Provides structured opportunities for students to practice, and consolidate new skills, concepts and vocabulary. • Students Orally Elaborate Concepts • Variety of Grouping Strategies • Students Use Content Language • Integrate More than One Language Skill • Writing in Content Areas • Students Practice Academic Language	Rating

REFERENCES

Abu-Rabia, S. (1998). The learning of Hebrew by Israeli Arab students in Israel. *Journal of Social Psychology, 138*(3), 331-341.

Adams, M., & Dutro, S. (2005). *A focused approach to frontloading English language instruction for Open Court Reading, K-6* (3rd ed.). San Diego, CA: University of California, California Reading and Literature Project.

Allington, R. (2002). You can't learn much from books you can't read. *Educational Leadership, 60*(3), 16-19.

Anstrom, K., DiCerbo, P., Butler, F., Katz, A., Millet, J., & Rivera, C. (2010). *A Review of the literature on Academic English: Implications for K-12 English Language Learners.* Arlington, VA: The George Washington University Center for Equity and Excellence in Education.

August, D., Carlo, M., Dressler, C., & Snow, C. (2005). The critical role of vocabulary development for English language learners. *Learning Disabilities Research & Practice, 20*(1), 50-57. doi:10.1111/j.1540-5826.2005.00120.x

Aukerman, M. (2007). A culpable CALP: Rethinking the conversational/academic language proficiency distinction in early literacy instruction. *The Reading Teacher, 60*(7), 626-635. doi:10.1598/RT.60.7.3

Bowers, E., Fitts, S., Quirk, M., & Jung, W. (2010). Effective strategies for developing academic English: A study of teacher practices and student achievement. *Bilingual Research Journal, 33*(1), 95-110. doi:10.1080/15235881003733407.

California Department of Education. (2005). Mathematics and reading professional development program final report. Retrieved from http://www.cde.ca.gov/pd/ca/ma/mard05execsumm.asp

Carlo, M. S., August, D., McLaughlin, B., Snow, C. E., Dressler, C., Lippman, D. N., Lively, T. J., & White, C. E. (2004). Closing the gap: Addressing the vocabulary needs of English-language learners in bilingual and mainstream classrooms. *Reading Research Quarterly, 39*(2), 188-216.

Cazden, C. B. (2001). *Classroom discourse: The language of teaching and learning.* Portsmouth, NH: Heinemann.

Chamot, A. U. (2009). *The CALLA handbook: Implementing the cognitive academic language learning approach* (2nd ed.). White Plains, NY: Pearson.

Chappius, S., Chappius, J., & Stiggins, R. (2009). Supporting teacher learning teams. *Educational Leadership, 66*(5), 56-60.

Corson, D. (1997). The learning and use of academic English words. *Language Learning, 47*(4), 671-718.

Cummins, J. (1979). Linguistic interdependence and the education development of bilingual children. *Review of Educational Research, 49*(2), 222-251.

Cummins, J. (1981). The role of primary language development in promoting educational success for language minority students. In California State Department of Education (Ed.), *Schooling and language minority students: A theoretical framework* (pp. 2-49). Los Angeles, CA: California State University, Evaluation, Dissemination and Assessment Center.

Doherty, R. W., Hilberg, R. S., Epaloose, G., & Tharp, R. G. (2002). Standards performance continuum: Development and validation of a measure of effective pedagogy. *Journal of Educational Research, 96*(2), 78-89.

Droop, M., & Verhoeven, L. T. (1998). Background knowledge, linguistic complexity, and second language reading comprehension. *Journal of Literacy Research, 30*(2), 253-271.

Duff, P. A. (2003). Intertextuality and hybrid discourses: The infusion of pop culture in educational discourse. *Linguistics and Education, 14,* 231-276.

Dutro, S., & Moran, C. (2003) Rethinking English language instruction: An architectural approach. In G. Garcia (Ed.), *English language learners: Reaching the highest level of English literacy* (pp. 227-258). Newark, DE: International Reading Association.

Echevarría, J., Vogt, M. E., & Short, D. (2008). *Making content comprehensible for elementary English learners: The SIOP model.* Boston, Ma: Allyn & Bacon.

Gee, J. (2002). Literacies, identities, and discourses. In M. J. Schleppegrell & M. C. Colombi (Eds.), *Developing advanced literacy in first and second languages: Meaning with power* (pp. 159-175). Mahwah, NJ: Lawrence Erlbaum.

Geva, E. (2006). Second-language oral proficiency and second-language literacy. In D. August & T. Shanahan (Eds.), *Developing literacy in second-language learners: Report of the national literacy panel on language-minority children and youth* (pp. 123-139). Mahwah, NJ: Lawrence Erlbaum.

Gibbons, P. (2002). *Scaffolding language, scaffolding learning: Teaching second language learners in the mainstream classroom.* Portsmouth, NH: Heinemann.

Goldenberg, C., Coleman, R., & Amabisca, A. (2008, March). *Standards-based differentiated ELD instruction to improve English Language Arts achievement for ELLs.*

Paper presented at the annual meeting of the American Educational Research Association, New York, NY.

Goldenberg, C., Rueda, R. S., & August, D. (2006). Sociocultural influences on literacy attainment of language-minority children and youth. In D. August & T. Shanahan (Eds.), *Developing literacy in second-language learners: Report of the national literacy panel on language-minority children and youth* (pp. 269-318). Mahwah, NJ: Lawrence Erlbaum.

González, N., Moll, L. C., & Amanti, C. (2005). *Funds of knowledge: Theorizing practice in households, communities, and classrooms*. Mahwah, NJ: Erlbaum.

Gottlieb, M., Cranley, M. E., & Oliver, A. R. (2007). *Understanding the WIDA English Language Proficiency Standards: A Resource Guide*. Madison, WI: WIDA Consortium.

Graves, A. W., Gersten, R., & Haager, D. (2004). Literacy instruction in multiple-language first-grade classrooms: Linking student outcomes to observed instructional practice. *Learning Disabilities Research & Practice, 19*(4), 262–272.

Harper, C., & De Jong, E. (2004). Misconceptions about teaching English-language learners. *Journal of Adolescent & Adult Literacy, 48*(2), 152-162.

Hawkins, M. R. (2004). Researching English language and literacy development in schools. *Educational Researcher, 33*(3), 14-25.

Hyerle, D. (1995). Thinking maps: Seeing is understanding. *Educational Leadership, 53*(4), 85.

Hymes, D. H. (1974). *Foundations in sociolinguistics: An ethnographic approach*. Philadelphia, PA: University of Pennsylvania.

Jiménez, R. T. (2000). Literacy and the identity development of Latina/o students. *American Educational Research Journal, 37*(4), 971-1000.

Jiménez, R. T., García, G. E., & Pearson, P. E. (1996). The reading strategies of bilingual Latina/o students who are successful English readers: Opportunities and obstacles. *Reading Research Quarterly, 31*(1), 90-112.

Kieffer, M. J., & Lesaux, N. K. (2007). Breaking down words to build meaning: Morphology, vocabulary, and reading comprehension in the urban classroom. *The Reading Teacher, 61*(2), 134-145.

Klingner, J. K., Vaughn, S., & Schumm, J. S. (1998). Collaborative strategic reading during social studies in heterogeneous fourth grade classrooms. *The Elementary School Journal, 99*, 1-22.

Lucas, T., & Grinberg, J. (2008). Responding to the linguistic reality of mainstream classrooms: Preparing all teachers to teach English language learners. In M. Cochran-Smith, S. Feiman-Nemser, D. J. McIntryre, & K. E. Demers (Eds.), *Handbook of research on teacher education: Enduring questions in changing contexts* (3rd ed., pp. 606-636). New York, NY: Routledge.

Marshall, C., & Rossman, G. B. (2006). *Designing qualitative research*. Thousands Oaks, CA: SAGE.

Martin-Beltrán, M. (2010). The two-way language bridge: Co-constructing bilingual language learning opportunities. *Modern Language Journal, 94*(2), 254-277. doi:10.1111/j.1540-4781.2010.01020.x

Martínez-Roldán, C. M., & Newcomer, S. (2011). Reading between the pictures: Immigrant students' interpretation of *The Arrival*. *Language Arts, 88*(3), 188-197.

McSwan, J. (2000). The threshold hypothesis, semilingualism, and other contributions to a deficit view of linguistic minorities. *Hispanic Journal of Behavioral Sciences, 22*(1), 3-45.

Miles, M. B., & Huberman, M. A. (1994). *Qualitative data analysis: An expanded sourcebook.* Thousand Oaks, CA: SAGE.

Mohan, B., & Beckett, G. H. (2003). A functional approach to research on content-based language learning: Recasts in causal explanations. *The Modern Language Journal, 87*(3), 421-432.

Moll, L. C. & Diaz, S. (1985). Ethnographic pedagogy: Promoting effective bilingual instruction. In E. E. Garcia & R. V. Padilla (Eds.), *Advances in bilingual education research* (pp. 127- 149). Tucson, AZ: University of Arizona.

Nagy, W., Garcia, G. E., Durgunoglu, A. Y., & Hancin-Bhatt, B. (1993). Spanish–English bilingual students' use of cognates in English reading. *Journal of Reading Behavior, 25,* 241-259.

Nation, I. S. P. (2005). Teaching and learning vocabulary. In E. Hinkel (Ed.), *Handbook of research in second language teaching and learning* (pp. 581-595). Mahwah, NJ: Lawrence Erlbaum.

Nieto, S. (2009). From surviving to thriving. *Educational Leadership, 66*(5), 8-13.

Saunders, W. M., & Goldenberg, C. (1999). *The effects of instructional conversations and literature logs on the story comprehension and thematic understanding of English proficient and limited English proficient students.* Research Report #6. Center for Research on Education, Diversity & Excellence. Santa Cruz: University of California.

Schleppegrell, M. J. (2004). *The language of schooling: A functional linguistic perspective.* Mahwah, NJ: Lawrence Erlbaum.

Schleppegrell, M. J., & Colombi, M. C. (Eds.). (2002). *Developing advanced literacy in first and second languages: Meaning with power.* Mahwah, NJ: Lawrence Erlbaum.

Schleppegrell, M. J., & Go, A. L. (2007). Analyzing the writing of English Learners: A functional approach. *Language Arts, 84*(6), 529-538.

Solomon, J. & Rhodes, N. (1995). *Assessing academic language of English language learners: Final report.* Washington, DC: Center for Applied Linguistics.

Swain, M. (2005). The output hypothesis: Theory and research. In E. Hinkel (Ed.), *Handbook of research in second language teaching and learning* (pp. 471-483). Mahwah, NJ: Lawrence Erlbaum.

Swain, M., & Lapkin, S. (1995). Problems in output and the cognitive processes they generate: A step towards second language learning. *Applied Linguistics, 6*(3), 371-391.

Swain, M., & Lapkin, S. (1998). Interaction and second language learning: Two adolescent French immersion students working together. *Modern Language Journal, 82*(3), 320-337.

Téllez, K., & Waxman, H. C. (2006). *Preparing quality educators for English language learners: Research, policies and practices.* Mahwah, NJ: L. Erlbaum Associates.

Tikunoff, W. J. (1983). *An emerging description of successful bilingual instruction: Executive summary of part I of the SBIF study.* San Francisco, CA: Far West Laboratory for Educational Research and Development. (ERIC Document Reproduction Service No. ED297561).

Townsend, D. R., & Lapp. D. (2010). Academic language, discourse communities, and technology: Building students' linguistic resources. *Teacher Education Quarterly, Special Online Edition*. Retrieved from http://teqjournal.org/townsend_lapp.html

Valdés, G. (2004). The teaching of academic language to minority second language learners. In A. F. Ball & S. W. Freedman (Eds.), *Bakhtinian perspectives on language, literacy, and learning* (pp. 66-98). Cambridge, England: Cambridge University Press.

Zwiers, J. (2007). Teacher practices and perspectives for developing academic language. *International Journal of Applied Linguistics, 17*(1), 93-116.

CHAPTER 3

PEDAGOGICAL LANGUAGE KNOWLEDGE AND THE INSTRUCTION OF ENGLISH LEARNERS

Audrey Lucero

The number of language minority children in our nation's public schools has grown tremendously over the past 20 years, and continues to increase annually. More than one in nine children nationwide qualified for ESL (English as a Second Language) services due to low English proficiency in 2008 (Goldenberg, 2008). These children speak more than 400 different home languages, and have varied schooling experiences, but more than 50% of qualified ELL (English language learner) students were born in the United States and nearly 80% speak Spanish at home (Capps, Fix, Murray, Passel, & Herwantoro, 2005). At all grade levels, Spanish-speaking ELL students compare unfavorably with native English speakers on tests such as the National Assessment of Educational Progress (NAEP) and state standardized tests (Cadelle Hemphill, Vanneman, & Rohman, 2011). They also do poorer in school and exhibit higher dropout rates than children from other immigrant groups (Rumberger & Rodríguez, 2011; Suárez-Orozco, Suárez-Orozco, & Todorova, 2008).

Academic Language in Second Language Learning, pp. 57–81

Multiple studies have underscored the importance of proficiency in *academic language*—the academic register of spoken and written language necessary to participate in the literate community of school—for the success of ELL children (Arreaga-Mayer & Perdomo-Rivera, 1996; Bunch, 2011; Freeman, 2000; Zwiers, 2008). However, we currently know little about how classroom teachers instructionally support academic language development or how teacher educators can prepare them to do so. This dearth of information stands in contrast to abundant research on general schoolwide practices that facilitate learning for ELL children (August & Hakuta, 1997; Faltis & Valdés, 2011; Goldenberg, 2008; Miramontes, Nadeau, & Commins, 1997), such that prominent scholars have begun conceptualize the specialized knowledge base that teachers of language minority learners need and to suggest ways for teacher education to address this need (Enright, 2011; Faltis, Arias, & Ramírez-Martín, 2010; Fillmore & Snow, 2002; Galguera, 2011; Harper & deJong, 2009). Galguera (2011) referred to this specialized knowledge base as "pedagogical language knowledge" and recognized it as a variation on the widely known construct of pedagogical content knowledge (Shulman, 1987), mirroring work that has been done in disciplines such as science and math (Bausmith & Barry, 2011).

In this chapter, I expand upon the notion of pedagogical language knowledge by reporting findings from a qualitative case study that investigated how teachers in one urban elementary school instructionally supported the academic language development of Spanish-speaking first graders, as well as the challenges they faced in doing so. I argue that elementary teachers of language minority students need pedagogical language knowledge, and therefore I suggest both theoretical and practical implications of these findings for the preservice preparation of elementary teachers

ACADEMIC LANGUAGE AND ITS DEVELOPMENT

I define academic language as the language that students need to understand and produce in order to be successful in school (Cummins, 2000; J. Gibbons & Lascar, 1998; P. Gibbons, 1993; Goldenberg, 2008; Scarcella, 2003; Stahl & Nagy, 2006). It encompasses content-specific vocabulary (Echevarría, Vogt, & Short, 2008; Goldenberg, 2008); complex grammatical structures (Cummins, 2003; Stahl & Nagy, 2006); morphological word parts (Echevarría et al., 2008); and linguistic features specific to particular academic disciplines (Cummins, 2000; Scarcella, 2003). Academic language is challenging for language minority students because it draws on vocabulary, sentence structures, and rhetorical forms that are not usually encountered in nonacademic settings.

Differences between conversational and academic language in school contexts also go beyond linguistic form and are heavily dependent on context, first in terms of the environmental support available for communication and second in terms of how people participate in various communities (Bunch, 2004; Gutierrez, 1993; Stahl & Nagy, 2006; Valdés, Bunch, Snow, Lee, & Matos, 2005). On the first point, Cummins' (1991, 2000, 2003) work has been highly influential. He conceptualized communication as existing along a continuum from context-embedded to context-reduced. In reality, of course, communication in school occurs all along the continuum, and rarely exists exclusively at one end or the other (C. E. Snow, 1987). Language that is more context-reduced, however, may be conceptually abstract as well as linguistically dense, including reference to people, events, or concepts that are not present or observable (J. Gibbons & Lascar, 1998; Goldenberg, 2008; Stahl & Nagy, 2006).

A second issue related to context is how proficiency enables someone to become part of a literate culture (Stahl & Nagy, 2006), to join the literacy club (Han & Ernst-Slavit, 1999; Smith, 1985). Speakers must understand the social requirements to participate in particular conversations or activities. In other words, "academic English arises not just from knowledge of the linguistic code ... but also from social practices in which academic English is used to accomplish communicative goals ... the particular conventions and norms that characterize the people who use it" (Scarcella, 2003, p. 29).

The distinction between conversational and academic language proficiency is sometimes confused as the difference between spoken and written language. It is true, particularly in primary classrooms, that spoken language is typically highly contextualized, but class discussions can be just as conceptually demanding as written work, and they may be more or less contextually supported. Even in primary classrooms, there are many situations that require children to have a solid grasp of academic language that is embedded in social language (C. E. Snow, 1987). Therefore, "it is clear that the contextualized/decontextualized distinction is not the same as the oral/written distinction" (Stahl & Nagy, 2006, p. 38).

Understanding these multiple elements of academic language can be difficult for classroom teachers who have little formal preparation in language acquisition and the social and academic dimensions of language, although they likely recognize the need for such knowledge. Recent research suggests that teachers need to have a much greater understanding of how the various genres of academic content interact with the language of texts and classroom discourse, one that takes them beyond an emphasis on vocabulary development and a focus on grammar. (Faltis et al., 2010, p. 321)

In this chapter, I argue that teachers' needs go beyond understanding language and into instructional practices that support social and academic language development.

INSTRUCTIONAL MOVES THAT
FACILITATE ACADEMIC LANGUAGE DEVELOPMENT

There are multiple challenges facing teacher educators who prepare teachers to support academic language development in classroom settings. One of the biggest obstacles teacher educators face is that, "no single approach or method has been proven effective in developing students' proficiency in all oral and written manifestations of academic language" (Galguera, 2011, p. 90). Galguera and others argue that the field should concentrate its efforts on preparing teachers to understand the functions that language plays in school settings (P. Gibbons, 1993; Schleppegrell, 2004). While the ability to analyze language demands is critical, I contend that it is important to pay equal attention to the actual instructional repertoire of approaches and methods teachers use to facilitate academic language development.

In a recent qualitative content analysis, Faltis and colleagues (2010) identified nine teacher competencies deemed essential for the education of ELL students. These competencies are framed in terms of what teachers both need to know and what they need to do. However, only two of the competencies could be considered instructional moves per se: "use small-group work and heterogeneous grouping of English learners and English speakers," and "direct students' attention to language forms" (p. 313). The others relate more to teacher knowledge or the process of coordinating and preparing for instruction (i.e., understand BICS/CALP distinction; use multiple assessments).

In contrast, in this study I investigated five instructional moves from second language and academic language theory and research on the premise that understanding their use could provide a framework for further theorizing pedagogical language knowledge. These moves were: simultaneous focus on language and content; instructional scaffolding; dialogic interactions; varying the amount of context; and providing explicit instruction of language.

Simultaneous Focus on Content and Language

It has generally gone uncontested in ESL education that language and content should be combined for instructional purposes (García, 1996; P. Gibbons, 2002; Lyster, 2007). Nevertheless, Bigelow and Ranney (2005) argued that the field has not adequately defined effective content and language integration, and proposed a set of criteria for such integration: "(1) the language instruction is contextualized in content; (2) the tasks in the lesson require that the form be used appropriately; (3) the language lesson fits with overall curriculum" (p. 185). However well established these are in principal, however, there has not yet been empirical research investigating how mainstream classroom teachers actually integrate the two disparate goals, especially if they are not knowledgeable about language acquisition.

Linguistic Scaffolding

It is widely accepted that young children need to be immersed in language and print-rich environments in which reading, writing and conversation are used for authentic purposes. However, it is also increasingly clear that simply immersing ELL students in such an environment is not enough (Freeman, 2004). Students also need frequent opportunities to engage in meaningful interaction with more proficient speakers of the target language (Genesee, Lindholm-Leary, Saunders, & Christian, 2006; P. Gibbons, 2002; Téllez & Waxman, 2006). The concept of linguistic scaffolding is particularly salient in terms of how teachers integrate "the current level of learners' knowledge and L2 abilities, and the broader knowledge and specialist language of the (academic) community into which the students are being apprenticed" (P. Gibbons, 2003, pp. 249-250).

The relationship between the language teachers use and that which students use can be conceptualized in terms of the zone of proximal development (Vygotsky, 1978)—too close a match between teachers and students would not provide students access to unknown language, while too large a difference might not enable students to understand at all (P. Gibbons, 2003). Students also need to use longer stretches of language where there is a 'press' on their linguistic abilities. This study investigated how teachers created classroom contexts that were facilitative of academic language learning by providing the appropriate scaffolding at the appropriate time.

Dialogic Interactions

Dialogic interactions are structured conversations facilitated by the teacher. Such discussions may take place as a whole class or in small groups, but they have as a defining feature that student contributions determine the course of the interaction to some extent (P. Gibbons, 2006; Haneda & Wells, 2008). They differ from the traditional IRF pattern in that teachers pose open-ended questions rather than those with pre-scribed answers and that their primary goal is to help students elaborate, articulate, and clarify their ideas; this makes them a fruitful venue for oral academic language development.

Movement Along the Context Continuum

There is evidence that the level of success language minority students achieve in developing academic language depends to a large extent on how contextualized their early instruction on a given topic is (P. Gibbons, 2002). At the most context-embedded level, small group interactions early in a lesson or unit permit students to understand key concepts in everyday, practical language. Later lessons could challenge children's thinking and also move them toward clear and appropriate decontextual-ized uses of language, often in the form of written work (Freeman, 2004; Lyster, 2007; Stahl & Nagy, 2006). Written work typically occupies the least contextualized spot on the continuum, as it reports on generaliza-tions rather than the specifics of any given experiment.

Explicit Instruction of Language

A final instructional move that may be significant for academic lan-guage development is explicit attention to language itself (Faltis et al., 2010). Goldenberg (2008) noted that, "effective second language instruc-tion provides ... explicit teaching that helps students directly and effi-ciently learn features of the second language such as syntax, grammar, vocabulary, pronunciation, and norms of social usage" (p. 13). To make connections between language and content explicit, teachers can give stu-dents frequent opportunities to investigate the language of academic texts in order to learn how various discourse communities use language and to learn to use decontextualized language (Freeman, 2004). Some scholars have argued that explicit instruction of linguistic forms and structures is one of the most effective ways to help second language learners acquire academic language (Fillmore & Snow, 2002).

METHODOLOGY

This chapter recounts findings from a qualitative case study of a team of first grade teachers over one school year. Data was collected during the 2009-2010 academic year in an urban public K-5 elementary school in the Pacific Northwest, Hurley Heights International School.[1] Approximately 25% of the school's 440 students spoke Spanish as a first language, and an additional 40% spoke other languages—notably Cantonese and Vietnamese. Forty-two percent of students received ESL services, and 69% were eligible for free and reduced lunch. It had the second largest ESL population in the district, and a dual immersion Spanish program.

Participants were selected using purposeful sampling methods (Glesne, 2006; Merriam, 1998; Patton, 2002) and included: first grade Spanish and English-medium teachers; the principal; a school-level ESL specialist; and a district-level ELL consulting teacher.

Señora Molly Gregor was the Spanish-medium classroom teacher and was in her second year of teaching at Hurley Heights. She taught literacy and social studies to kindergarten and first grade. She provided all instruction in Spanish. She was relatively new to teaching young children, but had almost 10 years of experience as a high school Spanish teacher in a nearby district. She was a White, native English speaker. The unit I observed in her class was a social studies unit on culture, which was developed by her and other teachers and incorporated a number of elements from GLAD (Guided Language Acquisition Design), a language-focused strategy program that is widely used throughout the district and school. This was the first time Sra. Gregor had taught this unit, which consisted of 10 lessons over 3 weeks.

Mr. Brad Riley was in his seventh year of teaching at Hurley Heights. He had previously taught third and fourth grade at the school, and had experience teaching second grade at another school in the district prior to that. He shared his job with another teacher, and was only responsible for teaching math and science. He was a White, monolingual English speaker who conducted all instruction in English. He had little formal knowledge about language acquisition, but had many questions and concerns about the language development of his students. He expressed frustration about his lack of knowledge and did not feel like he had anyone to ask. The unit I observed in his class was from the district inquiry-based science curriculum and focused on balls and ramps. It consisted of fourteen lessons, and I observed the first nine, which focused on balls and their properties. Mr. Riley taught those nine lessons in 23 sessions over 6 weeks. He had taught the unit every year since moving to first grade, so the content was very familiar to him, and he felt comfortable teaching it.

Ms. Rebecca Cortez had been teaching first grade at Hurley Heights for 7 years. Before that, she had several years of experience as a fourth grade teacher in the same district. She was a White, native English-speaker who was married to a Mexican man. She conducted her class primarily in English, but frequently used her low-intermediate Spanish to clarify and reinforce concepts for the Spanish-speaking children in her class. The unit I observed was from the Everyday Math curriculum. The unit consisted of eight lessons, which Ms. Cortez taught in 11 sessions over 3 weeks.

DATA COLLECTION AND ANALYSIS

Three primary sources of data informed this study: classroom, professional development, and meeting observations; semistructured interviews; and relevant documents. I conducted the study as a participant-observer (Becker & Geer, 1969; Emerson & Pollner, 2001), but the degree to which I participated in classroom activities varied throughout the year depending on immediate circumstances. I was most likely to engage with students during small group activities.

Because I wanted to explore how teachers scaffolded academic language over time and provided instruction along the context continuum, I observed entire units rather than only individual lessons. This enabled me to observe changes in the teachers' instruction as children became more proficient in the register of the content area and in academic language overall. The theoretical importance of observing sequences of lessons has been articulated in the research (Ball, Thames, & Phelps, 2008; Christie, 1995; P. Gibbons, 2003; Lin, 1993).

In my observation I focused on key events such as whole group instruction, interactions with individual students, and the facilitation of small group work. Bunch (2004) makes the compelling argument that focusing on group interactions allows researchers to gather information about language norms and opportunities for both ELL and English-proficient students as they learn academic language together. All observations were audiorecorded and I took descriptive written field notes (Dyson & Genishi, 2005). I often also audiorecorded postobservation reflections, which went beyond objectivity in the direction of perception and interpretation.

I conducted initial interviews with all participants in October 2009 to get an overview of their understanding of academic language and its development in young language minority students (Brenner, 2006; Seidman, 2006). Interviews were semi-structured using prepared interview guides (Patton, 2002). In addition, the three focal teachers were interviewed either once or twice more, usually at the beginning and end of their unit. The school-level ESL specialist was interviewed twice during the course of the study, but declined to be audiorecorded.

Finally, I collected fifty documents relevant to my research questions. These documents ranged from instructional and professional development materials to samples of student writing, and included materials given to me by all participants.

I engaged in ongoing analysis throughout the data collection period, in addition to conducting a focused analysis upon leaving the field (Glaser & Strauss, 1967). I began by open coding to identify emerging patterns related to teachers' instruction of academic language (Emerson, Fretz, & Shaw, 1995). In line with my research design, I only coded and counted the five instructional moves that fit my theoretical framework. At the whole class level, I coded all relevant instructional moves whether they were specifically targeted at Spanish speakers or not. At the pair and small group level, I only analyzed instruction the teacher provided to pairs or small groups that had Spanish speakers in them. I also conducted quantitative counts of each type of instructional move teachers made during classroom observations. Finally, I conducted member checks, sharing analytic memos with participants as appropriate and to the extent that they were interested (Brenner, 2006; Merriam, 1998).

FINDINGS

The first grade teachers at Hurley Heights undertook each of the five practices at different times and with varying degrees of confidence. Table 3.1 shows the total number of instructional moves that were coded for each teacher, as well as the mean number observed per session and per hour. I present the data in this way because simply counting the total number of moves would not be sufficient to understand teacher practice. For example, I observed more than twice as many hours in Mr. Riley's class as I did in either Sra. Gregor's or Ms. Cortez's (see Table 3.1), so it is not surprising that I observed many more instances of his academic language instruction.

Conversely, the table also shows that Sra. Gregor had both the lowest number of coded moves overall and the lowest mean number per hour. This data is somewhat deceptive because her classes tended to include more small group work and were less teacher-centered than those of Ms. Cortez, whose instruction was typically highly teacher-directed. I highlight other examples and give a more detailed analysis of these differences in the sections that follow.

Table 3.1.   Coded Instructional Moves by Teacher

	Total Number of Coded Moves	Mean Number of Coded Moves Per Session	Mean Number of Coded Moves Per Hour
Sra. Gregor	72	7.2 ($N = 10$)	10.8 (6.66 hours)
Mr. Riley	233	16.6 ($N = 14$)	16.6 (14 hours)
Ms. Cortez	156	19.5 ($N = 8$)	29.3 (5.33 hours)

"Go-to" Moves

In general, the teachers in this study were aware of their own level of understanding about academic language development and thoughtful about the limitations of the instruction they provided to Spanish-speaking students. However, it became apparent through both interviews and analysis of their practice that each teacher had moves they felt comfortable using to support academic language, and used those more frequently and confidently than others.

As Table 3.2 shows, the most widely used instructional move by far was linguistic scaffolding. All three teachers commonly provided linguistic scaffolding either in print or spoken form, for both specific vocabulary and for sentence structures.

I did not consider linguistic scaffolding to be any of the teachers' "go to" move, however, for several reasons.[2] I do not mean to suggest by this omission that linguistic scaffolding is not an important instructional practice, but simply that I found my analysis of "go to" moves to be richer when I attended to the other four moves instead. In the next few sections I describe and explain "go to" patterns of instruction for each teacher.

Señora Gregor

Of the three focal teachers, Señora Gregor most consistently provided instruction that integrated content and language goals (see Table 3.2). She felt strongly about the need for students to produce more, and more sophisticated, language as the unit and school year progressed. Therefore, she undertook instructional practices that were designed to support students as they participated in whole class and small group discussions. For example, she wanted students to be able to both define *cultura* and use it in appropriate descriptive sentences—"una oración completa con una letra mayuscula y un periodo" ["a complete sentence with a capital letter and a period"]. The following exchange, which occurred in a small group on the second day of the unit, illustrates this dual focus on content and language:

**Table 3.2. Percentage of Different Types of
Instructional Moves by Teacher**

	Total Number of Coded Moves	Integration of Content and Language	Dialogic Interactions	Movement Along the Context Continuum	Explicit Instruction	Linguistic Scaffolding
Sra. Gregor	72	36%	10%	17%	5%	32%
Mr. Riley	233	10%	10%	21%	2%[a]	57%
Ms. Cortez	156	18%	6%	26%	4%	46%
Overall (average)	461	(21%)	(9%)	(21%)	(4%)	(45%)

a. All of the Explicit instruction codes for Mr. Riley were negative, indicating that he was not explicit when I thought he could have been and it would have been beneficial to students.

Sra. Gregor:	(to small group): Cuál es una oración con la palabra *cultura*? Quién puede pensar en una oración completa?
Alicia:	Yo me como cereal para …
Abigail:	… antes de la escuela.
Abigail:	Sí, antes de la escuela.
Sra. Gregor:	Pero yo no escuché la palabra *cultura* … ustedes tienen que pensar en una oración con la palabra *cultura* en la oración, y 'como cereal antes de la escuela' no tiene la palabra *cultura*.
[Sra. Gregor:	What is a sentence with the word culture? Who can think of a complete sentence?
Alicia:	I eat cereal …
Abigail:	… before school.
Alicia:	Yes, before school.
Sra. Gregor:	But I didn't hear the word culture … you need to think of a complete sentence with the word culture in it, and "I eat cereal before school' doesn't have the word culture in it."]

This example illustrates how Sra. Gregor worked to elicit more oral language from children, which she considered one of her main responsibilities. It suggests that as a knowledgeable and experienced language teacher, she understood both the receptive and productive dimensions of language acquisition.

Despite this high level of awareness, however, Sra. Gregor struggled to fit both kinds of instruction into a limited amount of time. She explained the difficulty she had in prioritizing language development in the following way: "It seems simple, but a lot of times, for the sake of the time or the way that it's flowing, you say, 'oh, and who has been to California?' and kids say 'me! Me!' so I just write down their names instead of having them say 'I have been to California.'" Given that she was the most knowledgeable of the teachers about the role of language in learning, the difficulty she experienced in enacting instruction was notable.

Mr. Riley

In contrast to Señora Gregor, Mr. Riley's primary means of providing academic language instruction was by modeling its use in context-embedded interactions prior to moving to context-reduced ones (see Table 3.2). He saw it as his primary responsibility to, "show them (the students) that it works, model for them, and have them repeat it." In my observations of his instruction, I noted that he did frequently model academic language and make it accessible for students. For example, he often paraphrased general academic terms as in "how could you *describe* ... how could you *talk about* ... what could you *say* about these different kinds of balls?" or "What *affects* how it rolls? What *makes it* roll well or makes it roll not so well?"

In half of the lessons I observed, he followed an inquiry cycle similar to that described by Gibbons (2006). I considered this to be evidence of movement along the context continuum (Cummins, 1991, 2000) in the sense that he first introduced new language in a highly contextualized way, often using word cards, charts, and concrete materials like balls along with language. Then he guided students through pair and small group investigations to learn new information about the key concepts of the unit. Finally, he pulled students back together as a class to reflect on their learning. This process often resulted in the generation of new understandings about scientific concepts, if not always the use of more language without the support of here-and-now contexts.

In order to concretely illustrate this movement along the context continuum, I present here an in-depth analysis of one lesson taught during the 9th and 10th sessions of the unit. The focus of the sessions was on comparing the bounciness of two balls. Mr. Riley began the first session by reviewing with the whole class the definition of a "good bouncer" they had formulated the day before: a ball that bounces a lot of times. He then introduced the focus question from the district instructional manual, "How can we measure the bounciness of balls to find the best bouncer?" He then explained the notion of a fair test and modeled examples of unfair tests in order to solicit student ideas about fair test criteria. At this stage, he was the one who recontextualized students' contributions, as shown in the exchanges below:

Mr. Riley:	What did I do wrong in my test?
Erash:	Because you put the ping pong ball so up high and then you put the small rubber ball so down.
Mr. Riley:	So what could I have done to make this more … fair? What could I have done to make this more fair?
Erash:	By maybe putting them both down or putting them both up high.
Mr. Riley:	So I can't just drop them from anywhere. I have to make sure that I drop them from the same …
Student:	Height.
Mr. Riley:	The same height. The same distance from the ground. Okay. So I'm going to do a little change here. I'm not just going to say drop it. I'm going to say I have to drop it … from the same … drop from the same height.

(later in the same conversation)

Cyrus:	You need to do one only on the table, or actually, you should do both on the table and both, or both on the carpet.
Mr. Riley:	Okay, so we need to do them both … on the same surface.

These examples highlight the way in which Mr. Riley recontextualized students' contributions at the introductory stage of a lesson. He rephrased Erash's suggestion as "dropping them from the same height." Likewise, he rephrased Cyrus' contribution as a general statement about the need to bounce both balls on the same surface. This recontextualization was a frequent instructional move made by Mr. Riley, and lined up closely with his belief about the importance of modeling academic language.

Next, Mr. Riley thought aloud as he modeled conducting the investigation and completing a T-chart with the data from three trials. He then sent students off in pairs to conduct their own investigation. To conclude the first session of this lesson, the whole class met back at the rug with their recorded T-chart data in hand. Mr. Riley guided pairs as they orally added their data to a double line plot chart in order to establish which of the two balls was the better bouncer. This discussion presented an opportunity for increased linguistic complexity, as students were asked to explain their interpretation of the class data set. However, as the following examples from that discussion show, Mr. Riley did not provide enough press on student answers to truly increase the academic language demand:

Mr. Riley:	Did anybody notice anything about our line plot there? Xavier?

| Xavier: | Um, that, I found that it looked like the, um, the small rubber ball, um, bounced less. |
| Mr. Riley: | Bounced fewer times. Bounced less. |

(later in the same discussion)

Mr. Riley:	What else did you notice, Beatriz? (pause) Anything about how the ping pong ball, the small rubber ball, which one seemed to bounce more?
Beatriz:	Small rubber ball.
Mr. Riley:	Seemed to be more bouncy? Okay.

In these exchanges, Mr. Riley filled in most of the critical information himself, thus reducing the productive academic language demand on students. In the second session (the next day), he had students write in their science journals about the previous day's investigation. Theoretically, writing "relies primarily on linguistic cues to meaning, and … heavily on knowledge of the language itself" (Cummins, 2000, p. 68). To support students in this context-reduced task, Mr. Riley modeled completing a cloze paragraph on the whiteboard. When students went to independent writing time, the same paragraph was available at their tables so they could copy it, inserting terms as appropriate.

When I asked Mr. Riley about his reasons for structuring the lesson in this way, he said, "that was where I was like, oh my gosh, we don't understand any of the vocabulary, so what I'm going to do is I'm going to write a whole paragraph and you're just going to put in the word." He did not ultimately feel that the writing portion of the lesson was successful, however, explaining that "the problem was that … it was not as meaningful to them because it was just filling in the blank, just using one word. They weren't doing the connecting on their own."

This detailed description of one lesson elucidates the ways in which Mr. Riley sought to move his instruction along a context continuum both conceptually and linguistically, and why he thought it was important to do so. It also makes visible the challenges he faced as he attempted to address the language needs of his first grade Spanish-speaking students in science.

Ms. Cortez

Of the three focal teachers, Ms. Cortez devoted the most energy to language-specific instructional moves, especially in the way she supported students in making their oral language and writing more explicit (see Tables 3.1 and 3.2). In our final interview, she explained the value she placed on students being able to explain their thinking in the following way: "I try to show them all the information that they know already in

their head, and how to say it. And then later how to write it and draw it."
Thus, she mindfully built opportunities for this kind of learning to occur
in her classroom. The way she did so was through instruction that moved
along the context continuum, especially as it related to the language skill
of defining. As Snow, Cancino, DeTemple, and Schley (1991) noted, good
definitions require "analyzing one's own knowledge of word meaning to
distinguish 'definitional' from incidental information about the target
concept, as well as control of the conventional form for giving definitions"
(p. 90). Much of Ms. Cortez's language-specific instruction was aimed at
helping students develop that control.

Ms. Cortez shared the "go to" move of manipulating context with Mr.
Riley, and like him, she often rephrased students' oral contributions into
more general language. Her overall approach to instruction along the context continuum, however, was very different than that of Mr. Riley in that she
pressed students to be as explicit as possible in their own language, rather
than doing the work herself. The primary venue she used for such instruction was a weekly center she facilitated with small, heterogeneous groups of
students. On one occasion she talked students through the process of developing an oral definition of a rectangle and then writing it out. Like Mr.
Riley, Ms. Cortez did not use the word "define." Rather, she told them they
were going to write an answer to the question "what is a rectangle?":

> "What is a rectangle? What *is* a rectangle? You know what, you've seen lots of
> rectangles. But when you are writing about your math thinking, how do you
> explain what a rectangle is?"

Her instruction in this example was also related to one of the purposes
for using language I discussed earlier—to be an expert on a given topic.
She began by providing written scaffolds in the form of a model math
journal page and a list of key content-specific terms. She then facilitated a
conversation with the small group about what they understood about the
defining features of rectangles. The group collaboratively developed an
description, and then each student wrote his or her own math journal
entry. Through this process, Ms. Cortez sought to help students improve
not only the explicitness of their writing but also to deepen their understanding of the shape. The following conversation from one group provides evidence of this two-pronged goal:

Ms. Cortez: What can you say, here, if this was the rectangle we were
             looking at right here, what can you say about this rectangle,
             Javier?
Javier C.:   Um, um, …
Ms. Cortez: It's a shape.

Javier C.:	It's long.
Ms. Cortez:	It's long? What's long? Ah, he said it's long.
Javier C.:	The shape.
Ms. Cortez:	Javier said it's long. Do you know what he means by that?
AL:	Long means it's bigger.
RC:	Bigger, but ... but I want him to be more clear. I want him to really explain what he's thinking. What is long about this rectangle, Javier? Is this long right here? (points to short side of a drawn rectangle) And this, is that long?
Javier C.:	Short.
Ms. Cortez:	Oh, that's short. So these two ... sides are short. But what's this?
Javier C.:	Long.
Ms. Cortez:	Is this the part you were talking about?
Javier C.:	Uh, yeah.
Ms. Cortez:	And how many sides are like that?
Javier C.:	(long pause) Two?
Ms. Cortez:	Two sides. Two sides are ...
Javier C:	Um ... long.
Ms. Cortez:	And two sides are ...
Javier C.:	Short.
Ms. Cortez:	Okay, can you say that to me, Javier? Two sides ...
Javier C.:	Two side is long, long and two is ... short.

The math journal entries that Spanish-speaking students produced as a result of this conversation also closely approach what Snow and colleagues (1989, 1991) would characterize as a formal definition. Entries included:

> "a rectangle is a long shape an it has 4 sads"
> "A rectangle es a shape what has 4 angles and 4 sides"
> "A rectangle is a shape that has four corners and four angles and it is long and it is straight and it is sort of a polygon and it is a kind of square and 2 sides are long and the other two are short."

Clearly students were at different levels of English language proficiency and understanding of the essential elements of rectangles, but the fact that they were all able to write accurate (if incomplete) definitions after targeted contextualized instruction speaks to the influence of Ms. Cortez's "go to" move on her students. Specifically, students were able to write definitions that included only essential features of rectangles in a recognizable definitional structure.

Infrequently Used Moves

There were two instructional moves that were infrequently used by all three teachers: dialogic interactions and the explicit instruction of language, which together accounted for only about thirteen percent of all coded instructional moves (see Table 3.2).

Dialogic Interactions

Dialogic interactions were those in which teachers enacted conversations with clear academic goals with one or several students. Such interactions are designed to elicit student thinking and support their oral expression of that thinking (P. Gibbons, 2006; Goldenberg, 1991; Tharp & Gallimore, 1991). They are important because, "a classroom program that is supportive of second language learning must ... create opportunities for more varied and dialogic interactional patterns to occur" (P. Gibbons, 2002, p. 17).

Although I observed many instances of teachers leading discussions, they often fell short of true dialogic interactions because teachers did not press students enough to gauge or enrich learning. It seemed that knowing when and how to press on students' language ability was difficult. Mr. Riley, for example, felt strongly that language minority students should not be pushed to participate orally in the whole class context until they were ready to do so. In practice, this meant that he did not typically have extended interactions with students who struggled with English. The following exchange provides one of many examples in which Mr. Riley abandoned a potential dialogic interaction with Javier T., a struggling Spanish-speaker:

Mr. Riley: What else could affect how it bounces? Any of these properties. Javier, what do you think?
Javier T.: Size.
Mr. Riley: The size. So do big balls bounce well and small ba ... tell me more.
Javier T: Size ... (long pause). Um, I forgot.
Mr. Riley: Okay. Can we come back to you? Do you want to tell us, maybe think more about how the size affects it?

This interaction began with an open-ended question that could have been conducive to a dialogic interaction. However, it stopped short of being so because of Mr. Riley's unwillingness to push Javier beyond his current level of proficiency. Despite his suggestion that he would return to Javier later in the lesson to give him a chance to share, he did not. The exchange also shows linguistic scaffolding that did not fall within the student's zone of proximal development. Rather, the interaction kept Javier squarely within his comfort zone.

The same was true of Ms. Cortez' instruction. Outside of the weekly center mentioned earlier, she used dialogic interactions infrequently. She was the very conscious about the need for children to use oral language as much as possible, but her instruction tended to be heavy on teacher talk such that she often left little room for extended student contributions. On only a few occasions did she engage the class in lengthy conversations that could be considered dialogic.

Explicit Instruction of Language

Dutro and Moran (2003) and others have argued that metalinguistic awareness arises as a result of explicit teaching of language: "through instruction that makes explicit the tools needed for different academic language functions, students learn the vocabulary and sentence structures needed for a range of cognitive tasks and uses of language" (p. 234). In interviews, my focal teachers emphasized the importance of intentionality and explicitness in providing academic language instruction, but in practice, I rarely observed them explaining academic language to children beyond modeling its use. This suggests that even though these teachers were aware of some of the language needs of their students, they struggled to enact supportive instruction. Sra. Gregor, for example, was knowledgeable about second language development but new to working with young children and teaching content in addition to language. She provided various forms of linguistic scaffolding and much instruction that could be considered supportive of oral language development, but this infrequently meant explicit instruction. For his part, Mr. Riley was less convinced of the need to be explicit about language, or how he might go about doing so. He said that there were certain language "protocols" he wanted his students to understand, but when I asked him how he communicated important aspects of those protocol to them, he said "mostly by modeling the correct usage because, um … the sort of meta doesn't, they're not really into that … and it doesn't seem like it's developmentally appropriate."

IMPLICATIONS FOR PEDAGOGICAL LANGUAGE KNOWLEDGE

In this chapter, I seek to contribute to the growing pedagogical language knowledge base by providing qualitative data from three experienced teachers as they used their knowledge of academic language and instruction to support Spanish-speaking students' learning. Moving beyond the descriptive, I now echo Galguera's (2011) question of what these findings tell us about "how to foster clear and explicit links between theory and practice among preservice teachers" (p. 102). The findings from this study lead me to conclude that teacher education courses need to present theoretical and practical knowledge about academic language in an integrated way so that teachers are able to define it, identify it in their curricula, and plan and teach lessons accordingly. Three recommendations I propose as a result of this study are:

First, teacher education courses need to help teachers understand the multiple elements of academic language. Teachers in my study had differing depths of knowledge with regards to its components, social purposes, and cognitive dimensions, but the instructional moves they made were generally consistent with the beliefs and understandings they expressed. Practically, this meant that each of them had a relatively small repertoire of instructional moves they felt comfortable using rather than being able to flexibly use multiple strategies. For example, they privileged complete sentences over one-word answers, but had little awareness of what actually constituted the specialized academic language of their content areas, which some have considered critical knowledge for teachers (Gebhard, Harman, & Seger, 2007; Valdés et al., 2005). Therefore, they attempted to undertake dialogic interactions but were unable to follow through with them because they struggled to know exactly what they wanted students to say or how to guide them within their zones of proximal development. This highlights to the need for teachers to understand first and second language development, which Faltis et al. (2010) also found in their study. For example, Mr. Riley was concerned about the social well-being of his students, but a better understanding of the need for productive language use in developing a second language might have motivated him to press students more and provide appropriate support for them to be successful.

Second, pedagogical language knowledge requires that teachers be able to conduct linguistic analyses of their curricula because it is clear that, "content is not separate from the language through which it is presented" (Schleppegrell & Achugar, 2003, p. 21). My findings add to the argument that analyzing the language demands of a unit can be a productive first step to incorporating language into content teaching (Achugar, Schleppegrell, & Oteíza, 2007; Faltis et al., 2010). For Mr. Riley in particular, helping language minority children meet the language expectations of his unit was untenable given his inability to identify those demands. This was made all the more crucial by the fact that the district-provided curriculum materials (like others designed for mainstream English-speaking students) did a poor job of helping him decipher the purposes for using language in the unit. The teachers' manuals for both the science and geometry units used included suggestions for supporting language minority students, but they fell short of being truly useful resources because of their vagueness or because of teachers' limited ability to follow up on the suggestions.

Finally, a responsive teacher education program would explicitly teach pedagogical practices to develop academic language in concert with content learning. Since research has shown that the five instructional moves highlighted in this chapter may be effective, they provide a starting point for thinking about academic language instruction. In particular, the difficulty that teachers had in facilitating dialogic interactions and providing explicit instruction points to the kinds of practices that need to be especially supported in preservice teacher education.

AREAS FOR FUTURE RESEARCH

It is becoming increasingly common for university-based teacher education programs to offer (and in some cases even require) foundational and methods courses in second language acquisition and instruction. Therefore, a productive area for future research is to qualitatively and longitudinally follow new teachers graduating from such programs as they move into classroom placements and investigate how their practices are related to teacher education coursework. Will their practices look appreciably different from those of my focal teachers? What are the long-term academic language benefits to students of teacher education coursework in second language education, if any?

Additionally, Bigelow and Ranney (2005) have argued that the field has not adequately defined effective content and language integration in mainstream classrooms, and based on my study, I am inclined to agree. Like them, therefore, I argue that we need more qualitative research that brings us even closer to a clear set of measurable criteria for what constitutes effective instruction for academic language development. Designing research to address these questions can go a long way toward helping us incorporate meaningful coursework into teacher education programs, and to more fully flesh out the pedagogical language knowledge base proposed in this chapter.

NOTES

1. This and all other names are pesudonyms.
2. First, it was likely overrepresented in the data because it included written scaffolds such as charts, notes on the whiteboard, and sentence strips. For example, print scaffolding accounted for almost 50% of Sra. Gregor's coded moves. It also included instances of peer scaffolding such as when a more

proficient English-speaking partner clarified a concept for a Spanish-speaking peer in Spanish. Second, many instances of linguistic scaffolding occurred at the microlevel and therefore the code frequently overlapped with other instructional moves. An example of this would be when a teacher pressed for elaboration during a dialogic interaction. Third, micro level rephrasing, repetition, and prompting are somewhat natural behaviors for teachers and therefore were somewhat more likely than other instructional moves to be unconscious or unintentional on the part of the teacher.

REFERENCES

Achugar, M., Schleppegrell, M., & Oteíza, T. (2007). Engaging teachers in language analysis: A functional linguistics approach to reflective literacy. *English teaching: Practice and Critique, 6*(2), 8-24.

Arreaga-Mayer, C., & Perdomo-Rivera, C. (1996). Ecobehavioral Analysis of Instruction for At-Risk Language-Minority Students. *The Elementary School Journal, 96*(3), 245-258.

August, D., & Hakuta, K. (1997). Studies of school and classroom effectiveness *Improving schooling for language-minority students: A research agenda* (pp. 163-249). Washington, DC: National Academy Press.

Ball, D. L., Thames, M. H., & Phelps, G. (2008). Content knowledge for teaching: what makes it special? *Journal of Teacher Education, 59*(5), 389-407.

Bausmith, J. M., & Barry, C. (2011). Revisiting Professional Learning Communities to increase college readiness: The importance of pedagogical content knowledge. *Educational Researcher, 40*(4), 175-178.

Becker, H. S., & Geer, B. (1969). Participant observation and interviewing: A comparison. In G. J. McCall & J. L. Simmons (Eds.), *Issues in participant observation: A text and reader* (pp. 322-331). Reading, MA: Addison-Wesley.

Bigelow, M. H., & Ranney, S. E. (2005). Pre-service ESL teachers' knowledge about language and its transfer to lesson planning. In N. Bartels (Ed.), *Researching applied linguistics in language teachers education*. New York, NY: Springer.

Brenner, M. E. (2006). Interviewing in educational research. In J. L. Green, G. Camilli, & P. B. Elmore (Eds.), *Handbook of complementary methods in education research* (pp. 357-370). Mahwah, NJ: Erlbaum Associates.

Bunch, G. C. (2004). "But how do we say that?": Reconceptualizing academic language in linguistically diverse mainstream classrooms (PhD dissertation). Stanford University, Standford, California.

Bunch, G. (2011). Preparing mainstream secondary content-area teachers to facilitate English language learners' development of academic language. In C. J. Faltis & G. Valdés (Eds.), *Education, immigrant students, refugee students, and English learners* (Vol. 103, National Society for the Study of Education). New York, NY: Teachers College Press.

Cadelle Hemphill, F., Vanneman, A., & Y. Rahman. (2011). *Achievement gaps: How Hispanic and White students in public schools perform in mathematics and reading on* the *National Assessment of Education Progress*. Washington, DC: National Center for Education Statistics, Institute of Education Sciences.

Capps, R., Fix, M., Murray, J., Passel, J. S., & Herwantoro, S. (2005). *The new demography of America's schools: Immigration and the No Child Left Behind act*. Washington, DC: The Urban Institute.

Christie, F. (1995). Pedagogic discourse in the primary school. *Linguistics and Education, 7*, 221-242.

Cummins, J. (1991). Interdependence of first- and second-language proficiency in bilingual children. In E. Bialystok (Ed.), *Language processing in bilingual children* (pp. 70-89). Cambridge, England: Cambridge University Press.

Cummins, J. (2000). *Language, power, and pedagogy: Bilingual children in the crossfire*. Clevedon, England: Multilingual Matters.

Cummins, J. (2003). Reading and the bilingual student: Fact and friction. In G. G. Garcia (Ed.), *English learners: Reaching the highest level of English literacy* (pp. 2-33). Newark, DE: International Reading Association.

Dutro, S., & Moran, C. (2003). Rethinking English language instruction: An architectural approach. In G. G. García (Ed.), *English learners: Reaching the highest level of English literacy* (pp. 227-258). Newark, DE: International Reading Association.

Dyson, A. H., & Genishi, C. (2005). *On the case: Approaches to language and literacy research*. New York, NY: Teachers College Press.

Echevarría, J., Vogt, M., & Short, D. J. (2008). *Making Content Comprehensible for English Learners: The SIOP Model* (3rd ed.). Boston, MA: Pearson.

Emerson, R. M., Fretz, R. I., & Shaw, L. L. (1995). Processing fieldnotes: Coding and memoing *Writing ethnographic fieldnotes* (pp. 142-168). Chicago, IL: University of Chicago Press.

Emerson, R. M., & Pollner, M. (2001). Constructing participant/observation relations. In R. M. Emerson (Ed.), *Contemporary field research: Perspectives and formulations* (2nd ed.). Long Grove, IL: Waveland.

Enright, K. (2011). Language and literacy for a new mainstream. *American Educational Research Journal, 48*(1), 80-119.

Faltis, C., & Valdés, C. (Eds.). (2011). *Education, immigrant students, refugee students, and English learners*. National Society for the Study of Education (Vol. 103). New York, NY: Teachers College Press.

Faltis, C. J., Arias, M. B., & Ramírez-Martín, F. (2010). Identifying relevant competencies for secondary teachers of English learners. *Bilingual Research Journal, 33*(3), 307-328.

Fillmore, L. W., & Snow, C. E. (2002). What teachers need to know about language. In C. T. Adger, C. E. Snow, & D. Christian (Eds.), *What teachers need to know about language* (pp. 7-54). Washington, DC: Center for Applied Linguistics.

Freeman, R. D. (2000). Contextual challenges to dual-language education: A case study of a developing middle school program. *Anthropology & Education Quarterly, 31*(2), 202-229.

Freeman, R. D. (2004). *Building on community bilingualism*. Philadelphia, PA: Caslon.

Galguera, T. (2011). Participant structures as professional learning tasks and the development of pedagogical language knowledge among preservice teachers. *Teacher Education Quarterly, 38*(1), 85-106.

García, E. (1996). Preparing instructional professionals for linguistically and culturally diverse students. In J. P. Sikula, T. J. Buttery, & E. Guyton (Eds.), *Handbook of research on teacher education: A project of the Association of Teacher Educators* (pp. 801-813). New York, NY: MacMillan.

Gebhard, M., Harman, R., & Seger, W. (2007). Reclaiming recess: Learning the language of persuasion. *Language Arts, 84*(5), 419-430.

Genesee, F., Lindholm-Leary, K., Saunders, W. M., & Christian, D. (2006). *Educating English language learners: A synthesis of research evidence*. New York, NY: Cambridge University Press.

Gibbons, J., & Lascar, E. (1998). Operationalising academic language proficiency in bilingualism research. *Journal of Multilingual and Multicultural Development, 19*(1), 40-50.

Gibbons, P. (1993). *Learning to learn in a second language*. Portsmouth, NH: Heinemann.

Gibbons, P. (2002). *Scaffolding language, scaffolding learning: Teaching second language learners in the mainstream classroom*. Portsmouth, NH: Heinemann.

Gibbons, P. (2003). Mediating language learning: Teacher interactions with ESL students in a content-based classroom. *TESOL Quarterly, 37*(2), 247-273.

Gibbons, P. (2006). *Bridging discourses in the ESL classroom*. London, England: Continuum.

Glaser, B. G., & Strauss, A. L. (1967). *The discovery of grounded theory: Strategies for qualitative research*. Chicago, IL: Aldine.

Glesne, C. (2006). *Becoming qualitative researchers: An introduction* (3rd ed.). Boston, MA: Pearson.

Goldenberg, C. (1991). *Instructional conversations and their classroom applications*. Berkeley, CA: National Center for Research on Cultural Diversity and Second Language Learning.

Goldenberg, C. (2008, Summer). Teaching English language learners: What the research does—and does not—say. *American Educator*, 8-44.

Gutierrez, K. D. (1993). Biliteracy and the language-minority child. In B. Spodek & O. N. Saracho (Eds.), *Language and literacy in early childhood education* (pp. 82-101). New York, NY: Teachers College Press.

Han, J., & Ernst-Slavit, G. (1999). Come join the literacy club: One Chinese ESL child's literacy experience in a first grade classroom. *Journal of Research in Childhood Education, 13*(2), 144-154.

Haneda, M., & Wells, G. (2008). Learning an additional language through dialogic inquiry. *Language and Education, 22*(2), 114-136.

Harper, C., & deJong, E. (2009). English language teacher expertise: The elephant in the room. *Language and Education, 23*(2), 137-151.

Lin, L. (1993). Language of and in the classroom: Constructing the patterns of social life. *Linguistics and Education, 5*, 367-409.

Lyster, R. (2007). *Learning and teaching languages through content: A counterbalanced approach*. Amsterdam: John Benjamins.

Merriam, S. B. (1998). *Qualitative research and case study applications in education*. San Francisco, CA: Jossey-Bass.

Miramontes, O. B., Nadeau, A., & Commins, N. L. (1997). *Restructuring schools for linguistic diversity: Linking meaning to effective programs*. New York, NY: Teachers College Press.

Patton, M. Q. (2002). *Qualitative research and evaluation methods* (3rd ed.). Thousand Oaks, CA: SAGE.

Rumberger, R., & Rodríguez, G. (2011). Chicano Dropouts. In R. Valencia (Ed.). *Chicano school failure and success: Past, present and future* (pp. 76-96. New York, NY: Routledge.

Scarcella, R. (2003). *Academic English: A conceptual framework*. Santa Barbara, CA: Linguistic Minority Research Institute.

Schleppegrell, M. (2001). Linguistic features of the language of schooling. *Linguistics and Education, 12*(4), 431-459.

Schleppegrell, M., & Achugar, M. (2003). Learning language and learning history: A functional linguistics approach. *TESOL Journal, 12*(2), 21-27.

Schleppegrell, M. (2004). *The language of schooling: A functional linguistics perspective*. Mahwah, NJ: Lawrence Erlbaum Associates.

Seidman, I. (2006). *Interviewing as qualitative research* (3rd ed.). New York, NY: Teachers College Press.

Shulman, L. S. (1987). Knowledge and teaching: Foundations of the new reform. *Harvard Educational Review, 57*(1), 1-22.

Smith, F. (1985). *Reading without nonsense*. New York, NY: Teachers College Press.

Snow, C., Cancini, H., Gonzalez, P., & Shriberg, E. (1989). Giving formal definitions: An oral language correlate of school literacy. In D. Bloome (Ed.), *Classrooms and literacy* (pp. 233-249). Norwood, NJ: Ablex.

Snow, C. E. (1987). Beyond conversation: Second language learners' acquisition of description and explanation. In J. P. Lantolf & A. Labarca (Eds.), *Research in second language learning: Focus on the classroom*. Norwood, NJ: Ablex.

Snow, C. E., Cancino, H., DeTemple, J., & Schley, S. (1991). Giving formal definitions: a linguistic or metalinguistic skill? In E. Bialystok (Ed.), *Language processing in bilingual children* (pp. 90-112). Cambridge, England: Cambridge University Press.

Stahl, S. A., & Nagy, W. E. (2006). *Teaching word meanings*. Mahwah, NJ: Erlbaum.

Suárez-Orozco, C., Suárez-Orozco, M. M., & Todorova, I. (2008). *Learning a new land: Immigrant students in American society*. Cambridge, MA: Harvard University Press.

Téllez, K., & Waxman, H. C. (2006). A meta-synthesis of qualitative research on effective teaching practices for English language learners. In J. M. Norris & L. Ortega (Eds.), *Synthesizing research on language learning and teaching* (pp. 245-277). Philadelphia, PA: John Benjamins.

Tharp, R. G., & Gallimore, R. (1991). *The instructional conversation: Teaching and learning in social activity*. Berkeley, CA: National Center for Research on Cultural Diversity and Second Language Learning.

Valdés, G., Bunch, G., Snow, C., Lee, C., & Matos, L. (2005). Enhancing the development of students' language(s). In L. Darling-Hammond & J. Bransford

(Eds.), *Preparing teachers for a changing world: What teachers should learn and be able to do* (pp. 126-168). San Francisco, CA: Jossey-Bass.

Vygotsky, L. S. (1978). Interaction between learning and development *Mind in Society*. Cambridge, MA: Harvard University Press.

Zwiers, J. (2008). *Building academic language: Essential practices for content classrooms.* San Francisco, CA: Jossey-Bass.

SECTION II

ACADEMIC LANGUAGE IN LANGUAGE TEACHING

CHAPTER 4

EXPLORING ACADEMIC LANGUAGE IN EXEMPLARY BEGINNING TEACHERS THROUGH A CONSTRUCTIVIST INQUIRY APPROACH

**Barbara J. Merino, Al Mendle,
Rick Pomeroy, and M. Cecilia Gómez**

We explore how exemplary beginning teachers (EBTs) address academic language (AL) in their practice and describe how teacher educators informed by "constructivist" learning theory and a commitment to advocacy for equity through inquiry and reflection work to influence the professional development of beginning teachers in linking AL to the disciplines. We define exemplary as serving as an example or illustration of effective practices empirically derived, in this case via above average performance in a teaching assessment. This case study is nested within a 15 month credential/MA program serving between 225 to 300 post-baccalaureate students a year. The program has a long-standing commitment to using the tools of inquiry about teaching and learning as a pathway for the design of instruction responsive to students' needs in culturally/linguistically diverse settings. All students are placed in sites with

Academic Language in Second Language Learning, pp. 85–102

high numbers of English language learners (ELLs) and upon completion of the credential most work in highly diverse settings.

We outline how faculty shape instruction and practica to address (AL). We explore the influence of life history, discipline focus, instruction and program features on exemplary beginning teachers (EBTs) drawn from an elementary ($N = 55$) and a secondary cohort ($N = 56$) as they address the language demands of classroom tasks as seen through the Performance Assessment for California Teachers (PACT) PACT (www.pacttpa.org) consists of a teaching event, designed as a lesson cycle of three to five lessons. Responding to standardized prompts teacher credential candidates provide context information, plans, assessments, videotaped segments of instruction and write reflections on the lesson cycle and address AL in their responses. Through a standardized protocol, PACT is scored along the following dimensions: planning, instruction, assessment, reflection and academic language (Pechone & Chung, 2006). We discuss six illustrative cases to show approaches used to address AL across the disciplines in science, math and English language arts. Two of these cases, Alicia working in elementary math and Paula in secondary science are given a more focused treatment in this chapter. Here we briefly outline influences shaping these cases as reported by the EBTs and faculty and as inferred through an independent analysis of key program artifacts. Our main objective is to help to inform the meaning of highly qualified teachers in AL (Darling-Hammond & Youngs, 2002).

THEORETICAL FRAMEWORKS AND RELEVANT LITERATURE

Academic Language (AL): In relying on an integrated view of AL, we draw on several traditions that have shaped its instruction and assessment (Bunch, 2010; Hyland, 2004). Multiple views of AL have been proposed over the past 30 years (Valdés, 2004). Some scholars have given emphasis to the cognitive load and the degree of contextualization of the functions involved in school tasks. Others have targeted areas of language, most typically, academic vocabulary. Some have focused on the qualities of AL linked to the communication demands of the discipline, such as argument in scientific discourse (Lemke, 1990). In the tradition of ethnography of communication, AL has been studied most productively as a dynamic concept. We rely heavily on this approach, drawing from research from targeted disciplines, genres, and communities as resources but not as static entities (Bunch, 2010; Scarcella, 2003; Schleppegrell, 2004; Valdés, 2004).

Professional Development: Dall'Alba and Sandberg (2006) have challenged the dominant model of professional development representing the process as cumulative and stage-driven. They argue that because professional practice is situated in particular contexts with unique sociocultural norms, professionals as individual with complex life histories and experiences will develop in variable ways. They question discussing knowledge and beliefs as somehow separate from action. They propose "embodied understanding of practice" as an alternative theory for describing professional growth; "embodied" to capture how experiences in particular contexts shape practice and "understanding" to portray that individuals' vary in their perception about the nature of their role. This view suggests that teachers act out their understanding of practice as they participate in various contexts and disciplines. Clearly, personal experiences in learning other languages, in surmounting the challenge of learning in the discipline through a second language will also shape teachers' embodied understanding of their practice and perspectives on how to foster AL. Such understandings are important to consider as we address AL in each discipline. Probably one of the most important academic components of preservice education is the major. At the secondary level student teachers in this program typically have a major in their discipline and have had experience in addressing AL demands in the disicipline on their own. In some cases, most notably science and social science, student teachers might have a major in one of the disciplines addressed in their placement but not all. At the elementary level, most students do not major in math and must rely on their experiences with the discipline before college in most cases except for a single college level course in math as a prerequisite in this program.

Exemplary Teachers: The research on exemplary teachers has a long history in North American education. Faltis and Merino (1992) in a review of the literature on defining exemplary teaching in bilingual, multicultural classrooms explored four traditions: (a) the competency based tradition defined as standards or skills and knowledge based; (b) the teacher effectiveness or value added tradition drawn from analyses of teacher presage variables (eg. knowledge or experience), process variables (instructional strategies or behaviors) and student outcomes or process behaviors (c) the ethnographic or case study tradition and (d) the literary or folklore tradition. This analysis revealed that while there were some commonalities across traditions, each revealed some unique features and insights. Moreover, each tradition varied in the degree to which findings were generated through valid, rigorous procedures and in the power and clarity of the findings as these could be used to inform teacher education. The case study tradition has been shown to be especially powerful in offering student teachers multiple pathways for "being" an effective teacher in a variety of settings, disciplines and situations tackling specific learning goals. Wells (2001) offers an example of this genre through a collection of essays on building collaborative communities through inquiry across disciplines, grades and inquiry approaches.

Nomination Procedures: Typically exemplary teachers are nominated through a set of criteria and then observed and/or interviewed with a focus on unpacking how teachers plan, reflect, implement and investigate their teaching. Some researchers target teachers who reflect defined characteristics and experiences. Thus Michelle Foster (1989) used a community nomination approach to identify exemplary African American teachers who had taught in Black communities in segregated schools and who were perceived as effective teachers by parents. Almost all the teachers in this study lived in the communities in which they taught, knew students' families and interacted with them frequently. A more typical approach has been to target teachers nominated by school experts, most typically principals, usually using specific criteria. Peterson and McKay (2001) report on a study of 10 exemplary elementary first year teachers nominated for the E. Parr Teacher award by school district's superintendents in Alberta, Canada over a 21-year period. Criteria used in the nomination process included: (a) knowledge of learning styles (b) skill in using instructional and diagnostic assessments (c) communication skills (d) evidence of assisting students to develop a positive self-concept and (e) involvement in professional development, extracurricular and community activities. This study sought to determine what nominated teachers' beliefs about efficacious teacher education programs and to compare these beliefs to five models that predominate in research on teacher education (Calderhead & Shorrock, 1997). A very few studies have used students as the nominators for exemplary teachers and then compared nominated to typical teachers. Moskowitz (1976) conducted a study using this approach asking foreign language students to nominate exemplary foreign language teachers from their high school experiences. She found that nominated teachers performed in significantly different ways in the classroom when compared to "typical" or non-nominated teachers. To sum up then, the nomination protocol is one of the most critical decisions made in studies of exemplary teachers. Researchers vary a great deal in their approaches, the criteria used and in how they select nominators. The expert approach with criteria is the most frequent protocol but carries with it the burden of defining the criteria clearly and meaningfully. Nonetheless, nominators may vary in how they interpret or prioritize the criteria provided. Sampling can also play a role in influencing case selection. Nominees who vary in the number of years they have taught and in the contexts in which they have been teaching may represent historically or contextually biased exemplars.

METHODS

Case Selection: In this study we used a hybrid process using an empirical approach based on performance assessments and specified criteria that targeted academic language in the discipline and practices deemed pedagogically sound for the discipline and the context and students. First, scores were analyzed for each cohort and means were computed for by discipline and for the sample as a whole. All beginning teachers performing above the mean within their discipline were reviewed and discussed by the clinical supervisors in a focus group meeting. The meeting began with a general discussion of high performance for the cohorts of the targeted year and in comparison to previous years. Areas of general strength and weakness in performance were discussed. Teacher educators who are former experienced teachers in the targeted disciplines, have taught in linguistically and culturally diverse settings, teach methods courses and supervise student teachers were the nominators. After oral discussion of possible nominees in terms of all areas of performance, nominators were asked to focus especially on the domain of greatest strength and a discussion of high performance in AL. Nominations were then made in writing with areas of strength outlined to support each nomination. The secondary faculty working in each discipline made the final decision on whom to nominate (one per discipline) and the elementary faculty as a group made a decision on a slate of three.

    AL in the context and program: We define AL as the body of knowledge, strategies and skills necessary to accomplish the academic tasks of a specific discipline in a particular context at a particular point in time within a specified classroom community. Methods faculty explore the language demands of tasks via modeled demonstrations and on going feedback during supervision from their discipline perspective. These faculty who teach methods and supervise student teaching are all highly experienced teachers in the disciplines. They play a critical role in helping student teachers co-construct working definitions for AL in the field. Faculty teaching inquiry courses are typically former teachers who are actively engaged in research on teaching and learning in the disciplines. They present AL as informed by multiple traditions as well. At both the elementary and secondary levels, AL is addressed in a range of courses, including a course addressing effective teaching and English language learners (ELLs), literacy methods courses targeting reading and writing in the content areas, and methods courses in the disciplines. Each secondary program conducts a year-long methods course taught by an experienced teacher in that discipline. At the elementary level, students enroll in literacy, science, math, bilingual and social studies methods classes that target teaching and learning in the discipline including AL. AL is also addressed in the inquiry classes held in Year 1 and 2, when students explore an instructional approach or intervention. Student teachers at both elementary and secondary levels participate in two inquiry studies, a short-term assignment in the credential year and a two-quarter inquiry in their first year of teaching.

Overview of Data Sources: Principal data sources included: PACT student responses; PACT scored protocols for each case, PACT video clips; Notes/Protocol for the nomination discussion, written nomination for each case; Inquiry reports/theses; field notes for inquiry from Year 2; surveys (at exit and 2 years after completing the program); interview data from cases and their surpervisors; interview data with lead faculty teaching discipline methods and AL coursework; course syllabi.

In this chapter we use a nested case study design to investigate optimal cases (Patton, 2002) at the upper range across three disciplines: mathematics, English language arts and science (Alicia, Amelia and Kate, at elementary out of $N = 56$; Holly—English language arts—$N = 16$, Paula—science ($N = 16$) and Bob—math—$N = 10$). At the secondary, the total sample was $N = 66$. Agriculture, social studies and Spanish/foreign language students were not included in this study. We investigate the performance of these cases to determine how "language demands" are identified and scaffolded in the PACT lesson cycle completed during the credential year through a review by faculty teaching the methods classes. Briefly, we provide an overview of these six cases to illustrate AL across the disciplines. Next we conduct an independent review and present "Alicia" and "Paula", the elementary mathematics and science cases, as exemplars, demonstrating how they address AL in planning, instruction, assessment and reflection across a three day lesson cycle and over time as they move through the program. We then compare performance in other program artifacts, including surveys and interviews drawn from both the credential year and the first year of teaching and discuss what influences the work of "Alicia" and "Paula". A specific focus of this analysis is how key faculty working with them have identified and shaped their understandings of AL.

FINDINGS AND DISCUSSION

Discipline and Program: PACT performance levels in AL for all cohorts were generally lower than for other domains and mean performance ranged from 2.2 for English language arts—ELA ($N = 16$) at the secondary to 2.5 to 3.0 for elementary math and bilingual math on a scale of 1-4. Most EBTs attained ratings at the 3.0 level with some at the 4 level, most often in scaffolding to address language demands, one of the elements in AL in PACT (Table 4.1). Identifying language demands was generally the

**Table 4.1.   PACT Performance by Domain and
Element With Rationale for Cases***

Disc./Elem	Plan.	Instruct.	Assess.	Reflection	AL	Rationale
ELA—	3.6	3.5	3.0	3.0	3.0	AL "text to world
Holly	4	4	3	3	3	connections"—
	4	3	3	3	3	"access to literature
	3					at a deep level;
						evidence from text"
						Historical novel;
						Holocaust;
Science	3.0	3.0	2.5	3.0	2.5	"inquiry approach
Paula	3	3	3	3	2	to science—effect of
	3	3	2	3	3	mass on force"
	3					contextualized AL—
						"concepts, vocab &
						summary."
Math	3.6	2.5	3.5	2.5	2.5	"strongest
Bob	4	3	4	2	2	realization of
	4	2	3	3	3	constant daily
	3					assessment" AL as
						vocab. with
						effective use of
						"diagrams/pictures"
Math Elem.	2.7	3	3.5	4	2.5	"authentic practice
Alicia	3	3	4	4	2	combined with
2nd grade	2	3	3	4	3	realia & examples
34% IFEP	3					... actively engaged
						Ss understanding of
						= equals"
Amelia	3.7	3.5	3.5	3.5	3	"numerous scaffolds
5th gr. Dual	4	3	4	4	3	contextualized AL
Imm. Eng-	4	4	3	3	3	focus on concepts,
lish;	3					not just operations;
All EL or						initiated discovery
RFEP.						of cognates"
Kate	3	3	3	2.5	2.5	AL embedded
3rd grade;	3	3	3	2	2	"activities on angles
45% EL	3	3	3	3	3	with straws &
	3					gestures."

*Case names are pseudonyms as per IRB protocol.

most difficult element among both exemplary and typical beginning teachers. At the secondary, for the cohorts as a whole beginning teachers in disciplines with high language demands who had undergraduate preparation in language performed at higher levels; in ELA and social sciences in comparison to math and science, for example. At the elementary EBTs with bilingual preparation had the highest scores in AL. Here personal experience in developing proficiency in two languages combined with additional course work and experience with addressing language demands and opportunities to develop scaffolding techniques appeared to play a role in higher performance as reported by faculty and students. Students mentioned opportunities to observe expert bilingual teachers in the field, as well as techniques learned in methods and inquiry classes as factors that influenced their understanding of AL. A very strong influence in the understanding of math teaching and learning for all elementary EBTs included the math methods course. The Elementary Cohrot—"Alicia"—The role of the math methods course and AL. For Alicia this course exposed her to research on teaching and learning of mathematics that targeted math language not simply as vocabulary but also as discourse (Carpenter, Franke, & Levi, 2003). Her lesson cycle on developing a deep understanding of the term "equals" targeted authentic activities with realia to unpack students' misconceptions. The Carpenter et al. monograph is a key reading in the class, driving many class activities and these experiences clearly influenced Alicia as evidenced by interview/survey data and the PACT lesson cycle especially in the discussion of students' understandings and misunderstandings regarding a single word "equal." In the methods course, student teachers discussed how processing the term went beyond a definition of the word. The Carpenter study revealed how elementary students understood other mathematical notations and relationships. The section that follows illustrates how the findings of the study were made transparent to the student teachers through class discussion of research on student learning of mathematics and how Alicia built on that experience.

Consider the following equation: $2 + 3 = 5$. This placement of the equal sign on the right side of the equation is almost exclusively used in the elementary mathematics textbooks adopted by the state of California. Most students are familiar with the representation and they would readily accept that as a true statement. Transforming the same equation into $5 = 2 + 3$ is not met with the same degree of student acceptance. Carpenter et al. found that a significant number of students believed the second equation was wrong. The students did not think that the equal sign could be put on the left side of the equation. Looking for the missing addend in the equation, $7 + 6 = \_ + 5$, was also found to be problematic for many students. Incorrectly filling in the blank with 13 or 18 would be consistent with the researchers' findings about how the majority of elementary students responded. In the first case, the students simply added the 7 and 6; in the second, all three numbers, 7, 6, and 5, were added. Instead of thinking about equals as a relation, students though of equals as an operator, that is, a sign that some operation must be performed on the numbers (Carpenter et al., 2003, p. 9)

Alicia's Analysis of the Teaching Event: PACT protocols require a candidate to assess the work of three selected students as well as a profile of the entire class. With regard to the selected students, Alicia analyzed the work of four students. Two were from homoes where English was a second language. One of the four was a struggling learner with an IEP. Alicia shared these students' worksheets from all three lessons, and rated her intervention as successful. She found that at the end of the teaching event, all four students were not baffled by the placement of the equal sign, and they were generally able to demonstrate an understanding that a key idea was "balance" on both sides of the equal sign. Despite the apparent facility with the equal sign some students displayed, Alicia also found that some of these students were not using the "commutative" property to analyze their work. For example, instead of comprehending that 4 + 1 is the same as 1 + 4 for the following true/false query: 4 + 1 = 1 + 4, the student would use other strategies to verify that both sides were in balance. In her discussion of her students' performance Alicia related the performance of the focus students to the average performance of the class as seen through the daily worksheets. Alicia also looked toward the future and provided a template for this work.

> *Based on the majority of the class mastering the objectives, I would move into relational thinking which would propose a nice transition. This would ask students to build on the skills and understanding which they had just mastered by asking them to look at the relation between two expressions and determine an easy way to solve the problem without computing. Rather, students would recognize the relation of one side to the other (i.e. 11 + 4 = __ + 3, students would determine that 3 is less than one so they would simply add one to the missing variable which would then be 12) and then complete the number sentence with minimal computation. Students would be using relational thinking in order to prepare and support their algebraic thinking while* addressing arithmetic simultaneously." (PACT Reflection on Next Steps)

What makes Alicia's PACT exemplary or an illustration of commendable teacher performance is the fact that the entire focus was based on student understanding, student use and possible misuse of academic language. Although it is not the epitome of a perfect PACT and it did not receive the highest scores, it is an example of how academic language can be woven into the central focus of a teaching event. One characterization of academic language, "The body of knowledge, strategies and skills necessary to accomplish the academic tasks or genres of a specific discipline in a particular context" (Merino & Scarcella, 2005), is an appropriate descriptor of the candidate's thrust. The meaning of a single word was content specific, it connected to larger ideas that pervade arithmetic and algebra and it was embedded in student strategies and skill based work.

Implications of the Math Case: The potential to continue the development of academic language is found in Alicia's reflection about next steps. At the end of her Analysis of the Teaching Event section, Alicia's discussion of relational thinking as quoted verbatim above shows deep thinking about mathematical processes. This shows a mathematical dimension that looks beyond the meaning of the equal sign. This approach requires students to use problem-solving strategies and number properties in a way that can foster discussion and analysis. As noted by Alicia, it also parallels the type of reasoning involved in solving algebraic equations.

AL can be a part of the central focus of a mathematics lesson. These lessons as Alicia designed them were not part of the regular curriculum at her school site, but they did address some important conceptions and misconceptions. By focusing in on the meaning of one word and letting it radiate into a non-traditional look at equations, the pupils were able to use their skills to justify their work in content specific ways. Alicia shows us that there is value in discussing and extolling students' misconceptions for these can be an opportunity for students to use academic language and to think mathematically. Transforming parts of an equation and asking students to articulate what's is right and what is wrong can help facilitate this process. True/false sentences also provide this opportunity. The key is to have students use the academic language in ways that are meaningful for the discipline. Indeed focusing on the language demands of the discipline facilitated complex mathematical thinking. As Alicia made clear, this type of discourse and conceptual understanding is not just for the second grade. It is also an important connection to thinking algebraically.

Cross-Case Analysis: Next we compare cohort and case results and analyze them through competing theories of AL with examples from the secondary cohort. Findings are discussed from the perspective of an "embodied understanding" of practice to explore how life experiences, discipline knowledge and contextual features of the targeted credential programs influence performance. Students in the secondary program enroll in a course targeting AL and ELL issues from multiple perspectives including Scarcella's multitiered framework as well as others. Discipline specific methods also target AL where the emphasis is on language demands and ways of scaffolding these within the discipline. In addition, students enroll in a literacy course in the content areas with a special focus on reading. Despite the increased language demands of tasks in English literature lessons, EBTs who received extensive instruction to address AL and who also had a strong grounding in literature were able to support their ELs and could also identify language demands from multiple perspectives. As a group, English language arts students performed at the highest level in AL in comparison to the science and math cohorts. Holly, for example, drawing on Scarcella's multitiered framework of AL, built background knowledge on the Holocaust through clips and primary sources in her lesson cycle. She created scaffolded small group activities to support students' searching of text for textual evidence in response to prompts. She also provided models of ways to identify textual evidence.

"Paula"—The science elaborated case: Paula was selected as exemplary because of her high performance in scaffolding language demands, specifically her innovative approach to scaffolding inquiry through models, demonstrations and moving to authentic inquiry and discovery in small groups. AL targets included understanding "hypothesis" in science as a complex term involving understanding scientific concepts and for targeting key features of the discourse of a lab report with a focus on "data collection" procedural explanations and unpacking and distinguishing "results" and "conclusions". All beginning teachers in the science cohort demonstrated a similar trend in their ability to scaffold instruction, although the identification of language demands seemed more challenging. Paula showed a high level of understanding of her students' language levels and discipline knowledge in planning and reflecting on her lesson cycle on the concept "force" through a series of mini experiments with a toy train. Her objective was for students to "develop a testable hypothesis upon analysis of their data" and then to "conclude if their hypothesis was correct after conducting an investigation." (PACT Task 2)

> Prior to having students develop hypotheses, I will also need to reiterate the need to base those **hypotheses** on prior knowledge. Many students were making broad connections between what they did and what happened, but few saw how the specific **addition of mass changed the distance the train traveled**. Here as well, will be an opportunity to highlight the difference between the **results** section of a lab report (i.e., **data summaries"** and the **conclusions** section. (PACT Task 2)

Thus Paula in the planning commentary identified seven instances of scaffolding for the language demands related to the science concept of "force" targeted before implementation and two more after when she reflected on her instruction. She considered how to use multiple modalities in exposing her students to predictions and explanations.

> The lessons are structured together so that students first listen to, read, and discuss **predictions** and **explanations** about concepts of force using the

"talking to the text" strategy. They then participate in a simulated train experiment and report their findings. (PACT Task 2)

She gave less attention to the language demands related to the writing of a lab report as a genre, targeting "hypothesis" but not as much the complexities of the under-lying construct nor the discourse and scientific demands of procedural explanations. Nonetheless she recovers quite effectively resorting to a routine she described as: "model, read, define, use and apply." When one student asks what the term "baseline" means, she uses a constructivist approach (PACT data, personal communication).

To help him define the terms, I first asked other group members to help him and then to refer back to the text in which the term is introduced. (PACT Task 3).

Paula returns to the term during the data collection phases.

to help students collect their data" .... I discussed "the importance of being able to replicate data in an investigation. Eg. I asked one group if they had found their baseline and when they replied yes, had them prove it by repeating the trial. Ss had to repeat every trial three times to find an average distance. (PACT Task-3)

She does pay close attention to the selection of the key features of the demonstration and experiment that would help to build students understanding of the causal explanation with this concept but also as a text type.

Using the coins to add mass to the train set was a good demonstration to students about how mass changes the forces acting on an object. Most of the students intuitively know that and the change in distance was a way for them to see it. (PACT data, Personal communication)

Here Paula was influenced by the strong emphasis given in the methods and inquiry classes to foster the development of conceptual change about core concepts through inquiry (Syllabi review; faculty & student interview; class observation). She provided an authentic opportunity to investigate force in an experiment combined with reading from the textbook using the "talking to the text" reading strategy. Paula recognized missed opportunities during the lesson cycle and was able to compensate. She also noted quite specifically one important feature to improve on for the next time:

discussing the need to change only one variable at a time. Several groups, for example, added both the coins and the parachute in the same trial.

While this was within the realm of the objective, I missed an opportunity to develop this scientific concept." (PACT data; Reflection)

This integration of authentic experiences in science inquiry combined with demonstrations, reading and discussing in collaborative groups reflect the science, EL methods, and inquiry classes. Part of the science methods course takes students on a cycle of visits of cooperating science teachers to participate in mini lesson demonstrations that illustrate ways of approaching key concepts. Student teachers subsequently discuss what worked for them as learners and what they wonder about as teachers. It must be said that Paula was very ambitious in the goals she set out for the PACT short lesson cycle. She demonstrated sound planning before instruction and during implementation and upon reflection was able to point out specific areas where she missed opportunities but had developed ways to improve for the next time.

But Paula's approach was also influenced by her experience teaching at an outdoor school as an undergraduate where she reports she "fell in love with teaching" (Interview. Survey data). This experience she states helped her to define her role as a teacher as

> a person who exposes students to new ideas and experiences and then assists them as they make sense of those ideas and experiences. (Survey data two years post completion of the Credential/MA)

Paula's interest in developing AL related to explanations continued and was further developed in the inquiry she targeted in the thesis during her teacher research. Here again she targeted an ambitious agenda - the use of evidence in explanations—but was able to readjust and focus on elaborations and relevance when providing evidence proved to be too ambitious a goal. Paula reports learning much from the iterative process of the inquiry in the MA thesis. Paula's embodied understanding of practice was grounded in strong disciplinary knowledge with a major in genetics that served her well in understanding how to make authentic inquiry transparent to her students. Paula had limited exposure in learning another language herself. She had a mixed experience in one EL placement during the credential year but a productive second long-term placement that also included ELs. Perhaps some of her difficulty in identifying all the language demands of her cycle prior to teaching results from this limited experience. Paula showed great commitment to working with EL students and was hired to teach in a middle school with a high number of ELs. Her inquiry in Year 2 tapped extensively into practitioner research but not to so much to EL learning in science. These factors and her isolation as the only science teacher at her middle school seemed to have played a role in the challenges posed in her inquiry in Year 2. In sum,

Paula showed a deep understanding of AL as embedded within science as a discipline, indeed as a cultural community with specific values, understandings and protocols for communicating (Lemke, 1990). She shows understandings of the power of group work in a general way and indeed alludes to several research studies to support her approach for collaboration. She has not considered some of the nuances of implementing group work in how she assigns students and in how a mixed ability structure informed by a sociocultural view of the development of AL might yield additional benefits. Paula does not allude specifically to research on AL as seen through the lens of Systemic Functional Linguistics (Gibbons, 2002) but she uses some of the constructs and terminology of the theory quite profitably.

CONCLUSIONS

Understanding of AL development can be quite high in new teachers. Through the support of course work on methods and inquiry, the models provided by resident teachers, peers, faculty and supervisors, seemed to have helped these new teachers understand AL demands and provide appropriate scaffolds to support English learners' skills. Exposure to the concept of AL and appropriate instructional and inquiry methods in coursework offer a key pathway to deepen understanding through co-construction and independent inquiry. All EBTs exploited opportunities for engaging students in complex learning supported by strategic scaffolds designed to make the use of complex AL possible. These scaffolds as Holly demonstrated in her instruction of teaching how to use textual evidence were removed after applying the strategy with simpler text. Clearly Holly benefited from having majored in English and being able to draw from her own experiences with text and genre. But she also learned how to scaffold through a semester-long placement in an EL intermediate class and the mentoring by her supervisor, supervising teacher and faculty mentor in her inquiry. Paula saw her understanding of AL evolve with every major program assignment and continued this trajectory as she continued on her own. She developed a more nuanced understanding of vocabulary as she realized that some students, often ELLs could not access key ideas without explicit instruction and repeated opportunities to use key concepts.

Strategic reading of research on math learning and response to text when combined with models and opportunities for new teachers to develop their own discipline knowledge helped all elementary EBTs. Alicia understood that a word like "equals" is not just an isolated vocabulary term but that it is at the core of constructing the syntax of mathematics and thus worth the effort of expending valuable instructional time in scaffolding its development through multiple opportunities that allowed students to negotiate its meaning. Alicia a communications major benefited from additional opportunities in the program to understand more deeply how students learn mathematics and what misconceptions they can develop about critical concepts.

Strong discipline knowledge is an essential ingredient for a genuine integration of AL that facilitates conceptual change. This was true for all the EBTs. Some especially students at the elementary level who were not math majors benefited mightily from an opportunity to develop discipline knowledge in their methods course. Paula, a genetics major, exploited the opportunity to unpack the concept of force and through mentorship by faculty modeling of authentic inquiry created a similar opportunity for her students. Perhaps more could be done in linking discussion of AL and literacy as fundamental to the development of scientific literacy (Halliday, 2004; Kelly & Bazerman, 2003; Norris & Phillips, 2003). Connecting students explicitly to research on instructional approaches that help ELLs meet the challenges of language and cultural demands in complex learning tasks, like developing persuasive explanations would be beneficial as well (Smagorinzky, Johannessen, Kahn, & McCann, 2011)

Working directly with English learners accelerates understanding of how to implement strategies to support AL development. While coursework can provide the theoretical underpinnings to successful instruction, it is the direct contact with ELLs that allows new teachers to hone their skills—both in recognizing their students' needs and developing effective instructional approaches. All EBTs worked with ELs or former ELs, in schools in which mentoring teachers provided effective models.

Using models, such as examples from these cases, can demonstrate strong AL instruction to other new teachers. Watching and analyzing models of successful instruction by other novices make the concepts more clear and doable. Indeed new teachers can exhibit the skills of experienced teachers through viewing and discussing exemplary PACT performance. Indeed these models of early instances of exemplary practice challenge static stage models of professional development.

Scholarly Significance: In closing we revisit Dall'Alba and Sandberg's theory of embodied understanding of practice as regards the professional development of teachers in their perspectives on AL. In reviewing the instantiation of AL across cases, we see that discipline knowledge, whether through a major and/or through renewed attention to an analysis of how to develop key concepts in a lesson cycle, shape teachers' understanding of the nature of the linguistic demands of the tasks and concepts targeted for instruction. A general stance of inquiry about the concepts to be taught can be seen across cases. This general stance is fostered by the program and resonated with all the EBTs. All EBTs acted as advocates for the learners in their midst but some seem to have stronger awareness of the demands ELs than others. Those who did had many personal experiences with ELs, as friends, in their families or in their own experiences. Looking at PACT performance as an opportunity to see beliefs in action has many advantages but some limitations. Clearly the PACT protocols cue certain responses and the instructions related to AL play a role in drawing attention to language demands and scaffolding specifically. Because the program offers a variety of views on AL, EBTs drew from those that seem to apply to their particular situation and to those emphasized by their instructors.

Space limitations prevent an elaborate discussion of other artifacts but the inquiry projects required by the program suggest more continuities than discontinuities in how EBTs approach AL. Paula for example, continued to explore the development of AL through conceptual change in her year two inquiry. Her understanding of AL has evolved and she sees the need to unpack the cognitive and linguistic load of key vocabulary and concepts. Paula's PACT performance demonstrated many approaches to scaffolding language and most especially the discourse of authentic inquiry as seen in the pains she took to redirect her instruction and her students so that they could participate in multiple experiences that would illustrate core concepts and give them the opportunity to recycle the discourse of scientific explanations about their experiments. Cross-case common strategies seen in all EBTs included: scaffold use with AL key terms, accessing multiple modalities for presentation and responses, co constructed discussion with examples that are designed to unpack misconceptions, authentic inquiry, AL that targets core discipline concepts and AL as discourse and not just as decontextualized vocabulary.

A key advantage in using the embodied understanding framework is that researchers can tackle teacher beliefs integrated with action. Wideen, Mayer-Smith, and Moon (1998) and many others have explored teacher beliefs as sources of influence but typically these are analyzed as separate from action. Embodied understanding theory enabled us to see teaching performance addressing AL as an integrated whole. In the PACT artifacts EBTs tended to discuss theories of pedagogy rather than theories of AL. The language of AL theories does appear in the EBTs identification of language demands. Perhaps because the PACT rubrics and protocols do not emphasize AL as a sociocultural term and/or the limits of time and space in completing the PACT, some EBTs tended to discuss the AL demands in terms of language and cognitive demands. Clearly as teacher educators we have much to learn about how we can work to unpack the complexities of theories of AL as these are applied across disciplines.

REFERENCES

Bunch, G. C. (2010). Preparing mainstream secondary content-area teachers to facilitate English langague learners' development of academic language. *Yearbook of the National Society for the Study of Education, 109*(2), 351-383.

Calderhead, J., & Shorrock, S. B. (1997). *Understanding teacher education: Case studies in the professional development of beginning teachers*. London, England: Falmer Press.

Carpenter, T. P., Franke, M. L., & Levi, L. (2003) *Thinking mathematically: integrating arithmetic and algebra in elementary school*. Portsmouth, NH: Heinemann.

Dall'Alba, G., & Sandberg, J. (2006). Unveiling professional development: A critical review of stage models *RER, 76*, 383-412.

Darling-Hammond, L. & Youngs, P. (2002). Defining "highly-qualified teachers": What does scientifically-based research actually tell us? *Educational Researcher, 31*, 13-25.

Faltis, C., & Merino, B. (1992). Towards a definition of exemplary teachers in bilingual, multicultural school settings. In R.V. Padilla & A. H. Benavides (Eds.) *Critical perspectives on bilingual education research* (pp. 277-299). Tempe, AZ: Bilingual Review Press.

Foster, M. (1989). *Exemplary Black teachers in the segregated South*. Keynote Address at the Far West Regional Conference of the Holmes Group. Boulder, CO: University of Colorado.

Gibbons P. (2002). *Scaffolding language; scaffolding learning: Teaching second language learners in the mainstream classroom*. Portsmouth, NH: Heinemann.

Halliday, M. A. K. (2004) *The language of science*. London. England: Continuum.

Hyland, K. (2004). *Genre and second language writing*. Ann Arbor, MI: University of Michigan Press.

Kelly, G. J., & Bazerman, C. (2003). How students argue scientific claims: A rhetorical-semantic analysis. *Applied Linguistics, 24*, 28-55.

Lemke, J.L. (1990). *Talking science: Language learning and values*. Norwood, NJ: Ablex.

Merino, B. J. & Scarcella, R. (2005) Teaching science to English learners. *UC LMRI Newsletter, 14*(4), 1-5.

Moskowitz, G. (1976). The classroom interaction of outstanding foreign language teachers. *Foreign Language Annals, 9*, 135-143, 146-157.

Norris, S. & Phillips, L. (2003) How literacy in its fundamental sense is central to scientific literacy. *Science Education, 87*, 224-240.

Patton, M.Q., (2002) *Qualitative evaluation and research methods* (3rd ed.). Newbury Park, CA: SAGE.

Pechone, R. L., & Chung, R. (2006). Evidence in teacher education-PACT. *J. Of Teacher Education, 37*, 22-36.

Peterson, S., & McKay, R. (2001). Eminent classroom teachers join the dialogue on teacher education programs. *The Teacher Educator, 37*(2), 133-144.

Scarcella, R. (2003). *Academic English: A conceptual framework*. Santa Barbara, CA: UC Linguistic Minority Research Institute.

Schleppegrell, M. J. (2004). *The language of schooling*. Mahwah, NJ:Erlbaum.

Smagorinzky, P., Johannessen, L, Kahn, E., & McCann T. (2011). *Teaching students to write argument.* Portsmouth, NH: Heinemann.

Valdés, G. (2004). Between support and marginalization: The development of academic language in linguistic minority children. *Bilingual Education and Bilingualism, 7,* 102-132.

Wells, G. (Ed.). (2001). *Action, talk and text: Learning and teaching through inquiry.* New York, NY: Teachers College Press.

Wideen, M. Mayer-Smith, J., & Moon, B. (1998). A critical analysis on the research on learning to teach: Making the case for an ecological perspective. *Review of Educational Research, 68,* 130-178.

CHAPTER 5

DEVELOPING TEACHERS' CRITICAL LANGUAGE AWARENESS IN DIGITAL CONTEXTS

Tomás Galguera

A serious challenge for teachers required to teach and assess academic language emerges from the very complex and vast nature of their task. On the one hand, few would disagree with the premise that teachers ought to teach "academic language" to all students. How else are students to succeed in school unless they are skilled users of oral and written language? On the other hand, what exactly "academic language" sounds and looks like is rather difficult to determine in the fluid, dynamic setting of a most classrooms (Bunch, 2009). Should a teacher be concerned with students switching into their native language while discussing volcanic eruptions in small groups, when everyone in the group is bilingual? How much should she insist in students using "complete sentences" to answer questions? Should she require students not to use colloquialisms (e.g., *Hecka good!*) while chitchatting in the classroom, between classes? Are the *manga* books her students choose during silent reading likely to provide them with the skills needed to read academic texts? And is she squelching her students' creativity and voice by insisting that they follow linear academic written

Academic Language in Second Language Learning, pp. 103–124
Copyright © 2013 by Information Age Publishing

conventions, rather than the quirky, meandering style they favor? Questions such as these and many others add complexity to the decision-making process in a profession in which decisions are predominant and crucial (Jackson, 1968; Shavelson, 1973).

Standards and frameworks exist to guide teachers in deciding what to teach, the sequence in which the content ought to be taught, and the skills expected of students at each grade level. However, an examination of English standards yields few answers to teachers' pressing questions regarding language development. In California, the state with the majority of English learners in the United States, students performing at the "advanced" English language development (ELD) level for "organization and delivery of oral communication" are expected to "Negotiate and initiate social conversations by questioning, restating, soliciting information, and paraphrasing the communication of others" (California Department of Education, 2002, p. 3). A linguistic analysis of student conversations in most classrooms would yield evidence of these skills among most students, including most English learners at or above an intermediate level of English proficiency. Still, observers, teachers, and even linguists would agree that these conversations do not constitute advanced examples of academic language use. How are teachers expected to teach and assess language skills all students need to succeed in schools if, as I argue in this chapter, what counts as academic language is not immediately apparent even to proficient academic language users?

Information and communication technologies are the new literacies (Leu, Cairo, Kinder, & Commack, 2004) and as such offer excellent opportunities to demonstrate the power of scaffolding for language development (Lee, 2002). I argue for the need to foster in teachers of English learners (EL) critical language awareness toward issues of power and status for which language is both symbolic and instrumental. I see critical language awareness as a necessary precursor for the development of pedagogical language knowledge among teachers (Galguera, 2011). In this chapter I present two cases of developing critical language awareness among preservice teachers in the context of pedagogical tools I use in my preservice English language development methods courses for single and multiple subject beginning teachers. A foundational goal in the courses from which my self-study emerges is the development of critical language awareness among the preservice teachers enrolled in them. As Fairclough (1995), Gee (2007), and Alim (2005) remind us, our responsibility as educators and teacher educators is to foster among teachers and their students the ability to examine language and question the political structure for which such language is both symbolic and instrumental. As such, I hope that the preservice teachers in my courses gain the capacity to develop curricula and pedagogy that question existing dominant discourse and oppression while providing them with the linguistic and academic abilities required to participate in society. To achieve this goal, I adopt an experiential approach, requiring students to complete assignments that incorporate Web 2.0 tools and technologies. Though most of my students are familiar with these media as consumers, few have been producers of content, especially in an academic setting, a situation not at all dissimilar to that of most students they will teach. Students are familiar with books, charts, directions, posters, presentations, and other text types common in schools (Gibbons, 2002) and are capable of obtaining varying amounts of information from these sources. However, the challenge increases exponentially when they are required to produce sentences, paragraphs, essays, diagrams, labels, steps, procedures, demonstrations, or speeches that reflect academic norms and expectations. Evidence from my research points to the power of electronic media and Web 2.0 tools in fostering critical language awareness, empathy, and in furthering pedagogical skills for language development among preservice teachers.

TEACHER LANGUAGE AWARENESS AND PEDAGOGICAL LANGUAGE KNOWLEDGE

Awareness and knowledge are related constructs, though particularly in the case of language awareness and language knowledge, it is important to distinguish between explicit and implicit knowledge. Ellis (2010) describes these two types of knowledge as follows:

> Explicit knowledge [is] conscious, declarative, accessible only through controlled processing, verbalizable, learnable (in the sense that any piece of factual information is learnable), and typically employed when learners experience some kind of linguistic problem. Implicit knowledge, in contrast, is unconscious (i.e., we are not aware of what we know, implicitly), procedural, accessible for automatic processing, not verbalizable (except as an explicit representation), "acquirable" (i.e., can be internalized implicitly), and typically employed in unproblematic, free-flowing communication. (p. 440)

In a discussion of language awareness and second language pedagogy, Ellis (1997) further distinguishes between "analyzed knowledge" and "metalanguage" (p. 110). The former refers to knowledge about a second language that does not require conscious awareness; the latter refers to the language learners use to talk about the second language.

For teachers responsible for the language development of students, language awareness is an important contributor to the development of the content knowledge (Shulman, 1987) they must possess to fulfill their obligations. This is especially true when the language in question is academic English and the students are a mixture of native speakers of vernacular varieties of English and English language learners at an intermediate level of proficiency. This student composition is almost the norm in many U.S. public schools, particularly those in large urban metropolitan areas. It is precisely in these settings that developing language awareness can have a powerful effect on both teachers and students. Carter (2003) argues that, for teachers, language awareness can enhance their capacity to incorporate useful and meaningful learning tasks into their curricula, guide their assessment of students' learning and difficulties, inform their understanding of language varieties and appropriateness, and help them imagine links between language and learning in general. Carter notes that teaching practice that is informed by language awareness can also foster reflection and analysis in students, especially when it questions the relationship between language and power.

Fairclough (1995, 2001, 2003) has written extensively about the importance of recognizing the complex and pervasive links that exist between language, power, and ideology and the emancipating promise that exists in such work. Fairclough and others (e.g., Clark & Ivanic, 1997; Pennycook, 2001; Shor, 1992) have argued for the need to go beyond simply making teachers and students aware of language, in all its intricacies. Rather, they see it as crucial for educators to question the status quo of schools and society and notice the exploitation of some groups over others as well as social inequities built into systems and structures. The critical education movement capitalizes in the realization that language is both symbolic of and instrumental for power relations in society, a fact with direct implications for teachers of language, who often work with members of oppressed groups. It is no wonder then that much of the work associated with the education of language minority students and other disenfranchised groups is characterized by a political rhetoric rather than informed by educational research findings (Crawford, 2004; Hakuta, 1987).

Understanding the sociocultural and discourse-level features of the variety of language favored in academic settings is an essential component of the content knowledge required of teachers. Academic uses of language often requires describing abstract concepts and relations using figurative forms, explicitness for distant audiences, detachment and objectivity in tone, relying on evidence for support, and using modals and hedges to convey nuanced meanings, among other things (Zwiers, 2008). Knowing all these and other features of academic language requires both a linguistic analysis of language as well as awareness of our own uses of language in order to translate what is knowledge about language into curricula and pedagogy that is appropriate, engaging, and relevant to students and that leads to proficiency gains.

In a book devoted entirely to the subject of language awareness among language teachers, Andrews (2007) argues for the importance of teacher language awareness (TLA) as a particular type of content knowledge for teachers that may not be captured by test scores. Andrews does provide indirect evidence of TLA's importance on student learning, particularly as it relates to what is considered good practice among language teachers. Though Andrews's discussion concerns language teachers' practice and preparation, TLA is especially relevant for teachers of academic content. For them, noticing lexical, structural, and other discourse features associated with their respective subject is especially significant since such knowledge does not belong in most traditional preservice courses and often relies on each teacher's disposition and curiosity. It is for this reason too that it would be useful to create a category of teacher knowledge that recognizes not only the importance of TLA but that also identifies pedagogical practices intended to develop the proficiency of students to use language for academic purposes in all its dimensions and in ways that are both general and particular to academic subjects. Shulman (1987) coined the term "pedagogical content knowledge" (PCK) to describe "the blending of content and pedagogy into an understanding of how particular topics, problems or issues are organized, represented, and adapted to the diverse interests and abilities of learners, and presented for instruction" (p. 4). Building upon Lee Shulman's framework, I use "Pedagogical Language Knowledge" (PLK) (Galguera, 2011) as a construct to make it clear to the preservice teachers in my courses that the pedagogy I want them to begin developing is more than "just good teaching." Indeed, in a similar manner in which we must make a conscious effort to focus our attention on the structural and surface features of language, beyond meaning, it requires especial effort on the part of beginning teachers to notice the important, yet subtle characteristics of pedagogy for the development of language proficiency for academic purposes.

TECHNOLOGY AS NEW LITERACIES AND TEACHERS AS "TECHNOLOGY NATIVES"

Ong (2002) has argued that "writing and print and the computer are all ways of technologizing the word" (p. 79). According to this view, many of the features of thought and expression that we take for granted are not native and intrinsic to the human experience, regardless of our literacy skills and our awareness of ourselves as literate beings. The pervasive nature of literacy and other symbolic systems has resulted in redefinition of human identity, which assumes as given behaviors and ways of thinking that are consequences of technological advances—to the extent that literacy is indeed a technology. By implication, though none of us is a native user of written language, it is not easy to become aware of human discourse that is mediated by letters and other symbols. Recently, Palfrey and Gasser (2008) have used the term "digital native" to describe advanced users of technology born after 1980. Their use of the term was intended to draw a distinction between generations and the assumptions people make about information and representation as well as their roles as consumers and producers of digital media. Palfrey and Gasser are careful to point out that their designation is not necessarily inclusive, acknowledging that "participation gaps" (p. 15) exist among sectors of the population. In this chapter I argue that, in fact, even skilled users of ICTs lack the seamless relationship we have with spoken language.

Leu and colleagues (2009) have argued that ICTs are new literacies that go beyond simply technological skills. Rather, these are skills, strategies, and dispositions that allow us to use information and online content and communicate our understanding and experiences to others and favorably influence our lives and the lives of others. Therefore, there is an added benefit in using technology, particularly Web 2.0 tools to foster teacher language awareness and pedagogical language knowledge in preservice teachers. They are in fact becoming literate in "new literacies" Leu et al. (2004, p. 1572), an experience not at all dissimilar to those of their future students with traditional literacy. Gee (2007) agrees with this view, describing the exploding multimedia content, formats, and genres as discourse that emerges in a sociocultural milieu.

Though consuming digital media can feel like an effortless collection of clicks and quick skims, scans, and listening of content, fewer people have had opportunities to create digital content from scratch, specifically web pages and sites. The proliferation of online social media tools and web pages have made writing brief statements and uploading pictures or videos a familiar task for an increasing proportion of the U.S. population. However, even assiduous consumers of online content seldom have opportunities or demands to build entire websites or even pages. Even "digital natives" (Palfrey & Gasser, 2008) lack a native-like orientation toward producing Internet content. It is this non-native-like status that is at the core of the self-study I conducted in English language development methods courses I teach within a preservice teacher education program. I take advantage of the lack of familiarity most of my students have creating content for web pages to enhance their language awareness and, consequently, develop their pedagogical language knowledge (Galguera, 2011).

SCAFFOLDING IN ELECTRONIC CONTEXTS AS
PEDAGOGICAL LANGUAGE KNOWLEDGE

Aída Walqui (2006) builds upon Bruner and Sherwood's (1975) construct of scaffolding and provides a typology of pedagogical approaches that are intended to support the interaction between language learners and instruction. Walqui describes scaffolding that is continuous and provides opportunities to practice language through tasks that increase in complexity and difficulty; provides contextual support and enhances their willingness to take risks with language; provides opportunities for and supports the development of relationships among language learners; is contingent and flexible to respond to the students' development and growth as well as unexpected developments; encourages students to take over and teachers to hand over responsibility for language learners' learning; and fosters learners to be absorbed in the instructional tasks.

Walqui (2006) describes six types of scaffolding for language development that I both teach as content for the development of pedagogical language knowledge (Galguera, 2011) among preservice teachers. The pedagogy in the English language development methods preservice courses I teach is experiential in nature. Tigchelaar and Korthagen (2004, pp. 665-666) note that the predominant approach in preservice teacher education courses, a "technical-rationality approach," which aims to link theory-to-practice. The authors cite convincing research evidence that demonstrates that, even when student teachers recognize the value and importance of theories, the demands and immediacy of field experiences limit their ability to apply their theoretical knowledge to practice. Tigchelaar and Korthagen also mention an alternate "practice-based" approach that depends on guided induction of teacher candidates at school sites, sometimes in partnership with institutions of higher learning. Yet, this approach has also failed to integrate practice with theory, often resulting in teachers who are socialized into a profession that is viewed as a collection of technical know-how that rejects and devalues theory.

Tigchelaar and Korthagen's (2004) provide evidence for the potential of experience in preservice teacher preparation utilizing a "realistic approach" that incorporates preservice teachers' reflection on specific experiences and behaviors in a cooperative setting while examining "Gestalts," which are automatic teaching behaviors that make up the bulk of what teachers say and do and that have cultural origins (p. 677). My approach to developing critical language awareness (Alim, 2005; Gee, 2007; Fairclough, 1995, 2001) among preservice teachers is based on the assumption that providing them with opportunities to experience challenges and scaffolding in utilizing language for academic purposes on wikis, web pages, and other forms of electronic media provides me with the means to examine the manner in which they comprehend and produce content and the pedagogy that contributes to their success. Specifically, I ask students to participate in synchronous and asynchronous online discussions of tasks we complete during class, inquiry projects they complete at their field placements and reading assignments consisting primarily of research articles on language, language development, and pertinent instruction. I also adapt Walqui's six scaffolds for language development to help my students complete these tasks and specific experiences to examine their reactions and the reasons for utilizing these particular pedagogical approaches.

Walqui's (2006) six language development scaffolds are modeling, contexualization, text representation, schema-building, bridging, and metacognitive development. Modeling is the explicit presentation of examples of the products, learning processes, and the types of language that are most appropriate for each situation. In my courses, I provide students with examples of previous students' online comments, collaborative wikis, and web pages, discussing and highlighting important features and desirable qualities. Contextualization is scaffolding that links particular academic tasks with situated variables to enhance the students' ability to derive meaning from language and produce language that is both appropriate and effective. Therefore, I ask students to complete inquiry projects that are based on their field placements and ask them to reflect on the audience and the content, tone and structure of the online content they produce. Text representation can be thought of as helping students learn conventions associated with particular language uses by translating content across genres, engaging in genre transformation. To help them recognize the structure and features of wikis, web pages, and online contents, my students first write journal entries and a brief research paper and use these as starting points for comments, wikis, and web pages. Schema-building is related to text representation in that the goal is to help students organize knowledge according to subject-specific frameworks (e.g., cycles, cause-effects, contrasts, whole-parts) and norms and conventions associated with oral and written discourse. It is for this reason that I utilize prompts and online forms made up of content boxes requiring specific information to guide my students' content creation as well as utilizing conceptual frameworks to organize the content we cover. Bridging is scaffolding that aims to make clear and explicit links between content and each student's prior knowledge, experiences, and interests as well as previously taught content. Thus, my students and I document the work and learning in my courses on wikis that remain accessible to my them even after the semester ends, and I incorporate their comments and other written reflections into my lectures and discussions. Finally, metacognitive development is ensuring that students choose strategies consciously for each activity and evaluating their choices and future choices based on results. My students (and I) engage in metacognition by examining their experiences in consuming and producing online content, particularly regarding wikis and web pages. Small and whole-group discussions of challenging and successful approaches as well as discoveries make the learning process public and an important component of the course curriculum.

LANGUAGE AWARENESS AMONG PRESERVICE TEACHERS: TWO ILLUSTRATIVE CASES

The potential of ICTs to foster language awareness among preservice teachers has been evident to me in multiple manners. Building upon Tigchelaar and Korthagen's (2004) "realistic approach," I ask preservice teachers to examine their experiences as non-native producers of discourse associated with web pages, connecting their reflections and insights with both practical and theoretical aspects of teaching for language development. Over the years, I have collected sufficient evidence to convince me of the usefulness of this approach. However, two recent instances are especially remarkable in that they were unexpected and provided excellent teachable moments to discuss ways in which language development for academic purposes goes beyond the teaching of vocabulary. Both of these examples also allowed me to guide preservice teachers in an analysis of the relationship between discourse, power, and culture, essential elements of critical language awareness (Alim, 2005; Fairclough, 2001; Gee, 2007).

The first case illustrates the persistent power of schemas (Anderson, 1977; Bartlett, 1932) that influence our comprehension and production of spoken and written language, often without being aware of their existence. Despite providing my students with a template made up of pre-designated spaces for specific content and prompts describing the information they were required to represent according to web conventions, several added a "conclusion" section to their pages. These unexpected additions provided me with an excellent opportunity to discuss the organization of knowledge in memory as well as the structure of discourse into genres that serve normative functions for language use, especially in academic settings.

The second case represents a dilemma of practice (Cuban, 2001) that is not uncommon for teachers interested in developing the proficiency of students in using language for academic purposes, particularly with regard to production: overcoming the students' natural reluctance to say or write anything only to realize that the language produced is inappropriate or problematic in other ways. On the one hand, teachers are concerned with encouraging students to speak and write in a second language. On the other hand, they cannot ignore or allow language that is offensive, inappropriate, or that can be evidence of abuse or similarly dangerous situations. There are moral, ethical, and even legal consequences to any action (including no action at all). As I describe below, my use of technology in my teaching provided me with excellent opportunities to provide a real and immediate context to discuss important aspects of teaching for language development that are likely to have a lasting impact on the preservice teachers I work with.

Enduring Schemas and Conflicting Genres

The preservice teachers enrolled in my English Language Development Methods courses do not write conventional academic papers. In order to provide them with experiences that ground discussions of scaffolding and other important theories and constructs in my students' experiences, I require them to complete a website[1] that is made up of three pages: a home page with information about each student as a beginning teacher and two pages documenting separate but related inquiry projects. The first project is an inquiry on a child as a language learner based on one of the students they teach as part of their field practicum.[2] The project is framed as a case study, modeled after the four cases in Valdés's (2001) *Learning and Not Learning English: Latino Students in American Schools*, which my students read. The second project is an inquiry on their own teaching practice in which they choose a specific language skill to develop among the students they teach. On their respective "snapshots" (i.e., web pages), preservice teachers document the planning, teaching, assessment, and analysis associated with their teaching as well as discussing practical implications for developing language for academic purposes. For both assignments, I provide them with templates, an example of "schema-building" scaffolding (Walqui, 2006). Table 5.1 contains the sections and prompts for the second language learner inquiry project.

In asking students to model their inquiry after one of Valdés's (2001) case studies of a language learner, I am both relying on and modeling for them text representation, one of Walqui's (2006) types of scaffolding for language development. In addition, the template emphasizes differences between a traditional academic research paper and a web page both in content and structure. There are other ways in which I stress the conventions and norms associated with web pages besides devoting several class meetings for students to examine "snapshots" created by past students that I make accessible to them and that exemplify particular desirable characteristics. This is an example of a modeling scaffold (Walqui, 2006).

Table 5.1. Template for Second Language Learner Inquiry Project Website

Use a Descriptive Title

Provide a brief summary of the student case study you are presenting. Use a pseudonym and describe her/his class or grade level, language, ethnicity, and cultural backgrounds. Concisely, answer the question. What is this a case of? Provide the visitor with a frame to appreciate the information you present below. Also, though seemingly counterintuitive (remember, you are not writing a paper), make sure to comment on the implications that the results from this inquiry have for you in particular and for schools in general. In other words, address the "So what?" question. How will you change your present and future practice as a result of what you learned.

Your student's life away from school

Using Valdes as a model, summarize significant aspects of your focal student's life away from school (particularly information that can help you understand her/him better as a language learner). For instance, what have you been able to find out about your student's family situation? Is she/he responsible for younger siblings or elderly relatives (or both)? Does she/he work? How stable are things for her/him at home? Are there other children in the neighborhood with whom she/he spends time? What languages do close relatives speak? What are their educational level, and are they able to assist or support your focal student with school work? Summarize the assets and challenges you see in your focal student's life away from school as related to her/his academic future and proficiency is using language for academic purposes.

Past schooling

Provide the visitor with a synopsis of your students' past schooling, including U.S. schools and schools in other countries (if applicable). Please obtain this information both through official records (i.e., cumulative files) and/or anything your student tells you. Provide a summary of key experiences, such as how many schools she/he has attended and any events that are academically remarkable or significant. Are there past teachers that stand out in your student's memory? If so, why? Would she/he change any aspect of her/his schooling thus far? Why/

Current school experience

Describe your focal student's present schooling experiences with a focus on opportunities to use and develop language skills for academic purposes. For this piece of the assignment, you are required to shadow your focal student for at least half-a-day, documenting her or his participation in class and interactions with other students, teachers, and school staff.

Language assessment

Finds ways to assess your student's oral and written proficiency in using language for academic purposes. Make sure that your assessments does not come from a deficit perspective. In other words, describe what you believe are strengths and assets in your student's ability to use as well as needs and areas of future growth. Plan assessment tasks that are appropriate for your particular context. Also, make sure to upload the particular samples of student work or performance (e.g., retell, presentation, discussion, collaborative work) that you used as data for your assessment of both oral and written language proficiency. Finally, make sure to distinguish between your students' academic content knowledge and skills in a particular subject and her/his language abilities for academic purposes.

<u>Credential Students:</u> To prepare you for the assessment task in your teaching event, I encourage you to "discuss what [your focal student] appear[s] to understand well, and, if relevant, andy misunderstandings, confusion, or needs (including a need for greater challenge) that were apparent.... Cite evidence to support your analysis from the ... work samples you selected" (from task 4 in Teaching Event Handbook)

Another scaffolding example is an analytic rubric (Figure 5.2) I use to assess my students' web pages and to provide them with feedback as well as an opportunity for metacognitive development (Walqui, 2006). Finally, in weeks leading up to the deadline when their finished web pages are due, I provide my students with opportunities to share their work in progress and consult with each other and with me regarding specific issues or problems, often associated with format and electronic media. Yet, despite all the scaffolds and what I believed were explicit directions and instructions regarding the layered organization of content on web pages and the need to package content into manageable quanta available to the viewer to choose from, three students felt compelled to add a "conclusions" section to their templates. What follows is what Clarissa (pseudonym), a single-subject preservice teacher wrote and labeled as a "conclusion" for her language learner snapshot:

> I was very excited to interview and build a relationship with Serena. She is very comfortable with me and I have not seen her act up according to what other teachers have refereed her as a troublemaker. She is tangled and being pulled back and forth because of what she scores on her CST [California Standards Test]. She is very aware that she needs to pull them up but I'm concerned that there is not a conversation on why it's important to raise her CST scores or why she needs to be a better reader. I look forward to building a relationship with her and hopefully I would be able to help her comprehend why reading is important.

Two features in this preservice teacher's "conclusion" are noteworthy (in addition to the reasons for adding this piece, which I will discuss below): First, she follows conventions associated with conclusions in traditional essays. The conclusion is a chronological summary of Clarissa's experience in completing the inquiry, beginning with her initial positive expectations toward the student she chose to investigate, followed by a summary of what she believes are important issues concerning the students' academic success, and ending with a positive wish that has a future orientation. The second feature of this content is the presence of coding problems due to pasted text copied from a document created with word-processing software that supports "smart" quotes. I have included the original code as evidence that this student had, in fact, written the content for the language learner "snapshot" not by typing on the web page editor, but as a separate text. In a subsequent interview, Clarissa admitted using word-processing software to write the text for her language learner "snapshot" and then pasting segments onto each section. She described feeling the "need to write a short conclusion, almost without realizing it." When she noticed that there was no corresponding box on the web page, she decided to add it. I asked whether she considered using what she had

Table 5.2. Analytic Rubric for Language Learner Inquiry Web Page

Snapshot

Language Layers	Analytic Snapshop Rubric		
	Not Satisfactory (Yet)	Satisfactory	Excellent
Academic purposes	Snap shot appears rushed and unfinished, containing missing, inaccurate, or inappropriate information and irrelevant content. The overall tone and appearance are overly informal and/or feel disrespectful.	Snapshot provides visitor with a clear and easy view of relevant and useful information. The overall tone and appearance are both respectful and inviting.	Snapshot allows the visitor to glean the gist of information presented with ease and in an aesthetically pleasing way. The overall tone and appearance are appropriate and creatively contribute to the visitor's experience.
Structure of site and pages	Title and headings are missing, incomplete, or misleading. The visitor has to struggle to navigate each page. The information presented in each box is formatted without a sense of organization, often meandering away from the topic. Text is either not sufficient or excessive. Texts and graphics have a random quality in their organization.	Snapshot includes titles and headings, which, together with the relative position of boxes, facilitate navigation. Boxes contain distinguishable information. Succinct text and appropriate graphics are formatted following a sensible hierarchy. Snapshot includes multimedia and links to outside sites or pages.	Title and headings are not only clear and coherent but also help the visitor appreciate the nuances of the information presented. Graphics and text are formatted and used creatively to signal the relative importance of content. Snapshot not only includes links to outside sites or pages but also provides additional "layers" with relevant and innovative uses of multimedia.
Context and ideas	Snapshot contains incomplete or inaccurate information without a clear summary of main findings. The content seems incomplete or excessive. Pages appear unfocused, and content seems unrelated or digressing from the site's overall topic.	Snapshot contains complete and accurate information with a clear and succinct summary of main findings somewhere toward the top of each page. The information presented expands in complexity in a rational manner and relevant links follow an overall conceptual framework.	Snapshot contains accurate and complete information with a succinct summary of main findings toward top of each page demonstrates not only a clear understanding of the main points but also the ability to assume the visitor's perspective, anticipating possible questions and concerns.

(Table continues on next page)

Table 5.2. (Continued)

Snapshot _____

Language Layers	Analytic Snapshot Rubric		
	Not Satisfactory (Yet)	Satisfactory	Excellent
Style	Not controlled; flat tone; sentences halted or choppy containing basic vocabulary, not purposefully chosen. Graphics and other media are either absent or distracting because of quality and relevance.	Appropriate tone with varied sentence structure and vocabulary. The author's voice and perspective are noticeable. Aesthetic concerns are evident in the choice of media and formatting.	Purposefully and creatively chosen sentence structure and vocabulary. The author's voice and perspective are present without interfering with the site's main points. Choice of media and formatting is both aesthetically pleasing and supportive of the visitor's experience.
Sentence and paragraph structure	Frequent nonstandard word order, fragment and run-on sentences, and/or word omission. Isolated words resulting in cryptic content.	Standard word order without fragment or run-on sentences. Standard modifiers and coordinators are used appropriately. Transitions link sentences together.	In addition to standard sentences, simple complex, and compound sentences are used variedly and creatively to convey the main points and make reading enjoyable.
Usage and mechanics	Shifts from one tense or person to another; errors in conventions (them/ those, good/well, double negatives). Misspellings, punctuation errors or omissions, little or not formatting of text (e.g., bold, italic, color). Media used are poor in quality or unavailable (e.g., dead links).	The pages contain standard inflections, subject-verb agreement, and word meaning. Correct spelling punctuation, and formatting. Minor glitches do not interfere with meaning. Media are of acceptable quality and accessible.	The author uses metaphorical language and varied expressions creatively without losing standard usage. Besides using correct spelling, punctuation and formatting go beyond basic, enhancing the power of the site. Media quality, format, and availability provide options to the visitor for an optimal experience.

written for the title box, at the top of the page, where the prompt requested the following:

> Provide a brief summary of the student case study you are presenting. Use a pseudonym and describe her/his class or grade level, language, ethnicity, and cultural backgrounds. Concisely, answer the question, What is this a case of? Provide the visitor with a frame to appreciate the information you present below. Also, though seemingly counterintuitive (remember, you are not writing a paper), <u>make sure to comment on the implications that the results from this inquiry have for you in particular and for schools in general.</u> In other words, address the "So what?" question. How will you change your present and future practice as a result of what you learned from this inquiry project?

Clarissa described feeling confused because, though she realized that a web page has a different organization than a traditional academic paper, she still felt an almost inexplicable urge to include a conclusion. Her experience and those of her two other colleagues who, independently, had also included conclusions on her web pages provided me and other students in the class with an opportunity to discuss the power of schemas (Anderson, 1977) to influence the organization and structure of discourse beyond words. I was also able to emphasize the important role that discourse-level features of language, such as organization and structure, play in our ability to comprehend and create meaning through language. Research has shown that these large-scale features of language are more influential than words or particular sounds, though most of the attention to language development in school settings often stops at the sentence level (van Lier, 1995). Similarly, discourse-level features of language also influence teachers' perceptions of students' linguistic proficiency, which has direct implications for their academic achievement (Oliver, & Haig, 2005).

Language Production as a Dilemma of Practice

Cuban (2001) makes a distinction between "tame problems" and dilemmas in teaching as follows: "Tame problems are the familiar, routine, and frequent situations that practitioners face.... Dilemmas are messy, complicated, and conflict-filled situations that require undesirable choices between competing, highly prized values that cannot be simultaneously or fully satisfied" (p. 10). It is one such "messy, complicated, and conflict-filled situation" that provided me with an opportunity to discuss with students the emergence of a common type of dilemma in teaching for language development and the importance of managing such dilemmas.

To the extent that posting comments online in response to assigned readings is a relatively new pedagogical practice, the task provides me with an opportunity to discuss with students their feelings, reactions, and dispositions to this requirement for my course. In these discussions, I ask students to consider practical implications or lessons they may derive from their own and their classmates' experiences, which they might apply to their own teaching as well as theories we have read and discussed that might help them interpret their experiences and suggest useful ways to think of teaching for language development. Two features of online comments seem to be present particular challenges to my students: the public nature of the comments and the uncertainty as to the content, length, and tone of what they write. Typically, with every group, a portion of the students post regularly, and their comments are clearly thoughtful and pertinent. A few, tend to write comments more frequently than the rest of the class, and these comments are often considerably longer than others, although the topics addressed and tone of the comments may or may not be necessarily appropriate. These students could be considered to be fluent online producers. Finally, a minority of students, for multiple reasons, post infrequently, sometimes failing to meet the minimum number of required comments. These are reluctant producers.

The levels of participation I describe above are similar to those found in most classrooms for participation in whole-class discussions. This similarity provides me with ample opportunities to examine the reasons some students are reluctant to participate while others do it apparently with ease. I am also able to discuss practical arrangements to increase participation, such as setting aside time in class to begin discussions of the assigned readings in pairs and students agreeing to post comments on a topic of their choice they discussed. In other words, posting online comments allows them to continue the discussion they initiated in the classroom. We also engage in a discussion of theoretical lenses we might use to help us understand their reluctance and pedagogy we might use to ensure that everyone participates in the online discussions as well as lessons they might derive from this for their own teaching. In moving from a discussion of the experience itself, to practical concerns, and finally to relevant theories, we follow Tigchelaar and Korthagen's (2004) "realistic approach," which has proven to be useful. Nevertheless, I was not prepared to discuss the likelihood of dilemmas of practice related to language that may emerge while inviting and motivating students to produce language for academic purposes. A comment posted by Richard (pseudonym), one of the more prolific poster of comments, presented me with one such dilemma.

I had assigned one of the chapters in van Lier's (1995) extremely readable *Introducing language awareness* in which the author discusses appropriate language and the multiple social and political variables that determine what is considered appropriate and inappropriate in a variety of contexts. After a stimulating whole-class discussion, Richard approached me and asked me whether I had read his comment in response to the chapter, which he had posted a few minutes before class started. I told him I had not, and he said he was interested in my reaction, that he had followed my directions and posted a spontaneous and pertinent comment, both traits I had described as desirable for comments. When I read Richard's comment that night, I was startled to realize he had written about the etymology and usage of a vernacular term for vagina. My first impulse was to delete the comment, something that, as administrator of the content management system I utilize for my courses, I am able to do. But I also realized that doing so would run counter to my invitation (and requirement) for students to participate in these online discussions. I was in the proverbial horns of a dilemma similar to those described by Cuban (2001). This was not simply a problem in need of a solution; this was a dilemma I had to manage.

I proceeded to send an e-mail to Richard, explaining the reasons why his comment was problematic, particularly since the preservice program I teach in resides in a women's college, and most of Richard's classmates were women. I explained my dilemma and informed him that I would cut the body of his comment and paste it onto a separate wiki (i.e., web page), leaving only part of the initial sentence in it with a link to the rest. I also added a warning to the reader, informing her or him that, if they wished to read the rest of Richard's comment, they should know that some of the language he had used might be offensive to some. This might seem like a solution, but the truth is that I was worried that Richard would feel silenced, and that other students, upon finding about it, would be reluctant to post controversial comments for fear of being inappropriate. And yet, I could not simply ignore Richard's writing and run the risk of alienating the female majority of my students. What follows, is an excerpt from Richard's reply to my original message informing him of my actions and the reasons behind them:

> The double standard is that I am unable to talk about these things because I am a male? That hardly seems fair at all; and this is not your problem, but societies'. And when did anyone ever accomplish anything grand without being a bit controversial? (Not that I have delusions of grandeur, but I do think this topic has some deep issues and needs to be uncensored from society).

His apparent difficulties in understanding that appropriate uses of language depend on the particular social, political, and historical context of its use prompted me to exchange additional e-mail messages with him as well as speak with him in-person. I also recognized that the dilemma was a teachable moment not only for Richard but also for his classmates, especially since they needed to consider the possibility of a similar incident in their futures as teachers. The following excerpt from one of my e-mail messages to him conveys some of the issues I hoped he would understand:

> It is true that, as I mentioned in class, many aspects of language regarding correctness are arbitrary. That is one of the key universal features of language. It isn't a "double standard" that your gender colors the interpretation that readers derive from your comment. Language is always gendered in addition to subject to varying interpretations and meanings based on the class, race, ethnicity, age, and relationship (among other things) of the interlocutors. I can appreciate your interest to right wrongs, but I also know that discourse must remain within established norms for it to be conducive to communication and learning. Furthermore, as the teacher, I am especially responsible for ensuring that everyone shares in the discomfort equitably. And since I am male and there are fewer male students than female students, we are in a women's college, and are citizens of a nation who has codified aspects of language correctness and obscenity, I could not allow your comment to remain in its original form.

Throughout this experience, I was careful to reassure Richard that his posting and our ensuing electronic and in person conversation would not have a negative influence on his grade. At the same time, I realized the potential in this incident for him and his classmates to consider similar dilemmas they might face as teachers. I asked Richard for his consent to use his posting as an instance of unexpected and sometimes problematic outcomes when one asks students to write comments or similarly open-ended content. I wanted this group of beginning teachers to consider the possibility of their future students either saying or writing something that might be considered racist, homophobic, prejudiced, or otherwise inappropriate for a classroom situation and what they would do in response. I assured Richard that I would not discuss the particulars of his posting, referring to it only as an instance of a teaching dilemma related to language development. He graciously agreed.

CONCLUSION

I began this chapter by arguing that the task faced by teachers responsible for developing students? academic language proficiency is daunting in its complexity and uncertainty. No agreement exists as to what ?academic language? might be, especially in most present classrooms, where multiple linguistic, cultural, and situational layers make such definition difficult

(Bunch, 2006, 2009; Valdés, 2004). Similarly, there is no one approach or method that works for all language minority students, ensuring their linguistic proficiency and academic success (Hawkins, 2004). Finally, the "English learner" designation is problematic in that it conceals great heterogeneity of English proficiency levels, academic achievement, socioeconomic and immigration statuses, national origins, and schooling backgrounds (Batalova, Fix, & Murray, 2005).

I rely on information and communication technologies (ICTs) as tools and contexts to further preservice teachers' critical language awareness and, ultimately, their pedagogical language knowledge (Galguera, 2011). ICTs, despite their popularity and prevalence in all sectors of society, constitute new literacies (Leu et al., 2004) that afford teacher educators opportunities for experiential approaches in teacher education. Levin, Arafe, Lenhart, and Rainie (2002) make a compelling case for reducing the "digital disconnect" between schools and most students' experiences. Clearly, incorporating ICTs as a pedagogical context in teacher preparation begins to undo this disconnect. But perhaps more importantly, digital contexts in teacher education have the potential to transform the pedagogy of teacher education and prepare beginning teachers who understand the importance of defining learning outcomes as language development for academic purposes. It is my hope that this chapter will contribute to the discussion of language development practice and its corresponding efforts in teacher preparation as well as stimulate ideas and possibilities among other teacher educators.

NOTES

1. For this assignment, I rely on the online "Content Builder" tool that is available from the Multimedia Educational Resource for Learning and Online Teaching (MERLOT), "a program of the California State University, in partnership with higher education institutions, professional societies, and industry" (from the MERLOT site, http://www.merlot.org). "Snapshot" is what MERLOT calls each web page created with their tool.
2. All preservice teachers complete two semester-long student teaching field placements at one of the local public schools. They are required to spend mornings at their placements and attend courses in the afternoon.

REFERENCES

Alim, H. S. (2005). Critical language awareness in the United States: Revisiting issues and revising pedagogies in a resegregated society. *Educational Researcher, 34*(7), 24-31.

Anderson, R. C. (1977). The Notion of schemata and the educational enterprise. In R. C. Anderson, R. J. Spiro, & W. E. Monatague (1977). *Schooling and the acquisition of knowledge* (pp. 415-431). Hillsdale, NJ: Lawrence Erlbaum.

Andrews, S. (2007). *Teacher language awareness.* Cambridge, England: Cambridge University Press.

Bartlett, F. C. (1932). *Remembering.* Cambridge, England: Cambridge University Press.

Batalova, J., Fix, M., & Murray, J. (2005). *English language learner adolescents: Demographics and literacy achievements. Report to the Center for Applied Linguistics.* Washington, DC: Migration Policy Institute.

Bruner, J., & Sherwood, V. (1975). Peekaboo and the learning of rule structures. In J. S. Bruner, A. Jolly, & K. Sylva (Eds.), *Play: Its role in development and evolution* (pp. 277-285). Harmondsworth, England: Penguin Books.

Bunch, G. C. (2006). "Academic English" in the 7th grade: Broadening the lens, expanding access. *Journal of English for Academic Purposes, 5,* 284-301.

Bunch, G. C. (2009). "Going up There": Challenges and opportunities for language minority students during a mainstream classroom speech event. *Linguistics and Education: An International Research Journal, 20*(2), 81-108.

California Department of Education. (2002). *English-Language Development Standards For California Public Schools, Kindergarten Through Grade Twelve.* Sacramento, CA: Author.

Carter, R. (2003). Language awareness. *ELT Journal, 57*(1), 64-65.

Clark, R., & Ivanic, R. (1997). *The politics of writing.* London, England: Routledge.

Crawford, J. (2004). *Educating English learners:? Language diversity in the classroom* (5th ed.). Los Angeles, CA: Bilingual Education Services.

Cuban, L. (2001). *How can I fix it?: finding solutions and managing dilemmas: An educator's road map.* New York, NY: Teachers College Press.

Ellis, R. (1997). Explicit language and second language pedagogy. In L. van Lier & D. Corson (Eds.), *Encyclopedia of language and education: Knowledge about language* (Vol. 6, pp. 163-172). Dordrecht, The Netherlands: Kluwer Academic.

Ellis, R. (2010). Explicit form focused instruction and second language acquisition. In B. Spolsky & F. M. Hult (Eds.), *The Handbook of Educational Linguistics* (pp. 437-455). Hoboken, NJ: John Wiley & Sons.

Fairclough, N. (1995). *Critical discourse analysis. The critical study of language.* New York, NY: Longman.

Fairclough, N. (2001). *Language and power: Language in social life* (2nd ed.). London, England: Longman.

Fairclough, N. (2003). *Analysing Discourse: Textual Analysis for Social Research.* London, England: Routledge.

Galguera, T. (2011). Participant structures as professional learning tasks and the development of pedagogical language knowledge among preservice teachers. *Teacher Education Quarterly, 38*(1), 85-106.

Gee, J. P. (2007). *Social linguistics and literacies: Ideology in discourses.* London, England: Routledge.

Gibbons, P. (2002). *Scaffolding language, scaffolding learning: Teaching Second language learners in the mainstream classroom.* Portsmouth, NH: Heinemann.

Hakuta, K. (1987). *Mirror of language: The debate on bilingualism*. New York, NY: Basic Books.

Hawkins, M. R. (2004). Researching English language and literacy development in schools. *Educational Researcher, 33*(3), 14-25.

Jackson, P. W. (1968). *Life in the classroom*. New York, NY: Holt, Reinhart, & Winston.

Lee, L. (2002). Enhancing learners' communication skills through synchronous electronic interaction and task-based instruction. *Foreign Language Annals, 35*(1), 16-24.

Levin, D., Arafeh, S., Lenhart, A., & Rainie, L. (2002). *The digital disconnect: The widening gap between Internet-savvy students and their schools*. Washington, DC: Pew Internet and American Life Project. Retrieved August 12, from http://www.pewInternet.org/Reports/2002/The-Digital-Disconnect-The-widening-gap-between-Internetsavvy-students-and-their-schools.aspx

Leu, D. J., Kinzer, C. K., Coiro, J. L., & Cammack, D. W. (2004). Toward a theory of new literacies emerging from the Internet and other information and communication technologies. In R. B. Ruddell, & N. J. Unrau (Eds.), *Theoretical models and processes of reading* (5th ed., pp. 1570-1613). Newark, DE: International Reading Association.

Leu, D. J., O'Byrne, W. I., Zawilinski, L., McVerry, J. G., & Everett-Cacopardo, H. (2009). Expanding the new literacies conversation. *Educational Researcher, 38*(4), 264-269.

Oliver, R., & Haig, Y. (2005). Teacher perceptions of student speech: A quantitative study. *Australian Review of Applied Linguistics, 28*(2), 44-59.

Ong, W. J. (2002). *Orality and literacy: The technologizing of the word*. New York, NY: Routledge.

Palfrey, J., & Gasser, U. (2008). *Born digital: Understanding the first generation of digital natives*. New York, NY: Basic Books.

Pennycook, A. (2001). *Critical applied linguistics: A critical introduction*. Mahwah, NJ: Lawrence Erlbaum.

Schuck, S., & Russell, T. (2005). Self-study, critical friendship, and the complexities of teacher education. *Studying Teacher Education, 1*(2), 107-121.

Shavelson, R. J. (1973). *The basic teaching skill: Decision making*. Stanford, CA: Stanford University School of Education Center for Research and Development in Teaching.

Shor, I. (1992). *Empowering education: Critical teaching for social change*. Chicago, IL: University of Chicago Press.

Shulman, L. (1987). Knowledge and teaching: Foundations of the new reform. *Harvard Educational Review, 57*, 1-22.

Tigchelaar, A., & Korthagen, F. (2004). Deepening the exchange of student teaching experiences: Implications for the pedagogy of teacher education of recent insights into teacher behaviour. *Teaching and Teacher Education, 20*, 665-679.

Valdés, G. (2001). *Learning and not learning English: Latino students in American schools*. New York, NY: Teachers College Press.

Valdés, G. (2004). Between support and marginalization: The development of academic language in linguistic minority children. *Bilingual Education and Bilingualism, 7*(2 & 3), 102-132.

van Lier, L. (1995). *Introducing language awareness.* Harmondsworth, England: Penguin.

Walqui, A. (2006). Scaffolding instruction for English language learners: A conceptual framework. *The International Journal of Bilingual Education and Bilingualism, 9*(2), 159-180.

Zwiers, J. (2008). *Building academic language: Essential practices for content classrooms.* San Francisco, CA: Jossey-Bass.

CHAPTER 6

EDUCATORS' CONCEPTIONS OF ACADEMIC LITERACY AND LANGUAGE

Steven Z. Athanases and Juliet Michelsen Wahleithner

The work in understanding academic literacy and its application to instruction and learning must continue to be defined and redefined.

—Academic Literacy Summit participant

In response to the growing numbers of English language learners (ELLs) in U.S. schools, educational initiatives have developed to prepare teachers to meet the needs of ELLs in all classes. Among these efforts have been teacher education, development, and assessment projects focused on academic literacy and language (ALL). Pre- and in-service programs increasingly promote, develop, and assess capacity to teach ALL (Intersegmental Committee of the Academic Senates, 2002; National Council of Teachers of English, 2006; Pecheone & Chung, 2006).

Several problems often arise in these efforts. First, various, often competing, notions frame what *academic literacy* (or disciplinary literacy) and language mean and include, how they are best developed, and what challenges arise and supports are needed. Most projects use at least a basic

Academic Language in Second Language Learning, pp. 125–146

definition of academic literacy as the capacity to learn from, compose, and critically reflect on multiple forms of text, primarily in school content areas, P-16 (Moje, 2007). Schooling and the disciplines demand particular forms of language use (Schleppegrell, 2004), and *academic language* can serve the broader goals of academic literacy (Enright, 2010). Challenges grow as subjects diversify in upper grades, reading and writing demands intensify, and genres students read and compose gain complexity. For many, especially ELLs and nonstandard English speakers, such advanced literacy activity can be daunting (Schleppegrell & Colombi, 2002). Academic literacy and language are fields that may support such activity. However, what these fields entail varies widely from one theoretical conception to another, and such conceptions can have profound effects on what gets taught and learned.

A second problem is that educators' perspectives in ALL published work are rare. Without these perspectives in the work, initiatives run the risk of developing top-down models uninformed by practitioners. Such models, if not resonant for educators, can meet resistance or die out as passing fads. A third problem is that the interface between the published literature on ALL and actions teachers take to address such concerns can reveal a disconnect. Worse, work in the name of ALL can assume simplistic forms that undermine rather than support content learning (Bartolomé, 1998; Bruna, Vann, & Escudero, 2007). Academic literacy and language are terms fairly new in the education lexicon and need to be defined and redefined, as noted in our opening quote—with voices of thoughtful educators helping to shape those definitions.

Little research has featured teachers' conceptions and learning about ALL or perceptions of affordances and constraints in ALL development. To this end, we sought to understand perspectives of a diverse group of P-16 educators working in culturally and linguistically diverse schools and systems in northern California, many serving large numbers of students living in poverty. These educators' conceptions of need for these populations are a bellwether of national trends. Area students, many ELLs, speak various first languages—mostly Spanish, with many speaking Vietnamese, Hmong, Lao, and Russian/Ukrainian, among other first languages; and many others are nonstandard language users. The achievement gap is ever salient in the region, as educators strive to address urgent academic needs of students. Inviting these educators into ALL development work is essential and can help shape professional directions.

As part of an ongoing project, we have cohosted with university colleagues and local educational leaders an annual academic literacy summit. At these summits, academic language frequently has been embedded in larger discussions about academic literacy. For our first summit, we provided inputs and workshops, but also invitations to reflect on definitions, purposes, challenges, and supports related to the broader domain of academic literacy (hereafter, "AL"). Drawing upon data from the summit, we asked this research question: What are educators' conceptions of academic literacy in practice with culturally and linguistically diverse students, particularly in high need and often underperforming schools? We examined various dimensions of academic literacy, with academic language playing a key role.

FRAMEWORK

Competing Models of Academic Literacy

Basic conceptions of AL include learning from, composing, and critically reflecting on multiple text forms and linking literacy (reading, writing, speaking) with content area learning. For example, while many view reading instruction as exclusive to early grades, reports document dips in scores after this age, arguing that all teachers must provide reading support and instruction into adolescence (Biancarosa & Snow, 2006; Hall, 2005; Jacobs, 2008). Such work can include strategic approaches to reading for content area learning (e.g., Alvermann, Phelps, & Ridgeway, 2007; Greenleaf, Schoenbach, Cziko, & Mueller, 2001). Reports also document weak performances in analytic writing and explore how writing can support learning from content area source texts (Graham & Hebert, 2010; Sperling & Freedman, 2001). Despite these reports, those not designated language arts or reading teachers, especially in preservice, often resist AL work due to constraints of curriculum coverage and time, and a belief that they should not have to teach, for example, content area reading (Hall, 2005). Also, writing is used and taught relatively little beyond language arts, and in-school essay assessments remain uncommon, with selected response assessments dominating since the mid-20th century (Stiggins, 1994). Without occasions to develop reading and writing that meet demands of advanced literacy, students are disadvantaged.

Support and instruction in reading and writing may not suffice without teachers' attention to discipline-specific forms and functions. Noting the "every teacher a teacher of reading" model lacks a complex view of disciplinary literacy, Shanahan and Shanahan (2008) found content area experts' and secondary teachers' own comprehension strategies in math, chemistry, and history varied due to ways of knowing in different disciplines. The researchers also characterized an increasing specialization of literacy: The foundation was a basic level including decoding text. The intermediate level was activity generalizable across content areas and tasks. Finally, disciplinary literacy included engaging with text framed by subject-specific ways of knowing.

Some view the last of these as using different semiotic tools specific to varied discourse communities (Gee, 2003; Moje, Young, Readence, & Moore, 2000). Concerns here include types of text studied and constructed, kinds and methods of using evidence, norms for producing and communicating knowledge and for formulating and arranging arguments in reports. As they work with tools, individuals develop identities associated with particular discourses. Disciplines are dynamic, but ways of demonstrating knowledge assume discipline-specific representations in academic writing (Thaiss & Zawacki, 2006). Historical writing features causation, primary sources to build interpretation of events, and perspective; math features conjectures and proof; science features hypothesis-testing, experimental study, and evidence. Although meta-genres may cross disciplines (Carter, 2007), an important part of learning includes opportunities to participate in disciplinary communities in which particular discourses get used and developed. Teachers may need to provide apprenticeships so students can learn the "secret English," the kind of discourse that constructs meaning in a discipline (Martin, Wignell, & Rothery, 1993).

For teachers, managing such work can be a tall order. K-6 ELLs learning to write accounts of experience in science, for example, may require a range of supports (Merino & Hammond, 2002). Providing scaffolds for subject-specific writing requires care so they do not constrain but foster more heuristic forms of writing (Durst, 1984). Whether instructors articulate disciplinary rules or not, they may expect students to learn specific types of claims and warrants appropriate for a field, as well as disciplinary content and processes (Herrington, 1985). History teachers who integrate writing in courses may face problems of students' lack of adequate background knowledge and language proficiency for both processing and producing text (de Oliveira, 2008). Given lack of attention in scholarly work of disciplines and content area work in education to clarifying and articulating disciplinary rules of argument and evidence, a teacher is left with little guidance for deep evaluation of student writing (Langer, 1992). One study in high school history found a range of instructional strategies were needed to scaffold processes of interpreting historical events and generating evidence for claims about history (Monte-Sano, 2008).

These ways of knowing and displaying understanding that teachers must help students develop get marked in language. Language of schooling can be analyzed and taught, through attention to purposes and register features of general school genres and discipline-specific ways language functions. The latter category includes, for example, how language functions to link theory and practice in chemistry (Mohan &

Slater, 2006) or interpret experience in history (Schleppegrell, 2004). It also includes ways to enable students to explore genre conventions of academic tasks, play with language across registers, and develop meta-language in literature (Hammond, 2006). These practices and analyses are key to addressing needs of ELLs working to develop content area knowledge and English language proficiency and who may need guidance to crack academic codes. Much of the work, following Halliday (1993), assumes language is purposeful, constructs meaning in discipline-specific ways, and can serve as resource in content area learning. Varied grammatical constructions communicate different meanings in ways that can be made explicit so students learn how grammar can serve as a resource for meaning and effect (Schleppegrell, 1998).

Social perspectives also inform notions of AL. The discourse communities model foregrounds social engagement in ways of reasoning and using language. Social uses of literacy also can support in-school literacy development through students' informal group talk (Bunch, 2006) and through "hidden literacies" that tap social networks and linguistic resources (Villalva, 2006). Often such unofficial, social, hybrid literacies are not recognized for academic scaffolding potential in official school curricula (Dyson, 2008; Heath, 1983). AL initiatives need attention to out-of-school literacy practices that call for a more generative view of literacies and how they can be supported and taught (Alvermann, 2008; Flood, Heath, & Lapp, 2008; Hull & Schultz, 2002; Kress, 2008; Leander & Lovvorn, 2006; Lewis, 2008; Moje, Overby, Tysvaer, & Morris, 2008).

Institutions also inform AL conceptions. Accountability and testing demand documentation of achievement, and many see AL features as key to helping students make adequate progress in all subjects. Some teachers, however, strive to integrate AL work but resort to "negative and reductive examination of language errors alone" (Mohan & Slater, 2006, 315). Bruna et al. (2007) found such reduction in a ninth-grade English learner science class where academic-language-as-vocabulary minimized language production opportunities and science content knowledge development. Similarly working at cross purposes, a fifth-grade teacher in an English and Spanish bilingual class committed to students' academic language development focused 96% of remarks on student essays on spelling, punctuation, and grammar, and enacted cultural rapport building and immediacy in discourse events in ways that minimized students' need to produce and contextualize language (Bartolomé, 1998). These issues mark a need for deeper conceptualizations of AL and for engaging educators in articulating and shaping them.

The Need for P-16 Educators' Perspectives and Knowledge in Educational Innovations

Educational innovations such as AL need to include perspectives and knowledge of those working in the field. Only when we tap the range of educators engaged in the work of a field can we develop a representative and well-articulated knowledge base of effective teaching—in this case, of academic literacy. Tapping educators' conceptual knowledge is key—as a first step in articulating what educators currently know about AL, and what they need and want to know.

Educators' perspectives in AL professional and published work are rare. The problem originates in historic neglect of teacher perspectives in development of an educational field. Too often educational "knowledge" gets constructed in the academy, with too little attention to ways teachers' classroom-based inquiries and developing understandings can shape such knowledge (e.g., Cochran-Smith & Lytle, 2009). Much AL-related professional development (PD) positions teachers as recipients of authoritative discourses on research knowledge and best practices, failing to invite teachers to generate and possibly appropriate new conceptions of teaching and learners (Greenleaf & Katz, 2004). This stance is evidenced when reports cast teachers without agency, in passive voice: teachers *were given materials, provided with workshops*.

Our framework rests on this core assumption: Any line of work in education needs to include teachers' conceptions, understandings, and knowledge. For practitioner knowledge to become a professional knowledge base for teaching, it must be public, represented in a form enabling its cumulative and shared nature, and continually verified and improved (Hiebert, Gallimore, & Stigler, 2002). To develop a professional knowledge base for effective AL teaching, then, we need to engage P-16 educators in the work and to make public their AL conceptions, learning, and practices. This includes skills, knowledge, and dispositions necessary for effective teaching (Shulman, 1987). It also includes how such "knowledge" gets contextualized by the social surround, schooling conditions, and opportunities to teach and learn needed to make the work possible (Fenstermacher & Richardson, 2005). It is teachers' conceptions and practices that will help develop the knowledge base of effective AL teaching.

METHOD

Context for the Study: An Academic Literacy Summit

The purpose of our study was to tap regional educators' current conceptions of academic literacy. The study is part of a university-schools project to develop and study AL with regional educators working in culturally and linguistically diverse sites in the Sacramento Valley region of Northern California. The project is a partnership of the School of Education at the University of California, Davis, including the Cooperative Research and Extension Service for Schools (CRESS) Center, which houses many regional California Subject Matter Projects, and the nearby Yolo County Office of Education. The specific context for this study was the 2008 Academic Literacy Summit: A Call to Action in Practice and in Policy. Coplanned by university and P-16 leaders, the Summit attracted nearly 200 educators from the region. Schools serve a metropolitan area, as well as rural communities, with many students from families living in poverty and many ELLs.

AL content was threaded through all activities, with a range of theoretical perspectives, practical approaches, and entry points. To anchor the Summit in student achievement, an opening keynote examined the achievement gap in California and a need to address literacy in schools. Researchers spoke on the language of schooling, functions of content area text language, the social nature of language production, and out-of-school literacies and how they challenge us to learn what we can and cannot teach in schools. Breakout sessions targeted all schooling levels and subject areas. Presenters included education, linguistics, Spanish, and writing faculty of two universities, and science, history, and writing project directors from the California Subject Matter Projects (CSMP). Most breakouts included at least two presenters, often a campus-based researcher with a P-12 teacher. Sessions integrated research, practice, application, and reflection.

Participants

Participants included summit attendees, primarily 89 who completed questionnaires the day of the summit. Roles these participants played in education ranged from early childhood teacher through college instructor. *Current* specific roles were the following: elementary school teachers (18); middle school teachers (5); high school teachers (9); other unspecified K-12 teachers (10); literacy, reading, and bilingual education coaches and specialists (15); curriculum developers (8); school site administrators (9); district administrators (5); college/university faculty and staff (5); and graduate students (5). Participants also indicated *most recent* job responsibilities; here we noted that many coaches, curriculum developers, administrators, and graduate students recently had been classroom teachers. Also, 13 P-12 teachers, 2 CSMP leaders, and 12 university faculty/researchers led breakouts. The first author of this chapter served on the summit planning committee, and both authors (former K-12 teachers and experienced professional developers) participated in data collection and analysis.

Data Collection

We distributed open-ended questionnaires to Summit attendees at the opening of the day's events and encouraged participants to fill these out during morning sessions and later in the day, as well. Questionnaires ran four pages, with a range of items designed to elicit conceptions and illustrations of AL; challenges and successes of the work; ways summit events were prompting thinking; and efforts needed to sustain such work. Nearly all participants were observed filling out portions of the questionnaires; however, as predicted, many attendees did not complete the entire questionnaire and return it, no doubt due to its length. We received 89 completed for a 50% return rate, which represented all participant groups in terms of educational roles in approximately representative numbers. While selected response items may have yielded a higher return rate, open-ended responses yielded rich information in participants' language. Some participants noted appreciation for the design, including one who wrote, "Thank you for both posing and reading *constructed* responses." Research team members also kept fieldnotes of breakout and keynote speaker sessions, and collected session handouts and artifacts. A protocol guided note-taking to include participants' professional ideas and contexts, presenters' definitions or conceptions of AL, questions raised by participants, issues discussed, and ideas and practices participants accepted and resisted. Researchers also recorded fieldnotes in informal breaks and lunch discussions.

Data Analysis

Data analysis included several strands. First, we examined educators' questionnaire responses without a priori categories. Data collected from open-ended questionnaire items were typed into files verbatim. After preliminary review and analysis, research team members developed a coding scheme, practiced using it with data, and independently coded (and, in some cases, double coded) data per questionnaire item. The team reviewed all coded data together. We used grounded theory (Glaser & Strauss, 1967), recoding responses as necessary until we achieved intercoder agreement on all data, and revising categories and themes within them until they captured all available data. Coded data then were tabulated, and charts and data displays (Miles & Huberman, 1994) mapped response categories and themes within them.

Second, we considered the reviewed AL literature. We used published conceptions of AL as lenses through which to review data. We considered the degree to which conceptions of AL in the literature surfaced in our participants' responses. For example, we considered participants' AL conceptions, using Shanahan and Shanahan's (2008) model of levels of increasing specialization in AL (basic, intermediate, advanced). Third, we looked beyond questionnaire responses to participants' engagements in summit activities. Along with field notes and session artifacts, research team members wrote analytic memos on session activities, ideas and issues, and lingering AL questions. Memos were reviewed for emerging themes and for ideas referenced in the AL literature. Finally, we reviewed reports, figures, and tables of all results for crosscutting themes.

RESULTS

We begin by describing diverse foci of educators' reported conceptions of AL. We then turn to functions educators identified for AL. We also look closely at specific literacy features, their frequency of mention, and the levels of specificity in participants' AL conceptions.

Educators' Wide-Ranging Conceptions of Academic Literacy Foci

Educators' conceptions of AL were wide-ranging. Here we present a brief sampling of responses to illustrate how varied responses were in defining AL. First, there were general concerns of effective functioning within an academic context. For example, a community college instructor created a handbook "that outlines Academic Literacy for new students":

> It covers such things as what to do if you miss a class, are walking in late to class, have a disagreement with an instructor, and what various campus departments do. In addition, I polled a number of teachers for ways students can be successful in their classes. They gave me lists of equipment, attitude recommendations, time/place rules for questions, and study skills. We hope students can use this (I think counselors outline it at orientations).

These handbook tips feature ways one should behave, operate, and function within an academic culture. These may be particularly important, given the large numbers of community college students in California who are first generation college students, immigrants or children of immigrants, and non-native English speakers.

A second view of AL concerned the general language of academic work. One K-12 Reading Specialist described this as "Knowledge of academic vocabulary, common idioms, literary references." This conception highlights cultural literacy and perhaps the value of gaining access to cultures of power (Delpit, 1988). A third conception was the importance of possessing and using background knowledge as a means to enter the world of print text. A middle school EL Specialist highlighted this dimension of AL: "activating prior knowledge either to create new schema or to build on old—again, this is done to allow for access to core subjects." This response highlights contributions of schema theory to reading research and the role of prior knowledge in all content learning. A fourth conception of AL focused on vocabulary. One middle school teacher described the importance of "Having a strong expansive vocabulary (academic, but also social), and being able to speak in the different 'registers' of each content area—'speak science.'" This response highlights a discourse community (Gee, 2003; Moje, Young, Readence, & Moore, 2000) and specialized disciplinary languages (Schleppegrell, 2004; Shanahan & Shanahan, 2008).

Widely Varied Notions of the Functions and Dimensions of Academic Literacy

Varied functions of AL. Educators identified many functions of AL. Participants' dominant conception of AL was a knowledge domain students need to acquire in order to succeed at school literacy tasks.

Figure 6.1 shows in the left box that a range of AL knowledge dimensions (to be reported further in the next section) support engagement in and success with literacy tasks common to academic work. Educators described how the ability to apply that knowledge and perform varied tasks successfully provides access to short-term rewards, such as texts, ideas, course content, and deeper knowledge. Also, however, educators described longer-term outcomes (the right box in Figure 6.1), including effective communication, participation in communities and the larger

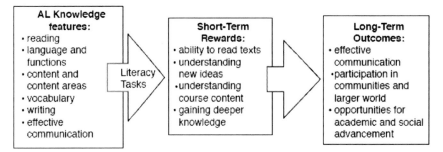

Figure 6.1.   Educators' conceptions of the features and functions of academic literacy

world, and opportunities for academic and social advancement. Responses were grounded in knowledge of learners, especially ELLs and underperforming students, who have a particular need to acquire AL to access learning opportunities and to reach achievement goals. In this way, the conception of AL as access was steeped in notions of equity and social justice.

Participants, however, repeatedly criticized diluting curriculum to make it accessible (e.g., "We need to raise kids to higher levels by adding support, not 'watering down'"; "All kids can learn rigorous material—it's our job to scaffold and support them"). There was urgency in responses. Referencing achievement gap data, a high school science teacher/bilingual resource instructor noted, "We must respond. *Every* teacher, not just English." Two ideas here are salient: The word *must* signals a social and professional imperative; *every teacher* highlights a *shared* responsibility of P-16 educators to promote *AL as access*. An administrator reported, "The development of academic language in all is contingent on how we as a society choose to provide access to ALL." This response highlights ways resources and societal commitments matter, as well as methods of delivery, and like other responses, it soundly rejects equating access with simplifying curriculum.

Range of literacy dimensions. We turn now to examine specifically the various *literacy* dimensions of educators' conceptions of AL. Participants' AL definitions included various features (those highlighted in the left box of Figure 6.1) elaborated more fully now in Table 6.1. Table 6.1 shows these varied features with the prominent themes that emerged. At the top of the list, just under two-thirds of respondents identified reading as central to AL, and these responses came from educators across the gradespan. Table 6.1 shows features in rank order by frequency of mention. However, in the next section we report the features in Figure 6.2, using an analytic scheme on degree of specialization.

Increasing Specialization of Academic Literacy Features in Educators' Conceptions

Here we use Shanahan and Shanahan's (2008) model of the increasing specialization of literacy. As noted earlier, their study involved content area experts and secondary teachers of math, chemistry, and history talking about processes they used to comprehend and produce texts in their fields. The researchers found participants' responses were widely varied. Across groups, participants identified a foundational set of basic skills upon which more complex skills are built. Building on top of these was a set of intermediate skills common across disciplines. Finally, each discipline, the

Table 6.1.   Important Features of Academic Literacy (and Themes) in Participants' Definitions

	Number (and %) of Respondents Reporting * (N = 75)
Literacy features	
Reading	49 (65)
General cognitive strategies	
Making connections	
"Going meta"	
Language and its functions	39 (52)
Academic/school language	
Language structure and functions	
Language of content	
Content and content areas	27 (36)
Specialized language	
Discipline specific ways of thinking, representing	
Vocabulary	23 (31)
Acquisition: persistence of vocabulary as foundational	
Pedagogy: prominence of "drill and kill" approaches	
Writing	21 (28)
General processes and skills	
Writing to learn	
Effective communication	18 (24)

* Participants had multiple opportunities to provide conceptions of academic literary, and some responses were double-coded.

authors noted, has both its own specialized language and its own specialized processes for constructing and displaying understanding. This is the top area of the triangle in Figure 6.2. Here we see reflected the different ways of knowing within disciplines.

Figure 6.2 uses this model to visually represent the central tendency of our participants' reports, per literacy feature. The Figure 6.2 shows that most of the literacy features in participants' responses were cast at the intermediate literacy level. We now discuss each of the literacy features. To do so, we begin at the more basic level, which, in our participants'

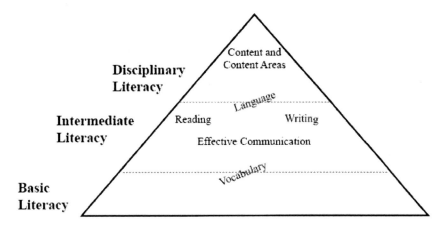

Source: Adapted from Shanahan and Shanahan (2008).

Figure 6.2.   The increasing specialization of academic literacy in educators' conceptions.

responses, was vocabulary. We also discuss themes within each literacy feature as identified in Table 6.1.

Vocabulary. Nearly a third of respondents identified vocabulary as a key AL feature (Table 6.1), and half of these reported this element first. Vocabulary teetered between basic and intermediate literacy work, up through high school. Responses featured learning words and occasionally word roots, using practice and repetition to expand vocabulary and "to access and process grade level content successfully." Reports noted vocabulary was important to understand "directions on worksheets, curriculum terms" and "to speak in the different 'registers' of each content area." Most responses about vocabulary were thin, naming vocabulary or school vocabulary without elaboration, unlike language and its functions (reported later), which featured word study in groups or classes of words tied to functional uses in content. Five participants, for example (three teachers, a reading specialist, and a bilingual resource educator) offered these conceptions of ways to address vocabulary: explicit vocabulary instruction; preview vocabulary needed to access content; repetition—encourage rereading; reread directions and rephrase; teach words/concepts as written in the text. Some responses emerged as little more than teach it and repeat it, "drill & kill."

Generalizable reading processes and skills. Figure 6.2 shows that several literacy features fell at the intermediate level. Most prominent among these was reading. Nearly two-thirds of participants identified reading as a key need in AL work (Table 6.1). Despite widespread local use of scripted reading programs, pacing guides, and multiple choice assessments of reading recall, educators offered more complex conceptions of reading for AL, even for young children, than *basic literacy* which Shanahan and Shanahan (2008) describe as "skills such as decoding and knowledge of high-frequency words that underlie virtually all reading tasks" (p. 44). Instead, participants cast reading skills and processes in AL primarily as *intermediate literacy*: "skills common to many tasks, including generic comprehension strategies, common word meanings, and basic fluency" (Shanahan & Shanahan, 2008, p. 44). According to participants, comprehension in AL included understanding text structure and content, how to "make connections with other texts, self and world," and how to activate prior knowledge "either to create new schema or build on old." Cognitive strategies included restructuring "information into manageable chunks," identifying significant passages, and "ability to paraphrase"—requiring "dissection of ideas/concepts." It also includes developing relevant "concepts, terms, habits of mind, graphic organizers, ways of thinking." Of particular importance for AL, several respondents specified students must "go meta" on cognition and language use, developing a conscious understanding of their processes, able to explain how they are learning.

Generalizable writing processes and skills. Conceptions of writing for AL also emerged as intermediate literacy—more than basic skills, primarily generalizable processes and skills equated with being academically literate. Respondents included organization and fluency, as well as ability to use "academic formal English." Several also wrote of writing to learn: "in all academic areas, as a way to solidify ideas and concepts (and) to increase higher level thinking skills." This included how writing guides students' knowledge-making and as a way for students "to demonstrate their grasp and understanding of the subject matter." However, few responses illustrated subject-specific functions and structures of writing.

Effective communication.   Though themes in this category were seeded already, especially in writing, just under a quarter of respondents specifically noted AL involves ability to communicate effectively, again characterized mostly as intermediate or generalizable literacy. Three themes emerged here. First, responses highlighted communication as purposeful and varied, or "the ability to function in society with all types of literacy." Second, responses attended to "show what you know." Part of this includes "learning more and more specific ways to describe what you learned," being able to articulate understanding of content, or "being able to communicate concepts." There is utilitarian value, marked in responses that highlighted, for example, "conveying knowledge of text to teacher" and success on assessment measures. However, several respondents also noted a third theme: the social dimension of communication as part of AL. This may require "self-identification as part of a community that uses academic language." This remark was rare in the data, but it links to issues of identity, identification, and engagement in discourses of a community (Gee, 2003; Moje, 2007).

Language and its functions. Another feature was language itself. As Figure 2 indicates, this literacy feature was cast at the level of intermediate literacy but transitioning to or approaching disciplinary literacy. Table 6.1 shows just over half of participants identified language and its functions as key to AL, with three themes emerging. The first theme was *academic/ school language* as distinct from other literacies. This related to learning and not just "doing school." One respondent reported AL "is not just an issue of vocabulary, it is about contextual knowledge, prior knowledge, language, how students learn, etc." Several participants highlighted various language "registers," academic versus others, including "street literacy." One highlighted the theme of AL as context-dependent: "The kind of language you use will be differentially powerful depending upon the expectations of the context in which you find yourself." Participants repeatedly reported urgency to develop ELLs' English language proficiency for academic success. A middle school ELL resource teacher noted AL means "Being literate/successful in the language of school. It's a third language for ELLs—1) native language, 2) English, 3) academic English." For some, AL for ELLs meant gaining access to academic capital, requiring that the teacher use what one participant called "consistency in effective implementation of instruction for all students regardless of their social-economic and linguistic barriers."

The second language theme was *language structures and functions*. Participants marked how understanding word functions contributes to AL, which is, one reported, the "ability to know how language is constructed. For example, connection, functional grammar, referrers." It involves "form and function--what language students need to understand, access, engage and produce texts, oral and written." Some noted metalinguistic awareness as key to AL, including knowing "how language is constructed" and "being able to control a language function." Transparency of AL processes with language was linked to access for ELLs. One participant noted, "Language must be unpacked for students, not left to natural discovery." A first-grade teacher noted having believed "students picked up structure of writing/reading naturally" but came to realize it needs to be "pointed out, practiced, talked about, and put to use."

Approaching Shanahan and Shanahan's (2008) top level of disciplinary literacy, the third theme, *language of content*, moved beyond language of academics to subject areas: "Language of a discipline used by practitioners in academic or professional settings." Several participants highlighted how once students learn discipline-specific languages, they can make connections among them, engaging a metadiscursive process, since "Each subject area is about literacy, it's just a different shade or color (history, science)." Making these various functions of language transparent to students was cast as fostering *access* to academic language, literacy, and content.

Content-specificity in academic literacy. Figure 6.2 shows that one literacy feature emerged at the top of the Shanahan and Shanahan (2008) triangle. Just over one-third of participants (Table 6.1) reported content-specificity, how AL is a domain beyond language arts and that it entails more than generalizable skills and processes. Participants reflected on "specialized language" of content areas—*disciplinary literacy* students need in adolescence and beyond, more sophisticated than basic and intermediate literacy and more specialized than generalizable routines (Shanahan & Shanahan, 2008). Two math instructors (one high school, one college) illustrated: (a) "ability to read a word problem, understand the context, understand what is being asked, draw appropriate conclusions from the information, write down appropriate notes, write an equation and solve the problem"; and (b) "represent a situation using tables, graphs, and (if reasonable) an algebraic or numeric expression or statement, and be able to move back and forth between representations." These examples highlight complex academic literacies a math instructor may expect, complicating AL definitions by adding comprehension and communication of algebraic and numeric expressions and multiple forms of representation to views of AL as strictly alphabetic. A few participants noted AL serves students in two other ways related to content area learning: participating in interdisciplinary discourse and effectively displaying learning in assessment contexts. While these tasks come easily for some, others need explicit instruction to develop knowledge to access such elements of advanced literacy.

Educators' Call for Professional Learning in Academic Literacy Development

Although not presented in Table 6.1, we report here that 32 participants (43%) named the teacher's role as key to AL, and this theme ran throughout Summit discussions among attendees beyond merely those who completed questionnaires. Within this theme was a call for supports for leaders to guide teachers in developing AL and with this focus: How do we learn to make the underlying processes and codes more transparent to ourselves as educators and then more transparent to students? There was a tension between desire for such knowledge and tools, and frustration with both institutional constraints on opportunities for teachers to learn and sociopolitical constraints of dictated scripted curricula with little space for such innovations. As one teacher remarked, "Pacing guides do *not* take the place of teacher knowledge." Another commented, "In California, many have been convinced that their job is to read the script, keep up with the pacing guide. If it's not in the script, they don't need to know it." The Summit renewed this participant's belief that teachers were "convinced that they needed to know *more* (always more) to help their kids." Reflecting on conventional institutional arrangements, one reading specialist stated: "Great to see researchers and frontline educators in one place." This statement echoes the argument in our framework that P-16 educators' voices need to be included in framing conceptions of AL.

DISCUSSION AND IMPLICATIONS FOR TEACHING AND TEACHER DEVELOPMENT

This study sought to understand educators' perspectives, in order to bring these into the complex and emerging conversation of conceptualizing academic literacy, its goals and purposes, its challenges, its knowledge base, and educators' needed supports for its development. We found wide variety in educators' conceptions of AL and in their notions of the functions of AL for students. Academic language emerged as a central part of educators' conceptions. Responses overall evidenced a preponderance of attention to deconstructing and constructing text, mostly through use of intermediate level or generalizable literacy strategies. There was far less attention in educators' responses to subject-specific ways of knowing, disciplinary reasoning, and literacy practices and conventions tied explicitly to particular content areas. In addition, while some recent work in academic literacy and language has explored the social dimensions of literacy, participants in our study rarely included such dimensions in their conceptions of AL.

Our study suggests that these last two areas, articulated in some recent research literature, may only rarely appear as dimensions of educators' current AL conceptions. Perhaps these dimensions do not yet hold resonance for many educators or may not hold center stage, due to contextual factors such as the pressures of scripted curricula, pacing guides, and high stakes assessments that place a premium on efficiency in attaining reading comprehension goals. Also, the accountability and testing climate constrains teachers' time and motivation to innovate, particularly in science and history, which students have learned to value less and multiple-subjects teachers may find less urgent to teach (de Oliveria, 2008; Lee, Luykx, Buxton, & Shaver, 2007). A policy climate of English-only also constrains efforts to support ELLs' home language use in schools (Lee et al., 2007), minimizing opportunities to access students' out-of-school literacies as resource. Broadly speaking, some resistance also frequently is due to teachers' lack of efficacy in integrating AL work and a need for collective efficacy (shared perception that one's school group can positively affect student performance) (Cantrell & Hughes, 2008).

The dearth of attention to social dimensions of AL also may point to the need for careful research and professional development on how being part of a semiotic domain (Gee, 2003), engaging in social practices of a disciplinary discourse community, really leads to, links with, and scaffolds AL development. As Moje (2007) notes, more clarification is needed for teachers and teacher educators on "how connections can be made from the everyday text practices of youth to the text practices they must engage in to learn at advanced levels in the disciplines" (p. 32).

Our framework presented the often-competing conceptions of AL in the literature but also highlighted the need for educators' voices in conversations and conceptions of AL. Data collection of the kind used in our study can surface wide-ranging conceptions of AL among P-16 educators and can point to areas of need. Our summit attendees reported the need for ongoing work to articulate and develop solid conceptions of AL and practices that align with these conceptions. Clearly, professional development needs ongoing opportunities to explore AL and should include conceptual clarity, whatever the particular emphases.

Our own work on the annual Academic Literacy Summit has used this examination of educators' conceptions, practices, discussions, and articulated needs as a means to understand what we as an educational community need to know and explore in the fields of academic literacy and language. Noting a dearth of attention in our work and Summit discussions to the "literacies" young people bring with them from their homes and communities, we focused our second annual Summit on this topic. In related work (Wahleithner & Athanases, 2010), we drew on data from that Summit to understand how educators perceive possibilities, practices, and challenges of tapping students' out of school literacies and cultural resources as support for academic learning.

This study holds potential to begin to clarify educators' conceptions of academic language and literacy and how they are distinct from other conceptions of language and literacy. Also, our analyses showed that conceptions of academic literacy, even when collected at an academic literacy summit which likely attracted educators with some knowledge about AL and possibly with some predisposition to address AL concerns in their work in schools, nonetheless were often "thin" and in need of conceptual clarification and content-specificity. If teachers are to be supported in designing more effective curriculum and instruction for linguistically and culturally diverse students in the climate of current school reforms, we as an educational community need to continually, as our opening quote argued, define and redefine conceptions of AL. To do this defining well requires a collaborative effort between educators working on these issues in the academy and those working to develop their students' ALL in P-16 classrooms.

Future efforts need conceptual clarity and grounding, whatever the particular emphases they feature. This is important so potentially strong development opportunities and programs do not go awry due to garbage can models that dump everything into the AL can, yielding, at best, a label for a fad that fades or, worse, a set of practices with conceptual underpinnings that work at cross-purposes with core instructional goals. Also needed, however, is flexibility and a norm of being responsive to evolving understandings not just in the academy but to those jointly constructed by academics and P-16 educators.

ACKNOWLEDGMENTS

An earlier version of this chapter was presented at the American Educational Research Association Annual Meeting in San Diego, 2009. We thank summit 2008 attendees who provided perspectives on academic literacy conceptions and practice, and summit coplanners, especially John Roina, Kerry Enright, Mary V. Sandy, and Edgar Lampkin. We also thank Kim Ferrario, Betsy Gilliland, Pamela Pan, and Jisel Vega for assistance with data collection, and Brenda Rinard for assistance with data collection and analysis.

REFERENCES

Alvermann, D. E. (2008). Why bother theorizing adolescents' online literacies for classroom practice and research? *Journal of Adolescent and Adult Literacy, 52*(1), 8-19.

Alvermann, D. E., Phelps, S. F., & Ridgeway, V. G. (2007). *Content area reading and literacy: Succeeding in today's diverse classrooms* (5th ed). New York, NY: Pearson/ Allyn & Bacon.

Bartolomé, L. I. (1998). *The misteaching of academic discourses.* Boulder, CO: Westview Press.

Biancarosa, C., & Snow, C. E. (2006). *Reading next—A vision for action and research in middle and high school literacy: A report to Carnegie Corporation of New York* (2nd ed.). Washington, DC: Alliance for Excellent Education.

Bruna, K. R., Vann, R., & Escudero, M. P. (2007). What's language got to do with it? A case study of academic language instruction in a high school "English Learner Science" class. *Journal of English for Academic Purposes, 6*(1), 36-54.

Bunch, G. C. (2006). "Academic English" in the 7th grade: Broadening the lens, expanding access. *Journal of English for Academic Purposes, 5*, 284-301.

Cantrell, S. C., & Hughes, H. K. (2008). Teacher efficacy and content literacy implementation: An exploration of the effects of extended professional development and coaching. *Journal of Literacy Research, 40*(1), 95-127.

Carter, M. (2007). Ways of knowing, doing, and writing in the disciplines. *College Composition and Communication, 58*(3), 385-418.

Cochran-Smith, M., & Lytle, S. L. (2009). *Inquiry as stance: Practitioner research for the next generation.* New York, NY: Teachers College Press.

de Oliveira, L. C. (2008). "History doesn't count": Challenges of teaching history in California schools. *The History Teacher, 41*(3), 363-378.

Delpit, L. D. (1988). The silenced dialogue: Power and pedagogy in educating other people's children. *Harvard Educational Review, 58*(3), 280-298.

Durst, R. (1984). The development of analytic writing. In A. N. Applebee (Ed.), *Contexts for learning to write: Studies of secondary school instruction* (pp. 79-102). Norwood, NJ: Ablex.

Dyson, A. H. (2008). Staying in the (curricular) lines: Practice constraints and possibilities in childhood writing. *Written Communication, 25*, 119-159.

Enright, K. A. (2010). Language and literacy for a new mainstream. *American Educational Research Journal.* doi: 10.3102/0002831210368989.

Fenstermacher, G. D., & Richardson, V. (2005). *On making determinations of quality in teaching. Teachers College Record, 107*(1), 186-215.

Flood, J., Heath, S. B., & Lapp, D. (Eds.). (2008). *Handbook of research on teaching literacy through the communicative and visual arts* (Vol. II). New York, NY: Lawrence Erlbaum.

Gee, J. P. (2003). Opportunity to learn: A language-based perspective on assessment. *Assessment in Education, 10*(1), 27-46.

Glaser, B. G., & Strauss, A. L. (1967). *The discovery of grounded theory: Strategies for qualitative research.* Chicago, IL: Aldine.

Graham, S., & Hebert, M. (2010). *Writing to read: Evidence for how writing can improve reading.* New York, NY: Carnegie Corporation of New York.

Greenleaf, C. L., & Katz, M. (2004). Ever newer ways to mean: Authoring pedagogical change in secondary subject-area classrooms. In A. F. Ball & S. W. Freedman (Eds.), *Bakhtinian perspectives on language, literacy, and learning* (pp. 172-202). Cambridge, England: Cambridge University Press.

Greenleaf, C. L., Schoenbach, R., Cziko, C., & Mueller, F. L. (2001). Apprenticing adolescent readers to academic literacy. *Harvard Educational Review, 71*(1), 79-129.

Hall, L. A. (2005). Teachers and content area reading: Attitudes, beliefs and change. *Teaching and Teacher Education, 21*, 403-414.

Halliday, M. A. K. (1993). Towards a language-based theory of learning. *Linguistics and Education, 5*, 93-116.

Hammond, J. (2006). High challenge, high support: Integrating language and content instruction for diverse learners in an English literature classroom. *Journal of English for Academic Purposes, 5*, 269-283.

Heath, S. B. (1983). *Ways with words: Language, life, and work in communities and classrooms.* Cambridge, England: Cambridge University Press.

Herrington, A. J. (1985). Writing in academic settings: A study of the context for writing in two college chemical engineering courses. *Research in the Teaching of English, 19,* 331-361.

Hiebert, J., Gallimore, R., & Stigler, J. W., (2002). A knowledge base for the teaching profession: What would it look like and how can we get one? *Educational Researcher, 31*(5), 3-15.

Hull, G., & Schultz, K. (Eds.). (2002). *School's out! Bridging out-of-school literacies with classroom practice.* New York, NY: Teachers College Press.

Intersegmental Committee of the Academic Senates. (2002, Spring). *Academic literacy: A statement of competencies expected of students entering California's public colleges and universities.* Intersegmental Committee of the Academic Senates of the California Community Colleges, the California State University, and the University of California.

Jacobs, V. A. (2008). Adolescent literacy: Putting the crisis in context. *Harvard Educational Review, 78*(1), 7-39.

Kress, G. (2008). "Literacy" in a multimodal environment of communication. In J. Flood, S. B. Heath, & D. Lapp (Eds.), *Handbook of research on teaching literacy through the communicative and visual arts* (Vol. II, pp. 91-100). New York, NY: Lawrence Erlbaum.

Langer, J. A. (1992). Speaking of knowing: Conceptions of understanding in academic disciplines. In A. Herrington & C. Moran (Eds.), *Writing, teaching, and learning in the disciplines* (pp. 69-85). New York, NY: The Modern Language Association of America.

Leander, K. M., & Lovvorn, J. F. (2006). Literacy networks: Following the circulation of texts, bodies, and objects in the schooling and online gaming of one youth. *Cognition and Instruction, 24,* 291-340.

Lee, O., Luykx, A., Buxton, C., & Shaver, A. (2007). The challenge of altering elementary school teachers' beliefs and practices regarding linguistic and cultural diversity in science instruction. *Journal of Research in Science Teaching, 44*(9), 1269-1291.

Lewis, C. (2008). Internet communication among youth: New practices and epistemologies. In J. Flood, S. B. Heath, & D. Lapp (Eds.), *Handbook of research on teaching literacy through the communicative and visual arts* (Vol. II. pp. 237-246). New York: Lawrence Erlbaum.

Martin, J. R., Wignell, P., Eggins, S., & Rothery, J. (1993). Secret English: Discourse technology in a junior secondary school. In L. Gerot, J. Oldenberg, & T. Van Leeuven (Eds.), *Genre approaches to literacy: Theories and practices* (pp. 143-176). Sydney, Australia: Common Ground.

Merino, B. J., & Hammond, L. (2001). How do teachers facilitate writing for bilingual learners in "sheltered constructivist" science? *Electronic Journal of Literacy Through Science, 1*(1). Retrieved http://ejlts.ucdavis.edu/

Miles, M. B., & Huberman, A. M. (1994). *Qualitative data analysis: An expanded sourcebook.* Thousand Oaks, CA: SAGE.

Mohan, B., & Slater, T. (2006). Examining the theory/practice relation in a high school science register: A functional linguistic perspective. *Journal of English for Academic Purposes, 5,* 302-316.

Moje, E. B. (2007). Developing socially just subject-matter instruction: A review of the literature on disciplinary literacy teaching. *Review of Research in Education, 31*, 1-44.

Moje, E. B., Overby, M., Tysvaer, N., & Morris, K. (2008). The complex world of adolescent literacy: Myths, motivations, and mysteries. *Harvard Educational Review, 78*(1).

Moje, E. B., Young, J. P., Readence, J. E., & Moore, D. W. (2000). Reinventing adolescent literacy for new times: Perennial and millenial issues. *Journal of Adolescent & Adult Literacy, 43*(5), 400-410.

Monte-Sano, C. (2008). Qualities of historical writing instruction: A comparative case study of two teachers' practices. *American Educational Research Journal, 45*(4), 1045-1079.

National Council of Teachers of English. (2006, April). *NCTE principles of adolescent literacy reform: A policy research brief.* Urbana, IL: NCTE. Retrieved from www.ncte.org

Pecheone, R. L., & Chung, R. R. (2006). Evidence in teacher education: The performance assessment for California teachers (PACT). *Journal of Teacher Education, 57*(1), 22-36.

Schleppegrell, M. J. (1998). Grammar as resource: Writing a description. *Research in the Teaching of English, 32*(2), 182-211.

Schleppegrell, M. J. (2004). *The language of schooling: A functional linguistics perspective.* Mahwah, NJ: Lawrence Erlbaum.

Schleppegrell, M. J., & Colombi, M. C. (2002). *Developing advanced literacy: Meaning with power.* Mahwah, NJ: Lawrence Erlbaum.

Shanahan, T., & Shanahan, C. (2008). Teaching disciplinary literacy to adolescents: Rethinking content-area literacy. *Harvard Educational Review, 78*(1), 40-59.

Shulman, L. S. (1987). Knowledge and teaching: Foundations of the new reform. *Harvard Educational Review, 57*(1), 1-22.

Sperling, M., & Freedman, S. W. (2001). Research on writing. In V. Richardson (Ed.), *Handbook of research on teaching* (4th ed., pp. 370-389). Washington, DC: American Educational Research Association.

Stiggins, R. (1994). *Student-centered classroom assessment.* New York, NY: Macmillan.

Thaiss, C., & Zawacki, T. M. (2006). *Engaged writers and dynamic disciplines: Research on the academic writing life.* London, England: Heinemann.

Villalva, K. E. (2006). Hidden literacies and inquiry approaches of bilingual high school writers. *Written Communication, 23(1), 91-129.*

Wahleithner, J., & Athanases, S. Z. (2010). *Linking classroom practices to students' home literacies: How do regional educators conceive of and utilize students' out of school literacies?* Paper presented at the American Educational Research Association Annual Meeting, Denver, CO.

SECTION III

ACADEMIC LANGUAGE IN SUBJECT-AREA CONTENT

CHAPTER 7

ACADEMIC LANGUAGE IN THE SOCIAL STUDIES FOR ENGLISH LEARNERS

Luciana C. de Oliveira

Academic language or the "language that stands in contrast to the everyday informal speech that students use outside the classroom environment" (Bailey & Butler, 2002, p. 7) is a "second" language for all students. The kind of language students learn at school is different from ordinary language for communicative purposes (Schleppegrell, 2001, 2004). Academic language is generally learned in school from teachers and textbooks, and only with proper instructional support (Fillmore & Snow, 2000; Schleppegrell, 2004). English learners (ELs) face a real challenge when reading and writing academic texts in English. This is especially relevant in the social studies.

Social studies is an umbrella term for several school subjects that represent social sciences: history, geography, economics, civics, sociology, psychology, philosophy, among others. Each of these school subjects has its own ways of presenting information and constructing knowledge. History is a key content area and a major focus in the social studies literature (e.g., Carretero & Voss, 1994; Leinhardt, Beck, & Stainton, 1994). Learning history is highly dependent on reading and writing texts, especially at the intermediate elementary grades and beyond.

Academic Language in Second Language Learning, pp. 149–170
Copyright © 2013 by Information Age Publishing

History has its own expectations and typical discipline-specific linguistic choices that present and represent historical interpretations and perspectives (de Oliveira, 2011; Schleppegrell & de Oliveira, 2006). A focus on these specialized ways of presenting and constructing historical content helps ELs see how language is used to construe particular contexts in this content area. Because of ELs' language needs, they need language support in history in order to be successful in the reading and writing tasks that require them to build connections, relationships, and interpretations.

Every text a historian writes is an interpretation in itself (Martin, 2003). The history texts that ELs are expected to read in school are a compilation of explanations. Historians interpret and explain what happened; they do not just record what happened. Interpretations and explanations involve the presentation of social values and different points of view (Martin & Wodak, 2003) which need to be recognized and understood. While history discourse is functional for its purposes, it also presents particular language demands for ELs.

English learners need to gain access to specialized history content which involves the use of academic language. Focusing on academic language in history requires a focus on meaning. This focus on meaning enables us to recognize how learning at school is dependent on language. Language is not the only means through which learning occurs, but it is certainly the most important element of learning, as *learning language* and *learning through language* occur concurrently (Halliday, 1993). A meaning-based theory of learning, systemic functional linguistics (SFL) offers a framework for analyzing how particular language choices of writers construct the meanings within a text and highlights how social contexts influence textual realizations. In any context, language realizes three kinds of meaning: *ideational meaning*—what is happening, or the content of the text, *interpersonal meaning*—who is taking part, the participants as well as their roles and relationships, and *textual meaning*—what part the language is playing. These three meanings are always present when language is used and their realization is dependent upon different situational contexts such as in schools. Understanding how the situational context of schooling uses language in particular ways helps us to see the linguistic demands and challenges of academic language for ELs. Analyzing the language of a particular text from this point of view can help us see what potential linguistic challenges ELs may face so they can understand what they read.

In order to address these potential challenges for ELs, mainstream content-area teachers must be *linguistically responsive* (Lucas, Villegas, & Freedson-Gonzalez, 2008). In order to be linguistically responsive, mainstream content area teachers must develop *linguistic knowledge* (LK) about how language works in different content areas. They need to develop knowledge about how to make content *accessible* to ELs. In this chapter, the word *accessible* takes a different connotation than in recent literature on modifying the language of texts to help ELs learn better from them (see Echevarria, Vogt, & Short, 2004). This chapter presents a different view of *accessible*: Making content accessible to ELs means providing them *access* to the ways in which knowledge is constructed in the content areas, as they are written, by not simplifying the texts, but by developing teachers' understanding about how disciplinary discourse is constructed. In the case of history teachers in particular, being linguistically responsive means understanding how the discourse of history is constructed so teachers can identify potential challenges that ELs may face when reading and writing about history. With this linguistic knowledge, history teachers can then address the linguistic needs of their ELs so that they can access discipline-specific meaning-making resources.

In this chapter, I provide a closer look at some potential linguistic challenges of the discourse of history for ELs in addition to vocabulary, using an eleventh grade example and an eighth grade example from two history textbook series. I argue that academic language is more than just vocabulary and draw on grammatical and lexical aspects of school history discourse. I then discuss what linguistic knowledge history teachers need in order to address the needs of ELs in their classes.

CONTENT-SPECIFIC LANGUAGE IN HISTORY AND ELs

Previous work on history discourse demonstrates that disciplinary knowledge in history is presented very differently from the ways in which meanings are constructed in students' everyday language (de Oliveira, 2010a, 2011 2012; Schleppegrell & de Oliveira, 2006). A close look at the grammatical choices that realize academic texts enables history teachers and students to see the differences between language used at school and the English language that students use every day in their lives outside of school. The concepts students must learn at higher levels at school increasingly become more difficult. In addition, the grammar that constructs these concepts becomes more distinctive and specialized. Knowledge about how academic language differs from everyday language is critical for history teachers who are preparing ELs for higher levels of schooling.

History has expectations for the way that it uses language to express interpretations of experience. Schleppegrell (2004) demonstrates that these expectations include: displaying knowledge by presenting and interpreting historical events; being authoritative by recording, interpreting, and judging; and organizing text in ways that enable explanation and interpretation (p. 128). These expectations are seen in the combination of grammatical and lexical features that the historian uses when writing about the past.

My work in K-12 classrooms has demonstrated that as ELs progress at school, they need to understand how history authors construct the abstract discourse of school history (de Oliveira, 2011). Compared to their English-speaking peers, ELs have an even more challenging task in reading history textbooks. Drawing on linguistic features of academic registers, the language of history textbooks has been described as dense and packed with information (Beck & McKeown, 1994). This language often becomes distanced from the everyday language of many students (Schleppegrell, 2004; Schleppegrell & de Oliveira, 2006). While recent work has attempted to produce more interesting history textbooks by adding vivid language and captivating details to make content more readily available to students, these additions did not necessarily lead to superior text comprehension (Paxton, 1999). Textbooks are a highly used resource in history classes (Ravitch & Finn, 1987; Thornton, 1991), so students need to be able to read and understand them to be successful in school history. The goal of history teaching in developing students' content knowledge and understanding has been linked to being able to access the language used by textbook authors and historians (Harniss, Dickson, Kinder, & Hollenbeck, 2001).

Many content area teachers of ELs draw on a variety of strategies and techniques to simplify the language of textbooks and to dilute textbook content in order to make textbook content comprehensible to ELs. While these strategies and techniques may be helpful for ELs at the beginning levels of language proficiency, they are not appropriate for ELs at intermediate to advanced levels, especially as they progress through the elementary grades and beyond and move out of special bilingual or English as a Second Language (ESL) programs into mainstream classes. Under a watered-down curriculum, ELs may never learn to read textbooks without modifications or adaptations if not taught how to deconstruct the language of content areas (Gibbons, 2006). At intermediate-advanced levels ELs commonly must read content area texts and so need to have additional strategies and be able to access difficult content (de Oliveira & Dodds, 2010). History teachers, then, have the dual responsibility of facilitating ELs' learning of historical events and concepts while also supporting their ongoing English language development.

More Than Just Vocabulary

Academic language in history involves more than just vocabulary. General academic vocabulary words occur across a range of content areas, but each content area has demands in terms of the academic vocabulary it often uses. Vocabulary is a significant component of academic language, but the challenges of academic language go beyond vocabulary challenges. Academic language consists of grammatical patterns through which meanings are made. Vocabulary knowledge is often described as an important element for ELs to comprehend information from texts (Scarcella, 2002), but knowing a word means knowing how to use it effectively in appropriate contexts. As will be shown in this chapter, knowledge of the academic vocabulary word is not enough to fully grasp the meaning of a history passage. Much more is needed than lexical understanding. Abstract terms typical of history, for example, occur within grammatical structures that will be difficult for ELs to understand even if they understand the academic vocabulary word. This is often the case with technical terms present in many science texts as well.

POTENTIAL CHALLENGES OF
ACADEMIC LANGUAGE IN HISTORY FOR ELs

English learners need to access specialized history content. They need to gain access to and participate in experiences involving the use of academic language. Although the academic language of history may present several challenges for ELs, it is functional for historians to present interpretations and generalizations through linguistic choices for expressing the historical content.

The two history series analyzed in this study were the 11th grade textbook *America: Pathways to the Present* (Cayton, Perry, Reed, & Winkler, 2000) and the 8th grade textbook *Call to Freedom* (Stuckey & Salvucci, 2003), two widely used textbooks throughout the United States. These grade levels were selected due to their focus on the teaching of U.S. history. I analyzed several passages from these two textbooks when I was a linguistics researcher for the history project at the University of California, Davis (http://historyproject.ucdavis.edu/), and also observed history teachers' applications of activities to help students develop their academic literacy skills in history. The linguistic approach used in this work focuses on applying language analysis to history teaching to support ELs' academic language development, developed by Schleppegrell and her collaborators and based on M.A.K. Halliday's Systemic Functional Grammar (see Achugar & Schleppegrell, 2005; Achugar, Schleppegrell, & Oteiza, 2007; Schleppegrell & Achugar, 2003; Schleppegrell, Achugar, & Oteiza, 2004; Schleppegrell & de Oliveira, 2006; Schleppegrell, Greer, & Taylor, 2008). I draw on that work as well as my new experiences in an Indiana school district with a high percentage of ELs to describe the potential challenges of academic language in history for ELs.

The categories of linguistic challenges found in the textbooks identified are drawn from recent scholarship on the language demands of schooling (e.g. Schleppegrell, 2004; Fang & Schleppegrell, 2008; de Oliveira, 2010a, 2011, 2012; de Oliveira & Dodds, 2010). I exemplify the challenges by using two text passages which are representative of other texts analyzed in this study. A total of 30 passages, 15 from the 11th grade textbook and 15 from the eighth grade textbook were part of the corpus analyzed in this study. The potential academic language challenges are exemplified with two text passages which are representative of other texts analyzed. The first text, presented in Figure 7.1, is a short passage about the consumer economy developed in the United States after World War I from *America: Pathways to the Present*. The second text, presented in Figures 7.2a and b, is a longer passage that describes the *Marbury v. Madison* case, the first to detail the Supreme Court's power of judicial review from *Call to Freedom*. Both passages illustrate some of the key linguistic challenges of the discourse of history for ELs.

More Than Real Actors: Abstractions That Occur as Participants

History uses both concrete entities in the form of individuals or groups, and abstract entities in the form of things, places, or ideas. These appear as <u>participants</u> in the *processes*—<u>who or what</u> is presented as *doing, thinking/ feeling,* or *saying,* or <u>what</u> is being *defined* or *described* (Fang & Schleppegrell,

---

Despite a year or so of uncertainty after World War I, the United States economy made a rapid adjustment. The rise in incomes that had begun during the war had resumed by 1920. Between 1914 and 1926, average wages rose more than 28 percent. The number of millionaires in the United States more than doubled in the same period. The main cause of this growth was the development of the **consumer economy**, one that depends on a large amount of buying by consumers - individuals who use (or "consume") products. During the 1920's, a consumer economy developed rapidly in the United States.

Source: Cayton, Perry, Reed, and Winkler (2000, pp. 347-348).

Figure 7.1.   Text 1: Passage from *America: Pathways to the Present*.

2008). For instance, in *Between 1914 and 1926, average wages rose more than 28%*, *average wages* is a participant in the *doing* process *rose*. In text 1, many abstractions are present as participants in different processes. Processes in this passage are mostly about actions: *made, had begun, had resumed, rose, more than doubled, developed*. Yet the participants functioning as actors doing these actions are abstractions realized in nominal groups: *the United States economy, the rise in incomes, average wages, the number of millionaires, a consumer economy*. These abstractions function as actors in these sentences and may cause difficulty for students who are not familiar with academic language used in historical texts. To focus on the meanings in the passage, ELs would need to recognize these processes and the abstractions that function as actors here, which pack a lot of information into this short paragraph. Another abstraction is *The main cause of this growth* which is then described through the describing process as *the development of the consumer economy*, another abstraction. As can be seen, these abstractions may be very difficult for ELs to understand.

The participants in text 2 are both concrete entities and abstractions, as this text presents a series of events unfolding to explain the *Marbury v. Madison* case. Text 2 can be described as a *historical account* that presents a series of events as naturally unfolding from the actions of historical actors, following Martin's (2002) description of historical genres. It presents the actions of historical actors such as John Adams, Jefferson, William Marbury, James Madison, and John Marshall to explain the main reasons for the events being recounted that led to the *Marbury v. Madison* case and the establishment of judicial review.

People are presented as doing or saying things, but also things are presented as doing or saying other things. For instance, in *The Supreme Court's decision in* **Marbury v. Madison** *surprised many people, including Jefferson*, it is *The Supreme Court's decision in* **Marbury v. Madison**, an abstraction, that is *surprising* many people. Another example of an abstraction functioning as a participant is in *The Judiciary Act of 1789 said the Court did*. It is *The Judiciary Act of 1789* that is "saying" something. This clause construction occurs right before *Chief Justice Marshall said the Court did not*. Here we see an individual functioning as a participant "saying" something. These constructions can be very confusing for an EL reading this text. These two constructions present different perspectives that are important for understanding what led to Marshall's decision about the *Marbury v. Madison* case and what led to the establishment of judicial review. But understanding the historical content that these constructions present is very important for understanding the meaning of this passage and the overall importance of the case.

Participants in the text occur as concrete entities presented as individuals (e.g. *President John Adams, Jefferson, Chief Justice Marshall*) and groups of people (e.g. *Federalists in Congress, other Republicans, all the justices*). Partici-

Marbury v. Madison

Early in 1801, before Jefferson took office, Federalists in Congress passed a new law that created many new judgeships and other court offices. Before his term ended, President John Adams had appointed dozens of Federalists to fill these positions. Jefferson accused Adams of filling these positions "till 9 o'clock of the night, at 12 o'clock of which he was to go out of office." Other Republicans called the people chosen by Adams "midnight judges."

When Jefferson entered office on March 4, 1801, some Federalists chosen by Adams had not yet received their special commissions. Without these forms they could not begin working as judges. Jefferson took advantage of this fact. He ordered Secretary of State James Madison not to give out the papers. **William Marbury** was one of the people affected by this decision. He demanded that the Supreme Court force the executive branch to hand over his commission. The Court had never done such a thing. However, Marbury claimed that the Judiciary Act of 1789 gave the Supreme Court the right to do so.

The chief justice of the United States was **John Marshall**, a Federalist appointed by Adams. Marshall and President Jefferson disagreed about many political issues. When Marshall agreed to hear Marbury's case, Jefferson protested, complaining that the Federalists "have retired into the judiciary as a stronghold." He was concerned that Marshall would make sure that "all the works of republicanism are to be beaten down and erased."

The Supreme Court's decision in ***Marbury v. Madison*** surprised many people, including Jefferson. All the justices agreed that Marbury had been treated unfairly. But did the Supreme Court have the power to force Madison to give Marbury his commission? The Judiciary Act of 1789 said the Court did. Chief Justice Marshall said the Court did not. His reason was simple. He did not think that the Constitution allowed Congress to give the Supreme Court new powers.

Source: Stuckey and Salvucci (2003, pp. 336-337)

Figure 7.2a.   Text 2: Passage from *Call to Freedom*. (Figure 7.2 continues on next page) pants also appear as abstractions (e.g., *The Supreme Court's decision, The Judiciary Act of 1789, his reason, the act, Marshall's ruling, this power, such a law*). Some of these abstractions present even more challenges for ELs, which will be described in more detail later in the chapter. Representing participants in these various ways can cause several challenges for ELs. ELs need to understand <u>who or what</u> is presented as *doing, thinking/feeling,* or *saying,* or <u>what</u> is being *defined* or *described.*

More Than Single Words: Dense Definitions That Require Explanations

Dense definitions and explanations are common features of the discourse of history. In text 1, three definitions occur within the same sentence:

The Judiciary Act of 1789, he believed, had wrongly given the Court such a power. In other words, the act was unconstitutional—meaning it did something not allowed by the Constitution. Therefore, the Supreme Court did not have the power to force the federal government to give Marbury his commission.

Marshall seemed to be giving up a power of the Supreme Court. But he was really claiming a much greater power. Marshall's ruling established the power of **judicial review**. This power allows the Supreme Court to declare an act of Congress to be unconstitutional. Such a law is then no longer in force. Marshall strongly defended judicial review in his written decision.

"It is, emphatically [absolutely], the province and duty of the Judicial Department to say what the law is. . . . The Constitution is superior to any ordinary act of the legislature."

—John Marshall, *Marbury v. Madison*

Judicial review greatly increased the Supreme Court's legal authority. As a result, the Court became a much stronger branch within the national government.

Source: Stuckey and Salvucci (2003, pp. 336-337).

Figure 7.2b.   Text 2: Passage from *Call to Freedom*. (Continued from previous page)

The main cause of this growth was the development of the consumer economy,
<u>one that depends on a large amount of buying by consumers—individuals</u>
<u>who use</u>

definition 1   definition 2

(or "consume") products.

definition 3

The term *consumer economy* is defined (see bolded definition 1) within the sentence and within its definition two other terms are further defined —*consumers* (definition 2) and *use* (definition 3). In addition to identifying the definitions, ELs have to recognize the markers that introduce these definitions, different for each one of them. The first definition is set out by a comma after *consumer economy*. The second definition is set out by a hyphen after *consumers* while the third definition is set out by parentheses and the connector *or.* These many ways of setting out definitions as well as the fact that these many definitions occur within the same sentence make it complex and difficult to understand and pose challenges for ELs. To get the full meanings presented in this packed sentence, ELs need to comprehend all of the definitions that are embedded here.

Even though the passage in text 2 is longer than text 1, only one definition occurs in text 2, in the following sentences:

Marshall's ruling established the power of **judicial review**. *This power allows the Supreme Court to declare an act of Congress to be unconstitutional. Such a law is then no longer in force.*

The power of judicial review which occurs in the first sentence is being defined in the sentence that follows. This definition presents a key historical concept that would need to be further clarified for students. There are two additional challenges in understanding this definition, which will be described in the following section, *cohesive devices*.

More Than Naming: Cohesive Devices That Create Links Within the Text

Cohesive devices are words or groups of words that create links within the text (Halliday & Matthiessen, 2004). These are commonly used in history discourse (notice my use of the demonstrative *these* as a cohesive device itself referring to *cohesive devices* from my previous sentence.) Rather than referring to items by name, cohesive devices are used to construct links between complex and abstract elements in both example texts.

In text 1, *this growth* functions as a cohesive device to connect to the previous three sentences and move the discourse forward. Figure 7.3 shows the cohesive devices connected to the parts of the text to which they refer. Some words that represent the meaning of *growth* (*rise, rose, more than doubled*) are <u>underlined</u>. It is important for an EL to make these connections between *this growth* and other words that represent growth and for teachers of ELs to explicitly point out how these links are made internally in the text. The pronoun *one* is substituting *economy* in "*…the development of the **consumer economy**, <u>one</u> that depends on a large amount of buying by consumers…*," functioning as a kind of cohesive device called *ellipsis*, as it leaves out a word that can be presumed from what appeared before (Halliday & Matthiessen, 2004).

Cohesive devices are pervasive in text 2. A range of cohesive devices is found:

- Personal pronouns (*they, he*) and possessive pronouns (*his, their*) refer forward or back to different participants.
- Demonstratives (*this, these*) occurring with substitutes (*positions, forms*)—or words that stand for other words—refer back to things or ideas already named.
- Demonstratives occurring with substitutes (*this fact; this decision*) refer back to entire clauses (e.g. *this fact* refers back to the clause *Without these forms they could not begin working as judges*).
- Ellipsis is used after naming (e.g. *The Judiciary Act of 1789, The Supreme Court*) when information can be retrieved from a previous clause (e.g. *The Judiciary Act of 1789* is referred to as *the act; act* is used with lower case as readers are supposed to know which *act* it is; *The Supreme Court* is referred to as *the Court*).
- *Such a* construction functions as a comparative device that refers to a particular class. For instance, the constructions *such a thing, such a*

[The <u>rise</u> in incomes that had begun during the war had resumed by 1920.] [Between 1914 and 1926, average wages <u>rose more than 28 percent.</u>] [The number of millionaires in the United States <u>more than doubled</u> in the same period.] The main cause of *this growth* was the development of the **consumer economy**, one that depends on a large amount of buying by consumers - individuals who use (or "consume") products.

Figure 7.3.   Cohesive devices in text 1.

power, such a law imply that the reference is to a particular *thing, power,* and *law* and no other. These are cohesive ties between the whole cohesive device and what precedes it.

Figures 7.4a and b show the cohesive devices in text 2. The arrows show the connections between the cohesive devices and previous discourse, especially the words, groups of words, or full sentences to which they refer. The cohesive devices are underlined and the words and groups of words to which they refer are italicized. If cohesive devices refer to full sentences, these sentences are in bold and in brackets.

Cohesive devices help identify and keep track of what or who is being discussed in a particular text. They have an important function in history, constructing links between complex and abstract elements that need to be

Early in 1801, before Jefferson took office, Federalists in Congress passed a new law that created *many new judgeships and other court offices.* Before his term ended, *President John Adams* had appointed dozens of Federalists to fill these positions. Jefferson accused Adams of filling these positions "till 9 o'clock of *the night,* at 12 o'clock of which he was to go out of office." Other Republicans called the people chosen by Adams "midnight judges."

When Jefferson entered office on March 4, 1801, *some Federalists chosen by Adams* had not yet received *their special commissions.* [**Without these forms they could not begin working as judges.**] *Jefferson* took advantage of this fact. [**He ordered Secretary of State James Madison not to give out the papers.**] *William Marbury* was one of the people affected by this decision. [**He demanded that *the Supreme Court* force the executive branch to hand over his commission.**] The Court had never done such a thing. However, Marbury claimed that the Judiciary Act of 1789 gave the Supreme Court the right to do so.

The chief justice of the United States was ***John Marshall***, a Federalist appointed by Adams. Marshall and President Jefferson disagreed about many political issues. When Marshall agreed to hear Marbury's case, *Jefferson* protested, complaining that the Federalists "have retired into the judiciary as a stronghold." He was concerned that Marshall would make sure that "all the works of republicanism are to be beaten down and erased."

Figure 7.4a.   Cohesive devices in text 2. (Figure 7.4 continues on next page)

understood in the context of a passage. The next section focuses on another important feature of history discourse: *causality*.

More Than Connectors: Series of Events and Actions That Construct Causality

Understanding causality is particularly important for ELs' understanding of historical events. Cause and effect relationships are an essential part of history learning (Achugar & Schleppegrell, 2005; Ciardello, 2002; Coffin, 2006). The construction of causality in history

The Supreme Court's decision in ***Marbury v. Madison*** surprised many people, including Jefferson. [All the justices agreed that Marbury had been treated unfairly.] But did *the Supreme Court* have *the power to force Madison to give Marbury his commission?* The Judiciary Act of 1789 said the Court did. *Chief Justice Marshall* said the Court did not. His reason was simple. [He did not think that the Constitution allowed Congress to give the Supreme Court new powers.] *The Judiciary Act of 1789*, he believed, had wrongly given the Court such a power. In other words, the act was unconstitutional—meaning it did something not allowed by the Constitution. Therefore, the Supreme Court did not have the power to force the federal government to give Marbury his commission.

Marshall seemed to be giving up a power of the Supreme Court. But he was really claiming a much greater power. Marshall's ruling established *the power of judicial review*. This power allows the Supreme Court to declare *an act of Congress* to be unconstitutional. Such a law is then no longer in force. Marshall strongly defended judicial review in his written decision.

"It is, emphatically [absolutely], the province and duty of the Judicial Department to say what the law is. . . . The Constitution is superior to any ordinary act of the legislature."

—John Marshall, *Marbury v. Madison*

Judicial review greatly increased the Supreme Court's legal authority. As a result, the Court became a much stronger branch within the national government.

Figure 7.4b.   Cohesive devices in text 2. (Figure 7.4 continued from previous page)

texts includes indirect linguistic choices to mark the motivation of actions (Achugar & Schleppegrell, 2005; Achugar & Stainton, 2010). As shown in de Oliveira (2010b), cause and effect is not just marked between clauses through connectors, but it occurs within clauses through the use of other causal markers, making understanding the connections between events more difficult for ELs to comprehend. In addition, causality may occur implicitly without clear markers, as will be explained in this section. Explicit and implicit markings of causality can be found in different texts.

Causality is expressed explicitly in text 1, but not through connectors. In text 1, the noun *cause* in *the main cause of this growth* marks a causal relationship between the sentence where it appears and the sentences prior to that. The entire nominal group *the main cause of this growth* introduces a very important historical concept that is then established in *the development of the **consumer economy**, one that depends on a large amount of buying by consumers—individuals who use (or "consume") products*. This entire clause contributes important meanings, constructing the causal relationship and the definition of the "consumer economy" concept.

Causal relationships are not marked explicitly in text 2, except in one instance, the connector *as a result* in the last sentence of the passage. The historians who wrote this text used linguistic resources to present a series of events as causes for the *Marbury v. Madison* case, and presented both concrete and abstract "participants" as the agents causing them. These series of events establish the causes for the case and causality is constructed implicitly as the events unfold. These linguistic choices construct causal reasoning by enabling the history author to elaborate on the motivation of the historical actors' actions as the series of events is developed.

Figures 7.5a and b present the series of events and implicit causal chains present in text 2[1]. Actions and events are numbered and represented through the "chain" shapes on the left side of the table. These actions and events have to be understood as building up the motivation for the *Marbury v. Madison* case. Number 19, *Marshall's ruling established the power of **judicial review***, establishes the main effect of the case, the most significant result from this causal chain constructed in the text.

English learners' understanding of how these actions and events create the causal organization of the text depends on their ability to identify cause-and-effect relationships. A common task found in textbooks is asking students to find cause and effect in history passages and drawing diagrams that show cause and effect relationships (e.g., Beck, Black, Krieger, Naylor, & Shabaka, 2003; Deverell & White 2006; Stuckey & Salvucci, 2003). In *Call to Freedom*'s teacher edition (Stuckey & Salvucci, 2003), a social studies skills workshop focuses on identifying cause and effect. In this section, students are advised to "look for clues," "identify the relationship" (either cause or effect), and "check for complex connections"

Marbury v. Madison

1. Early in 1801, before Jefferson took office, Federalists in Congress passed a new law that created many new judgeships and other court offices.

2. Before his term ended, President John Adams had appointed dozens of Federalists to fill these positions.

3. When Jefferson entered office on March 4, 1801, some Federalists chosen by Adams had not yet received their special commissions.

4. Without these forms they could not begin working as judges.

5. Jefferson took advantage of this fact.

6. He ordered Secretary of State James Madison not to give out the papers.

7. **William Marbury** was one of the people affected by this decision. He demanded that the Supreme Court force the executive branch to hand over his commission.

8. The Court had never done such a thing.

9. However, Marbury claimed that the Judiciary Act of 1789 gave the Supreme Court the right to do so.

10. When Marshall agreed to hear Marbury's case,

11. Jefferson protested, complaining that the Federalists "have retired into the judiciary as a stronghold."

12. He was concerned that Marshall would make sure that "all the works of republicanism are to be beaten down and erased."

13. The Supreme Court's decision in *Marbury v. Madison* surprised many people, including Jefferson.

32

Figure 7.5a   Series of events constructing implicit causal chains in text 2. (Figure 7.5 continues on next page) when reading a passage that contains cause and effect (p. 392). Students are given a short version of the *Marbury v. Madison* case and provided a diagram that presents cause and effect relationships from the short passage. But this shorter version rephrases the text so it can assist students to identify some "clue words" such as *led to* and *produced*. In the section labeled "Teach, All Levels, English Language Learners," teachers are advised to:

> Explain to students that cause and effect is rarely simple and that few effects have only one cause. Have students review the material on *Marbury v. Madison* on textbook pages 336-337. Ask them to copy the cause-and-effect chart about

14. All the justices agreed that Marbury had been treated unfairly.

(But did the Supreme Court have the power to force Madison to give Marbury his commission?)

15. The Judiciary Act of 1789 said the Court did.

16. Chief Justice Marshall said the Court did not. His reason was simple. He did not think that the Constitution allowed Congress to give the Supreme Court new powers. The Judiciary Act of 1789, he believed, had wrongly given the Court such a power. In other words, the act was unconstitutional—meaning it did something not allowed by the Constitution.

17. Therefore, the Supreme Court did not have the power to force the federal government to give Marbury his commission.

18. Marshall seemed to be giving up a power of the Supreme Court. But he was really claiming a much greater power.

19. Marshall's ruling established the power of **judicial review**. This power allows the Supreme Court to declare an act of Congress to be unconstitutional. Such a law is then no longer in force.

20. Judicial review greatly increased the Supreme Court's legal authority.

21. As a result, the Court became a much stronger branch within the national government.

Figure 7.5b.   Series of events constructing implicit causal chains in text 2. (Figure 7.5 continued from next page) the case from this page and to use the material from the text to expand it. Encourage students to reflect the fact that many causes led to the case and that the case itself had a number of other effects. Once they have expanded the chart, have students search the text for the clue words and phrases that helped them identify the relationships they showed in their charts. Ask them to finalize their cause-and-effect charts by adding the clue words and phrases on the lines to show the connections between events (p. 392).

As was shown in the causal chain analysis, only one clue word appears in the text. Other causality markers are absent and causality is realized as the series of events unfolds. Completing the task of identifying clue words and completing a cause-and-effect chart would pose several challenges for ELs. This would also pose challenges for their teachers, who may look for explicit clues without finding them in the passage. ELs, as well as their teachers, need additional support in recognizing the implicit construction of cause and effect in the texts they read.

The challenges described in this section clearly go beyond vocabulary. To fully grasp the meaning of a history passage, ELs need to understand how abstractions are constructed as participants, how cohesive devices create links within the text, and how a series of events and actions construct causality. Analysis of the author's use of these linguistic resources can help ELs see how language constructs historical meanings. But to accomplish this, ELs need the support of their history teachers.

LINGUISTICALLY RESPONSIVE HISTORY TEACHING: DEVELOPING LINGUISTIC KNOWLEDGE ABOUT HISTORY

Understanding the ways in which language constructs historical meanings enables teachers to anticipate potential challenges that ELs may encounter when reading history. Lucas et al. (2008) identify one of six essential understandings of second language learning for linguistically responsive teachers: "Explicit attention to linguistic form and function ... is essential to second language learning" (p. 363). The integrated analysis of form and function facilitates teachers' recognition of how historical meanings are constructed in texts. History teachers can develop *linguistic knowledge* (LK) about how language works in history while remaining experts in their content area.

History teachers are typically experts in their content area and often read texts without much difficulty as they are familiar with the textual constructions of history. To be linguistically responsive, history teachers need to develop knowledge about how to make content *accessible* to ELs by giving them *access* to the ways in which knowledge is constructed in history, not by simplifying the texts, but by keeping a focus on forms, functions, and meanings present in these texts. Being linguistically responsive involves developing knowledge about how to engage ELs to help them learn the content better. In mainstream classes, mere exposure to academic language is not enough to help ELs develop their content knowledge. The challenge for ELs in mainstream classes is to have their language needs explicitly addressed. The challenge for history teachers of ELs is to ensure access to grade-level content and materials by addressing these language needs.

Developing their linguistic knowledge about history enables history teachers to take up a dual responsibility of facilitating ELs' learning of historical events and concepts while also supporting their ongoing English language development. The situational context of history teaching and learning uses language in particular ways. Analysis of the language of a particular text can help teachers see the potential demands and challenges of academic language for ELs so they can understand what they read and learn content more effectively. For history teachers, this is a tall order. They may feel uncomfortable seeing themselves as responsible for addressing the linguistic needs of the ELs in their classes. But history teachers are in the best position to do so. They often know about their disciplinary practices and would be best able to develop ELs' ability to read and write the texts in history.

The linguistic knowledge that history teachers need to develop in order to teach academic language to ELs includes knowledge about how abstractions function in different kinds of texts, how cohesive devices work to organize historical meanings, and how causality is expressed through other linguistic means besides connectors. These are only some features of the academic language of history highlighted here as potential challenges for ELs (for more information about history discourse, see Coffin, 2006; de Oliveira, 2010a, 2011; Fang & Schleppegrell, 2008; Martin, 2002, 2003).

Developing history teachers' linguistic knowledge requires consistent and focused professional development such as the one offered through the literacy work by The California History-Social Science Project. By making visible and explicit the literacy demands of history, teachers can learn how to focus on language while still teaching historical content in a meaningful way.

CONCLUSION

A key aspect for all teachers is knowledge about how discourses of a specific discipline differ from other disciplines. Every discipline uses academic language in specific ways. These differences have to do with the nature of the discipline itself. Enabling ELs to recognize the different meanings presented through different language choices highlights the importance of focusing on the role of language in developing disciplinary knowledge in different content areas.

Being *linguistically responsive* means more than responding to ELs' needs; it involves having the linguistic knowledge necessary to identify potential academic language demands and address them in teaching. To help ELs gain access to and participate in experiences involving the use of academic language, history teachers can engage in closer reading of their materials and develop a better understanding of the language through which historical meanings are expressed.

Academic language is more than vocabulary. Knowledge of an academic vocabulary word is not enough for ELs to fully grasp the range of meanings presented in a history text. As shown through the examples presented, it is important for history teachers to understand that the ways in which history texts are constructed can be made explicit to ELs so they can see how language works in this content area. Teachers can engage all students in discussions about text in meaningful ways. As the analysis of text 1 highlighted, even short passages can contain relevant historical information that can be brought up with students through a close look at language. A history teacher does not have to engage in linguistic analysis of the entire textbook. This would be impossible. But even deconstructing a short passage such as text 1 can assist ELs in their reading of history. A functional analysis supports history learning as ELs continue to develop their language skills.

One of the major points presented in this chapter is the idea of accessibility. Making texts more accessible means more than simplifying the language through which content is manifested. History textbooks can definitely be written more clearly; however, ELs still need access to the dense and abstract language of history, as this language enables the expression of the interpretation and explanation given by historians. This is a matter of social justice; if ELs are not given opportunities to engage and participate in experiences involving the use of academic language, they will continue to be at a disadvantage and the so-called "achievement gap" between ELs and English-only speakers will likely remain a reality for these kids.

One of the main goals of this work is to enable teachers to make grade-level content accessible to ELs so they can be more proactive in helping ELs learn the ways language is used to construe historical knowledge. Efforts to change the academic language of the content areas are counterproductive, as *all* students will need to deal with the specialized knowledge presented in the disciplines to fully participate in school. Learning the language of the academic community allows individuals to have access to this community's meaning-making practices.

NOTE

1. Some sentences were removed from the text because they provide additional information and do not appear as part of the causal chains presented in the text.

REFERENCES

Achugar, M., & Schleppegrell, M. (2005). Beyond connectors: The construction of *cause* in history textbooks. *Linguistics and Education, 16*(3), 298-318.

Achugar, M., Schleppegrell, M. J., & Oteiza, T. (2007). Engaging teachers in language analysis: a functional linguistics approach to reflective literacy. *English Teaching: Practice and Critique, 6*(2), 8–24.

Achugar, M., & Stainton, C. (2010). Learning history and learning language: Focusing on language in historical explanations to support English language learners. In M. K. Stein & L. Kucan (Eds.), *Instructional Explanations in the Disciplines* (pp. 145-159). New York, NY: Springer.

Bailey, A. L., & Butler, F. A. (2002). *An evidentiary framework for operationalizing academic language for broad application to K-12 education: A design document.* Los Angeles, CA: University of California.

Beck, I. L., & McKeown, M. G. (1994). Outcomes of history instruction: Paste-up accounts. In M. Carretero & J. F. Voss (Eds.), *Cognitive and instructional processes in history and the social sciences* (pp. 237-256). Hillsdale, NJ: Erlbaum Associates.

Beck, R. B., Black, L., Krieger, L. S., Naylor, P. C., & Shabaka, D. I. (2003). *Modern world history: Patterns of interaction*. Evanston, IL: McDougal Littell.

Carretero, M., & Voss, J. F. (Eds.). (1994). *Cognitive and instructional processes in history and the social sciences*. Hillsdale, MI: Erlbaum.

Cayton, A., Perry, E. I., Reed, L., & Winkler, A. M. (2000). *America: Pathways to the present.* Upper Saddle River, N.J.: Prentice-Hall.

Ciardello, A. V. (2002). Helping adolescents understand cause/effect text structure in social studies. *The Social Studies, 93*(1): 31–36.

Coffin, C. (2006). *Historical discourse: The language of time, cause, and evaluation.* London, England: Continuum.

de Oliveira, L. C. (2011). *Knowing and writing school history: The language of students' expository writing and teachers' expectations.* Charlotte, NC: Information Age Publishing.

de Oliveira, L. C. (2010a). Nouns in history: Packaging information, expanding explanations, and structuring reasoning. *The History Teacher, 43*(2), 191-203.

de Oliveira, L. C. (2010b). Focusing on language and content by examining cause and effect in historical texts. *The Indiana Reading Journal, 42*(12), 14-19.

de Oliveira, L. C., & Dodds, K. N. (2010). Beyond general strategies for English Language Learners: Language dissection in science. *The Electronic Journal of Literacy Through Science, 9*(1), 1-14. Retrieved from http://ejlts.ucdavis.edu/

article/2010/9/1/beyond-general-strategies-english-language-learners-language-dissection-science.

de Oliveira, L. C. (2012). *What history teachers need to know about academic language to teach English language learners. The Social Studies Review, 51*(1), 76-79.

Deverell, W., & White, D. G. (2006). *United States History: Independence to 1914.* Austin, TX: Holt, Rinehart, and Winston.

Echevarria, J., Vogt, M. E., & Short, D. J. (2004). *Making content comprehensible for English learners. The SIOP model* (2nd ed.). Needham Heights, MA: Allyn & Bacon.

Fang, Z., & Schleppegrell, M. J. (2008). *Reading in secondary content areas: A language-based pedagogy.* Ann Arbor, MI: University of Michigan Press.

Fillmore, L. W., & Snow, C. (2000). *What teachers need to know about language.* Special report for the Center for Applied Linguistics (ERIC Clearinghouse on Languages and Linguistics).

Gibbons, P. (2006). *Bridging discourses in the ESL classroom: Students, teachers, and researchers.* London, England: Continuum.

Halliday, M. A. K. (1993). Towards a language-based theory of learning. *Linguistics and Education, 5*(2), 93-116.

Halliday, M. A. K., & Matthiessen, C. M. (2004). *An introduction to functional grammar.* London, England: Arnold.

Harniss, M. K., Dickson, S. V., Kinder, D., & Hollenbeck, K. L. (2001). Textual problems and instructional solutions: Strategies for enhancing learning from published history textbooks. *Reading & Writing Quarterly, 17*(2), 127-150.

Leinhardt, G., Beck, I. L., & Stainton, C. (1994). *Teaching and learning in history.* Hillsdale, NJ: Erlbaum.

Lucas, T., Villegas, A. M., & Freedson-Gonzalez, M. (2008). Linguistically responsive teacher education: Preparing classroom teachers to teach English language learners. *Journal of Teacher Education, 59*(4), 361-373.

Martin, J. R. (2002). Writing history: Construing time and value in discourses of the past. In M. J. Schleppegrell & M. C. Colombi (Eds.), *Developing advanced literacy in first and second languages: Meaning with power* (pp. 87-118). Mahwah, NJ: Erlbaum.

Martin, J.R. (2003) Making history: Grammar for interpretation. In J. R. Martin & R. Wodak (Eds.) *Re/reading the past: Critical and functional perspectives on time and value*(pp. 19-57). Amsterdam, The Netherlands: John Benjamins.

Martin, J. R., & Wodak, R. (2003). Introduction. In J. R. Martin & R. Wodak (Eds.), *Re/reading the past: Critical and functional perspectives on time and value* (pp. 1-16). Philadelphia, PA: John Benjamins.

Paxton, R. J. (1999). A deafening silence: History textbooks and the students who read them. *Review of Educational Research, 69*(3), 315-339.

Ravitch, D. R., & Finn, C. E. (1987). *What do our 17-year-olds know? A report on the first national assessment of history and literature.* New York: Harper & Row.

Scarcella, R. (2002). Some key factors affecting English learners' development of advanced literacy. In M. J. Schleppegrell & M. C. Colombi (Eds), *Developing advanced literacy in first and second languages: Meaning with power* (pp. 209-226). Mahwah, NJ: Erlbaum.

Schleppegrell, M. (2001). Linguistic features of the language of schooling. *Linguistics and Education, 12*(4), 431-459.

Schleppegrell, M. J. (2004). *The language of schooling: A functional linguistics perspective*. Mahwah, NJ: Erlbaum.

Schleppegrell, M., & Achugar, M. (2003.) Learning language and learning history: A functional linguistics approach. *TESOL Journal, 12*(2), 21-27.

Schleppegrell, M., Achugar, M., & Oteíza, T. (2004). The grammar of history: Enhancing content-based instruction through a functional focus on language. *TESOL Quarterly, 38*(1), 67-93.

Schleppegrell, M. J., & de Oliveira, L. C. (2006). An integrated language and content approach for history teachers. *Journal of English for Academic Purposes, 5*(4), 254-268.

Schleppegrell, M. J., Greer, S., & Taylor, S. (2008) Literacy in history: language and meaning. *Australian Journal of Language and Literacy, 31*(2), 174-187.

Stuckey, S., & Salvucci, L. K. (2003). *Call to Freedom: Beginnings to 1914* (Annotated Teacher's Edition). Austin, TX: Holt, Rinehart, and Winston.

Thornton, S. J. (1991). Teacher as curriculum-instructional gatekeeper in social studies. In J. P. Shaver (Ed.), *Handbook of research on social studies teaching and learning* (pp. 237-248). New York, NY: Macmillan.

CHAPTER 8

SCAFFOLDING ACADEMIC LANGUAGE IN SCIENCE EDUCATION FOR ENGLISH LANGUAGE LEARNERS

Frank Ramírez-Marín and Douglas B. Clark

INTRODUCTION

The linguistic landscape in U.S. schools has changed dramatically in the last 3 decades. According to the U.S. Department of Education (2007), the number of school age children (ages 5-17) who spoke a language other than English at home increased from 3.8 million to 10.6 million (the equivalent of 9% to 20% of students) between 1979 and 2005. The data indicate that Spanish was the native language of the great majority of students whose language proficiency was considered to be limited (79.2%), followed by Vietnamese (2%), Hmong (1.6%), Cantonese (1%), and Korean (1%). In 2005, 42% of public school students were considered to be part of a racial or ethnic minority group, which represents a significant increase from 22% of students in 1972 (U.S. Department of Education, 2007).

Academic Language in Second Language Learning, pp. 171–199
Copyright © 2013 by Information Age Publishing
All rights of reproduction in any form reserved.

While there is general agreement on the need for high standards and achievement expectations for all students in core curriculum, there is also strong disagreement on how best to bring about high academic achievement for English language learners (ELLs) (Crawford, 2004). This debate has grown increasingly heated between proponents of English-only instruction and those who promote the use of the students' home languages for instruction. The fact that educators and policymakers differ in opinions on how to best help ELL students obtain high levels of proficiency and literacy in English deserves careful consideration because this debate has resulted in the restriction or virtual elimination in some states (i.e. California, Arizona, and Massachusetts) of program alternatives and instructional approaches, such as bilingual and English as a second language (ESL) programs, that may meet the diverse and complex needs of English language learners (Crawford, 2004).

The convergence of cultural and linguistic diversity of the student population and language policies that promote English-only instruction has impacted schools and the instructional practices of content-area teachers across the United States. In this complex educational context, Hart and Lee (2003) assert that teachers of ELLs, including science teachers, face several challenges, such as helping their students acquire academic content and English language and literacy (August & Hakuta, 1997; Chamot & O'Malley, 1994; García, 1999). However, content area teachers are often not prepared to address these challenges because English for speakers of other languages (ESOL) training may not necessarily include the content-specific instructional strategies teachers require to effectively deliver challenging academic work and help ELLs learn English (Hart & Lee, 2003). In addition, based on what research indicates, Hart and Lee (2003) conclude that there may be a lack of the support and time that teachers need to develop the complex set of beliefs and practices that will enable them to assist ELLs in attaining challenging academic standards while developing English language and literacy (García, 1999; McLaughlin, Shepard, & O'Day, 1995).

Nevertheless, efforts have been made to address the rapid changes in cultural and linguistic diversity, as well as in language policies, and their impact on approaches to science education in the United States. Researchers and educators have focused their work on providing teachers with theoretical and conceptual guidance and pedagogical practices to support student achievement of high academic standards in science while simultaneously developing English language proficiency and literacy.

This chapter reviews literature in science education related to cultural and linguistic diversity, including English language learners, in the United States. Further, two prevalent frameworks for teacher preparation and development in science education (the instructional congruence framework and the effective science teaching for English language learners framework) are broadly described with the purpose of illustrating the theoretical and pedagogical practices advocated by researchers for content, language, and literacy learning in science education. Based on the literature reviewed, we argue that the *systemic functional linguistic* (SFL) approach to the study of language (Halliday, 1973, 1980, 1994) could synergistically augment these models for science education. SFL has not been widely considered in the science education literature, but SFL can provide teachers with a clear understanding of what academic language entails and at the same time highlight the importance of providing students with access to the specialized language embedded in the practices through which scientific knowledge is construed and represented. We also argue that SFL as a framework is extremely useful for teachers to identify the potential linguistic demands of school language and literacy. SFL, therefore, offers great potential for augmenting exemplary approaches in science education for supporting teachers of English language learners. Based on these discussions, we conclude the chapter with recommendations for further research and educational interventions in science education for culturally and linguistically student populations.

SCIENCE EDUCATION AND CULTURAL AND LINGUISTIC DIVERSITY IN THE UNITED STATES

Lemke (2001) explains that science, as a cooperative activity, is only possible because people grow up and live within social organizations or institutions (family, school, church, research lab, etc.) that provide meaning-making tools, such as language, beliefs systems, discourse practices, representational systems, and other specialized practices that constitute the culture of a community (e.g., American scientists). In the case of the United States, science educators have privileged the nature of science and science education, as well as the scientific and cultural practices associated with them, as they have traditionally been defined in Western science. Thus, Western or mainstream cultural values have permeated the American society and are favored and reflected in schools as sanctioned behaviors and expectations that many minority students, including English language learners, experience in their classrooms (Lee, 1999; Loving, 1997).

Tyler et al. (2008) based on the work of Sue and Sue (2003) point out that the public school as an institution is also permeated by the dominant group's cultural heritage and practices in a given society and embedded in this social dynamics is the belief that the dominant cultural heritage is superior to that of minority students. For these reasons, nonmainstream cultural values and practices (including linguistic practices) are many times discouraged or prohibited since they are considered inappropriate (Tyler et al., 2008).

In a synthesis of research Lee (2005) reviewed relevant research on multicultural learning environments. The studies included in the review show the culturally sensitive nature of science learning (e.g., Brickhouse, 1994; Driver, Asko, & Leach, Mortimer, & Scott, 1994; Gilbert & Yerrick, 2001), and the need to conceptualize science learning as a cultural process that requires the development of specialized language and procedures (e.g., Lemke, 1990, Lee & Fradd, 1998; Brickhouse, 1994; Gilbert & Yerrick, 2001; Rosebery, Warren, & Conant, 1992; Wellington & Osborne, 2001).

Based on what research indicates, Lee (2001) suggests that students in science classrooms sometimes display ways of knowing that are incompatible with the nature of science as it is taught in U.S. schools—including science content, teaching, and assessment—which has resulted in poor educational experiences and low academic performance for many culturally and linguistically diverse students (Atwater, 1994; Brickhouse, 1998; Calabrese Barton, 1998; Lee & Fradd, 1998; Rosebery, Warren, & Conant, 1992; Solano-Flores & Nelson-Barber , 2001). Thus, a body of research has tried to explain patterns of low academic achievement of these student populations in the United States as a result of *cultural discontinuity* between these students' home experiences and their classroom-based learning and social and institutional expectations (Deyhle, 1995; Gay, 2000; Ndura, 2004; Nieto, 1999; Parsons, 2001, 2003; Parsons, Travis, & Simpson, 2005; Solano-Flores & Nelson-Barber, 2001; Webb-Johnson, 2003).

Cultural discontinuity is represented in the educational research literature by different terms including *cultural conflict* (e.g., Vega, Khoury, Zimmerman, Gil, & Warheit, 1995), *cultural dissonance* (e.g., Bell & Clark, 1998; Garrett, 1995; Hale, 2001; Gordon & Yowell, 1992; Hollins & Spencer, 1990; Ladson-Billings, 1995; Portes, 2001; Tharp, 1989; Tillman, 2002), and *cultural misalignment* (e.g., Tyler, Boykin, & Walton, 2006), but *cultural discontinuity* can be broadly defined as "a school-based behavioral process where the cultural value–based learning preferences and practices of many ethnic minority students—those typically originating from home or parental socialization activities—are discontinued at school" (Tyler et al., 2008. p. 281).

Guided by the notion of cultural discontinuity, Lee (2001, 2005) asserts that due to the fact that science has been taught to be consistent with Western tradition, alternative ways of knowing, thinking, and interacting, as well as cultural and linguistic resources, have been ignored in science classrooms. As a result, teachers may ignore or fail to recognize the linguistic resources that language learners bring to the classroom. Lee (2001) points out that paying attention to issues related to the increasing diversity in U.S. classrooms is particularly important in science, considering low science performance and underrepresentation of students from diverse backgrounds in science.

INTEGRATION OF SCIENCE TEACHING, LANGUAGE, AND LITERACY

We now present two prevalent frameworks for teacher preparation to support diverse students studying science (the instructional congruence framework and the effective science teaching for English language learners framework) with the purpose of broadly illustrating the pedagogical practices identified by researchers to promote content, language, and literacy learning in science education. After presenting the two frameworks, we outline consensus between the frameworks and other research in the field to provide a foundation for subsequent discussions of the potential contributions of SFL to approaches in science education for supporting diverse science learners.

The Instructional Congruence Framework

The *instructional congruence* (IC) model (Lee & Fradd, 1998, 2001) builds on theoretical views of *cultural discontinuity*. The IC framework is grounded on the tenet that it is essential to incorporate ELL students' home languages and cultures in the educational process to provide meaningful context for the construction of new understandings. Lee and Fradd (1998, 2001) argue that effective science education incorporates students' prior linguistic and cultural knowledge in relation to science disciplines. Thus, the researchers propose the IC framework as a way to integrate specific scaffolding for language and literacy into standards-based science inquiry and learning.

According to Lee and Fradd (1998, 2001), teachers make academic content and inquiry (e.g., science) accessible, meaningful, and relevant for diverse students (e.g. linguistically diverse students) through *instructional congruence*. To achieve effective science and literacy instruction within the IC framework, "teachers need to integrate knowledge of (a) the students' language and cultural experiences, (b) science learning, and (c) literacy development" (Lee & Fradd, 2001, p. 111). Through instructional congruence, teachers make academic content and inquiry (e.g., science) accessible, meaningful, and relevant for diverse students (e.g., linguistically diverse students).

The IC framework includes four central foci. First, IC emphasizes the role of teachers in the instructional process. Relevant to this feature are the insights and practices of teachers who share the languages and cultures of their students and also understand science. Second, IC implements "subject-specific" pedagogies for diverse students to be used as referents to indicate congruence with both academic content and students language ("culturally relevant," "culturally appropriate," "culturally congruent," "culturally responsive," and "culturally compatible" pedagogies. For a summary, see Ladson-Billings, 1995). Third, IC promotes student learning in both science and literacy through students' development of the academic discourse proficiencies required to meet academic standards. Thus, effective science instruction for linguistically diverse students also promotes literacy development and English language learning in a systematic and explicit manner. Fourth, and finally, constructivism is at the core of the IC framework. Instructional congruence enables students to construct knowledge of academic content and inquiry within their language and cultural contexts.

According to Lee and Fradd (2001), within the IC framework, science and literacy are broadly defined based on standards documents, which specify what students need to know and do within the context of science learning. In addition, those documents include the science discourse and multiple representations using various written and oral communication formats students need to learn, as well as the scientific habits of mind in terms of the values, attitudes, and world views in science (National Research Council [NRC], 1996; American Association for the Advancement of Science [AAAS], 1989, 1993) (for detailed descriptions, see Lee & Fradd, 1999a, 1999b, 1998).

Lee and Fradd (1998, 2001) adopted a view of academic language as follows "[academic language] is characterized as the language of school instruction where understanding depends on knowledge of academic content and genre. Social language is characterized as interpersonal and dependent on the culture of the communication (tone of voice, facial expressions, body movements, turn taking, and other aspects of interactional styles), as opposed to academic language, which is characterized as linguistically complex, decontextualized and cognitively demanding. Similarly, literacy development includes social and academic discourse in formal and informal settings (Cummins, 1984; Fradd & Larrinaga-McGee, 1994; O'Malley & Valdez Pierce 1996; Wong-Fillmore & Snow, 2002).

An example of instruction in the IC framework is described in Lee and Fradd (2001). The researchers developed two instructional units—*The Water Cycle* and *Weather*—based on standards documents in science (AAAS, 1989, 1993; NRC, 1996) and literacy (American Council on the Teaching of Foreign Languages [ACTFL], 1996; International Reading Association and the National Council of Teachers of English [IRA & NCTE], 1994; Teachers of English to Speakers of Other Languages [TESOL], 1997). According to the researchers, instructional strategies and activities were developed to foster students' literacy skills, including those that encourage reading and writing and provide linguistic scaffolding to enhance students' understanding of science topics (IRA & NCTE, 1994).

Narrative vignettes are included to open the water cycle and weather units in order to activate students' prior knowledge on the science topic. Specific comprehension questions about inquiry activities are used in each lesson to make sure students are on track. Students record data and report results in multiple formats, including oral, written, and graphic (such as in data tables, graphs, drawings, and prose). Strategies to enhance comprehension of expository text about science information at the end of each lesson are provided. Also, a variety of language functions (e.g., describe, explain, report, draw a conclusion) are used in the context of science inquiry (Casteel & Isom, 1994).

Instructional strategies also involved following TESOL (1997) recommendations, such as the explicit introduction of key vocabulary to address the needs of ELLs. For instance, some strategies to provide ELLs with access to scientific support involved explicit attention given to particular words to support precision in describing and explaining objects and events, such as positional words (e.g., above, below, inside, outside), comparative terms (e.g., cold, colder, coldest), and affixes (e.g., *in* for increase or inflate as opposed to *de* in decrease or deflate). Instruction also included activities and tasks that promoted communication through the use of hands-on materials, cooperative groups, narrative vignettes, and expository texts.

The Effective Science Teaching for English Language Learners (ESTELL) Framework

A second prominent framework is the effective science teaching for English language learners (ESTELL) framework (Stoddart, Solis, Tolbert, & Bravo, 2010). ESTELL is an instructional approach that integrates the teaching of scientific inquiry, science discourse, and language and literacy development in a contextualized curriculum that is culturally, socially, and linguistically responsive. Stoddart et al. (2010) outline a set of socially, culturally, and linguistically responsive instructional practices that are effective in teaching science to ELL students. The framework is founded in sociocultural and Vygotskyan theory (Bakhtin, 1981; Rogoff, 1990, 1995; Rogoff & Wertsch, 1984; Tharp, 1997; Tharp & Gallimore,

1988; Vygotsky, 1978; Wertsch, 1985, 1991) with particular focus on two bodies of recent research based on sociocultural theory.

The first of these bodies of research was developed by the Center for Research on Education, Diversity and Excellence (CREDE) (Doherty & Pinal, 2004; Estrada & Imhoff, 2001; Hilberg, Tharp, & DeGeest, 2000; Saunders & Goldenberg, 1999a; Saunders, O'Brien, Lennon, & McLean, 1998; Tharp & Dalton, 2007). The Center for Research on Education, Diversity and Excellence (CREDE) identified the CREDE Five Standards for Effective Pedagogy (CFSEP):

1. Facilitate learning through joint productive activity among teachers and students (Moll, 1990; Rogoff, 1991; Tharp & Gallimore, 1988; Wertsch, 1985).

2. Develop competence in the language and literacy of instruction throughout all instructional activities.

3. Contextualize teaching and curriculum in the experiences and skills of home and community (pedagogical level, at the curriculum level, at the policy level).

4. Challenge students toward cognitive complexity wherein teachers elicit and model complex reasoning of science concepts.

5. Engage students through dialogue, especially *instructional conversation,* involving teacher initiation of conversation that requires student scientific reasoning and dialogue.

Research on the CFSEP approach has shown significant gains in science, reading and mathematics achievement and teachers use of this pedagogy has been positively linked to factors critical to student performance in school such as motivation, perceptions, attitudes, and inclusion (Doherty & Pinal, 2004; Estrada & Imhoff, 2001; Hilberg, Tharp, & DeGeest, 2000; Saunders & Goldenberg, 1999b; Saunders, O'Brien, Lennon & McLean, 1998; Stoddart, 1999, 2005; Stoddart, Pinal, Latzke & Canaday, 2002; Stoddart, Abrams, Canaday, & Gasper, 2000).

The second body of research that informs the ESTELL framework is comprised five NSF-funded research and development projects that produced findings on the relationship of the integration of science, language, and literacy instruction and ELL student achievement in science, language development, reading, and writing.

1. LASERS (language acquisition through science education in rural schools) used inquiry science as a context for the implementation of pedagogy that integrated language and literacy development into cognitively demanding science learning using and instruc-

tional approach that emphasized cooperative learning and cultural and linguistic contextualization (Stoddart, 1999, 2005; Stoddart et al., 2002).

2. The Seeds of Science, Roots of Reading project coordinated the efforts of science educators and literacy educators to create and test an integrated literacy-science curriculum for second and third grade elementary school classrooms (Cervetti, Pearson, Barber, Hiebert, & Bravo 2007).

3. The science instruction for all (SIFA) looked into the impact of a multiyear instructional intervention designed and implemented to promote achievement of science and literacy among culturally and linguistically diverse students in the San Francisco Bay area (Boquedano-López, Solis, & Kattan 2005; Garcia & Boquedano-López, 2007; Ku, Bravo, & Garcia, 2004; Ku, Garcia, & Corkins, 2005; Solis, 2005).

4. The Imperial Valley Project in Science focused on the effects of instruction that allowed students to conduct science projects as investigations and develop their writing proficiency by keeping a journal to reflect on their science activities (Amaral et al., 2002). The study was implemented over the course of 4 years with 4th fourth and sixth graders in a large school district in Southern California.

5. The P-SELL project consisted on the implementation of an integrated science and literacy curriculum for third graders in urban elementary schools in Florida. According to Lee, Maerten-Rivera, Penfield, LeRoy, and Secada (2008) the study involved 1,134 third graders at seven treatment schools and 966 third grade students at eight comparison schools. Another aspect involved in the NSF-funded P-SELL project inspected the results of integrating the teaching of science with English language development for ELLs in 7 urban elementary schools in the Southeast of the United States.

The common driving principles under which these body of research and development studies is that the relationship between science learning and language and literacy learning is reciprocal and synergistic. Stoddart et al. (2010) explain

Through the contextualized use of language and science inquiry, students develop and practice complex language forms and functions. Through the use of language functions such as description, explanation, and discussion in inquiry science, students enhance their conceptual understanding. This is a synergistic approach to teaching and learning in which language and literacy development is contextualized in scientific inquiry projects that promote understanding through collaborative work and discourse between teachers and students. (p. 157)

Based on the empirical evidence Stoddart et al. (2010) state that "findings from these five research and development projects all indicate that these integrated curriculum has a positive impact on the science learning and language and literacy development of ELL students" (Stoddart et al., 2010. p. 159.).

In sum, the theoretical views and the empirical evidence from CREDE and the NSF research projects and studies on the integration of science, language, and literacy contribute to the ESTELL framework in terms of the development of pedagogical practices (for examples see Stoddart et al., 2010). Specifically, ESTELL has distilled and integrated these findings into a framework focusing on the five issues listed below.

1. The integration of science, language, and literacy development.
2. The engagement of students in the use of scientific discourse.
3. The development of scientific understanding through complex thinking.
4. The implementation of collaborative inquiry in science learning.
5. The contextualization of science learning.

The ESTELL framework conceptualizes language in this framework in sociocultural terms as a (symbolic) tool that mediates and structures the ways in which scientists think and communicate with one another. The use of this mediating symbolic tool is realized within particular cultural contexts in which communities of people realize specialized practices (i.e., scientists doing science). In this context, academic language is better characterized through the concept of "discourse" (see Lemke, 1990; Gee, 1996, 2008). Stoddart et al. (2010), for example, cite Cervetti et al.'s (2007) assertion that "science activities are achieved through a social process where the language used for competent participation requires specialized ways of talking, writing, and thinking about the world in scientific ways" (p. 164). Thus, the language used by scientist is better described as discourse. Stoddart et al. (2010) explains:

The discourse of science goes beyond speaking, reading, and writing. It involves learning, talking, and doing science using discourse forms that have their own vocabulary and organization that are embodied in the ways scientists think and communicate. In fact, "learning and doing science is not just a process of acquiring a set of facts, principles, and procedures; it also involves using the language of science in ways of talking and representing the natural world through discourse, interaction and collaboration. (p. 164).

From ESTELL's perspective, teacher talk within *instructional conversations* is a pedagogical practice through which teachers engage students in scientific discourse and the instructional conversation is the means by which teachers and students relate formal, schooled knowledge to the student's individual, community, and family knowledge. The development of language and literacy within the ESTELL framework occurs through the "*contextualization of the use of language*" (Cummins, 1981; Swain & Lapkin, 1995). That is, the provision of meaningful cues that ELL students interpret what is being communicated. To achieve this, the use of visual cues, concrete objects, and hands-o-activities is a way to explicitly link the study of scientific phenomena with language learning. To promote the integration of language and literacy within this framework there is emphasis on the use of "authentic science literacy" through graphing data, recording observations, reading and writing expository texts, illustrations, and so on. In addition, the use of science reading materials and references and illustrations for learning science is emphasized. For verbal or written opportunities and development, students collaborate with peers and teachers. The latter assist students through questioning, listening, rephrasing, or modeling. According to Stoddart et al. (2010) "opportunities for literacy practices germane to science provide a context for authentic uses of literacy and increase the likelihood that students will build fluency in these literacy practices (p. 161)".

Summary: General Agreement in Science Education Research on Core Issues for Supporting Diverse Students

In relation to pedagogical practices, Lee (2005) and Stoddart and colleagues (2010) review an extensive body of research on approaches to science teaching that integrate language and literacy into contextualized science inquiry instruction (e.g., Dalton, 1998; Lee, 2005; Lee & Luykx, 2004; Palincsar & Magnusson, 2001; Rosebery, Warren, & Conant, 1992; Stoddart, 1999, 2005; Stoddart, Pinal, Latzkem & Canaday, 2002; Stoddart, Abrams, Gasper, & Canaday, 2000; Tharp, 1997; Tharp, Estrada, Dalton, & Yamauchi, 2000). These studies, as well as both the IC and the ESTELL frameworks, suggest that diverse students, including ELL students, need content-specific language supports as they progress in school (e.g., Rosebery, Warren, & Conant, 1992; Warren, Ballenger, Ogonowski, Rosebery, & Hudicourt-Barnes, 2001), which emphasize the discipline specific aspects of scientific discourse within science learning with culturally and linguistically diverse students, including ELLs. Studies that have contributed to these consensus views have explored, among other issues, the types of science instruction that ELLs receive (Barba, 1993); science teachers' preparedness to teach ELLs (Hart & Lee, 2003; Stoddart, Pinal, Latzke, & Canaday, 2002), the scientific discourse in bilingual classrooms (Ballenger, 1997; Buxton, 1999; Kelly & Breton, 2001; Rosebery, Warren, & Conant, 1992; Warren, Ballenger, Ogonowski, Rosebery, & Hudicourt-Barnes, 2001), and the impact of other specific educational interventions such as those implemented to overcome cultural discontinuity to promote equitable opportunities by leveraging students' linguistic and cultural resources (Solano-Flores & Nelson-Barber, 2001; Warren et al., 2001; Amaral, Garrison, & Klentschy, 2002; Lee, Deaktor, Hart, Cuevas, & Enders, 2005; Rodriguez & Bethel, 1983). Across these science education frameworks and studies, several points of consensus arise in terms of scaffolding ELLs studying science:

1. There is a need to provide language minority students, including ELLs, with pedagogical approaches that promote ELL's achievement in content areas while simultaneously developing literacy and language proficiency in English (e.g., Lee & Fradd, 1998; Rosebery, Warren, & Conant, 1992; Stoddart 1999, 2005; Stoddart et al., 2002; Tharp, 1997; Tharp et. al, 2000).

2. Content-area instruction provides a meaningful context for English language and literacy development, while the language processes provide the medium for analysis and communication of subject matter knowledge (e.g., Casteel & Isom, 1994; Hart & Lee, 2003; Lee & Fradd, 1996; Stoddart et al., 2002).

3. Hands-on and inquiry-based science instruction can help students develop scientific understanding and engage in inquiry practices while also supporting academic language and literacy development (e.g., Lee, 2002; Lee & Fradd, 1998; Rosebery, Warren, & Conant, 1992).

4. Integrating language and literacy research into contextualized science inquiry instruction has a positive effect for ELL students (e.g., Lee, 2005; Stoddart et al., 2010).

SUPPORTING ACADEMIC LANGUAGE: CHALLENGES FOR SCIENCE TEACHERS

Teachers need support to conceptualize academic language as a *discourse type*. Traditional language professional development or/and teacher training practices do not provide this support. More specifically, academic language is

> a socially accepted association among ways of using language, other symbolic expressions, and artifacts of thinking, feeling, believing, valuing, and acting that can be used to identify oneself as a member of a socially meaningful group or social network, or to signal (that one is playing) a socially meaningful role. (Gee, 1996, p. 131)

Furthermore, academic language is the language children encounter in schooling from the earliest years (Schleppegrell, 2004). It includes a range of *registers* across grade levels and the subject matters. These registers become highly structured conduits through which knowledge is authoritatively presented. Based on Halliday (1978), Schleppegrell (2004) indicates that registers are what people use to contextualize language. That is, academic language can be conceptualized as knowledge of the formal language system embedded in the situated social contexts in which linguistic choices are realized (Halliday, 1994; Martin, 1992; Schleppegrell, 2004).

While the instructional congruence, ESTELL, and other science frameworks outlined above provide a solid foundation for supporting diverse students learning science, science teachers need further support so that they can scaffold their students into these discipline specific discourse types and registers. Content-area teachers face challenges regarding the nature of academic language teaching and learning. Many content-area teachers do not receive training related to linguistic and multicultural issues, including the study of language used in their academic disciplines. And when training is provided, this is usually done from theoretical views that tend to conceptualize academic language as explicit, decontextualized, complex, and cognitively demanding (see Cummins, 1981; Snow, 1983, 1987).

As a result, language training for content-area teachers working with ELL students tends to focus on psycholinguistic aspects of the concept. This in turn downplays the need to understand and study the sociocultural practices that academic language embodies (and which thus organize and structure the linguistic choices required in each academic discipline). Consequently, there is a lack of information for content-area teachers about the nature and the types of registers used in academic disciplines and school contexts.

These challenges relate to broader English language education issues in their everyday practice. There is a heated debate in the fields of applied linguistics, language and literacy, and language policy as to how to approach English language education in settings where there is a large population of linguistically diverse students. Broadly speaking, some approaches are grounded on the assumption that providing ample opportunities for *comprehensible input* should allow language learners to "*pick up*" the language as "*meaning.*" These approaches often emphasize "meaning" over "*form*" (see Krashen, 1981, 1982, 1985). On the other hand, some instructional approaches favor the teaching of the formal language system (*language forms*), which students must "master" by taking English language classes until they are proficient enough (as determined by standardized tests) to be enrolled in content-area courses (e.g., the English education model of the state of Arizona).

Critiques of both instructional positions have been posed. Some researchers argue that instructional approaches grounded on the emphasis of "*meaning*" do not pay attention to the grammatical structures nor to the language forms that are expected in school contexts (see review by Lightbown & Spada, 2006). They also argue that this approach takes for granted that access to "native speakers" and ample opportunities for comprehensible input are readily available for language learners in school contexts, which is not always the case (Harklau, 1994; Miller, 2000; Olsen, 1996, 1997; Ramirez-Marin, 2010; Valdés, 1999, 2001). Conversely, it is argued that approaches that focus on *form* decontextualize those *linguistic forms* from their *usage* within social practices, such as those realized in academic and other social contexts (see Block, 2003, for a critique on these issues). In addition, it is argued that form-focused approaches may delay ELL students' access to the type of language and practices associated with the subject matter of their content classes, as well as to "native speakers," because ELL students are grouped together in ESL classes until they are "ready to transition" to mainstream classes.

Science teachers, as content area teacher, are caught up in the middle of this debate. In school districts where a large number of ELL students are placed in content-area classes, content-area teachers are expected to be well prepared to use supportive instructional and language strategies that will facilitate the conveyance of comprehensible input and prompt students' interactions thus facilitating the acquisition of the language while they learn the content of their courses. In contrast, in schools where ELL students are grouped together until they reach English language proficiency, content teachers may not interact with culturally and linguistically diverse students at all; and if they do, teacher may assume that their students are proficient enough to understand the content of their classes and thus the needs of those students may be ignored.

Challenges for content-area teachers also relate to the use, or lack thereof, of resources that ELL students bring into their content-area classrooms. Language policies addressed to this student population have restricted or virtually eliminated approaches to English language education that include a language other than English for instruction to meet the needs of culturally and linguistically diverse students. Those approaches include bilingual education, some forms of English as a second language programs, and other program alternatives that build upon the linguistic resources that students bring to school (see the cases of California, Arizona, and Massachusetts).

In some states, approaches that include the students' home languages for instruction have been replaced by what is referred to in the literature as sheltered english immersion (SEI). This approach emphasizes the use of general instructional strategies (such as creating collaborative groups, using visuals, and building on students' background knowledge) (see SIOP) and a variety of language teaching techniques to support content and language instruction for English language learners. Nevertheless, researchers such as de Oliveira (2010) state that without the necessary adaptations required in content-area courses the use of general instructional strategies often result in the simplification of the content and language for students. In this vein, de Oliveira concludes that "while these strategies may be helpful for ELLs at the beginning levels of language proficiency, they are not appropriate for ELLs at intermediate or advanced levels, especially as they progress through the elementary grades." More importantly, Schleppegrell (2004) states that general instructional language strategies do not allow ELL students access to learning the specialized linguistic features of the academic disciplines they find at school.

POSSIBLE SOLUTION: THE SYSTEMIC FUNCTIONAL LINGUISTICS APPROACH TO LANGUAGE

In light of these challenges, science teachers need further theoretical and instructional support in terms of academic language to augment the supports provided by the instructional congruence, ESTELL, and other science education frameworks. Essentially, the instructional congruence, ESTELL, and other related science education frameworks provide an excellent foundation, but teachers also require explicit supports in terms of academic language.

Research on systemic functional linguistics (Halliday, 1978, 1980; Schleppegrell, 2001, 2004) could provide specific approaches to such language supports that would synergistically augment and enhance the current frameworks in science education, such as the IC and ESTELL frameworks. The systemic functional linguistics (SFL) approach to language analysis would provide significant assistance to content-area teachers and English language learners in identifying linguistic features common to "*school language.*" SFL also illuminates how those features are intrinsically related to the specialized knowledge constructed within academic disciplines. More specifically, SFL should prove useful within teacher preparation and professional development because SFL:

- highlights how the context of schooling is realized through the language used in texts and tasks that constitute classroom practices
- demonstrates how school contexts differ from home contexts of language in terms of features (i.e., registers) used in reading and writing school-based texts
- highlights the potential linguistic demands and challenges of school language and literacy in the content areas (especially on middle through tertiary education).
- emphasizes the importance of structuring access to registers used in academic disciplines and the practices in which these registers are used

Schleppegrell's (2004) work on SFL addresses the aspects outlined above, particularly within the context of the development of language and literacy in the content areas. In her work, Schleppegrell demonstrates how particular linguistic features are used in science texts to display knowledge, organize information, and to convey an authoritative voice, all of which comprises features of scientific discourse. To do so, Schleppegrell provides empirical data to demonstrate that academic language is dense with technical language to construct texts according to the conventions established by a specific audience (i.e., a scientific community). Thus, teachers working from a SFL language analysis foundation could scaffold students, particularly language learners, so that they can identify they type of linguistic registers they are expected to use at school and the different kinds of texts they are expected to produce.

In her seminal work, Schleppegrell (2004) presents a set of pedagogical implications supported by the SFL approach to language analysis that could guide instruction in content-area classrooms. A selection of these implications include:

- pedagogical approaches, such as content-based language instruction, should view the teaching-learning process as a form of socialization for many English learners who may not have social experience with academic registers. As a result, pedagogical approaches to teach language and content should be grounded in the reality that the development of academic registers typically does not occur unscaffolded in students' ordinary language development. In fact, English learner students may need explicit focus on form in the context of purposeful learning of the registers and genres of school.

- theoretically, approaches to content-based language instruction can be enriched through an understanding that language and content are never separate; that "content" in school contexts is always presented and assessed through language; and that as the difficulty of the concepts students need to learn increases, the language that construes those concepts also become more complex and distanced from ordinary uses of language. Schleppegrell (2004) states that "such an understanding implies that focus on language itself is important for helping students learn the concepts of school subjects" (p. 155).

- approaches to teaching content while developing language and literacy with English learners should emphasize the use of academic registers to help students understand new ways of using language. Schleppegrell points out that often students whose reading and writing skills are weak are assigned simplified texts that do not present the technicality nor the content their grade-level requires. Instead, it is a common practice to simplify the language presented to those students, which deprive them of access to learning opportunities. Therefore, teachers should be supported to select and use instructional texts that represent good examples of real academic genres.

In terms of instructional practices drawing on SFL, important work is already underway. de Oliveira and Dodds (2010), for example, provide specific instructional sequences used to assist ELL students identify challenges they can encounter, specifically when reading science textbooks. de Oliveira and Dodds demonstrate that a *language dissection approach in science* can be applied in teaching science to ELLs. Based on de Oliveira (2010), the language dissection approach focuses on revealing language demands that science discourse may include. Specifically, de Oliveira and Dodds' approach focuses on highlighting the following linguistic aspects of science discourse (see Oliveira & Dodds, 2010 for broader examples and explanations):

1. Identification of technical terms and definitions
2. Conjunctions with specific roles (e.g., *or*)
3. Everyday questions and words with specialized meanings
4. Noun groups presented in a zigzag structure

These SFL ideas extend across the K-12 curriculum. de Oliveira (2010) demonstrates this through fourth grade examples from two science textbook series to show that key linguistic features found in science at the secondary level are already present at the fourth grade level. de Oliveira concludes that the linguistic demands found in her analysis should be addressed in elementary science methods courses. Oliveira argues that there is a need to pay explicit attention to language in elementary science methods science, so that both teachers and students develop linguistic awareness of some typical discourse features of science. SFL would provide this foundation to support students throughout their K-12 experience.

Similarly, Richardson-Bruna, Van, and Perales-Escudero (2007) implemented a case study of academic language instruction in a high school "English Learner Science" course. The study was part of a larger exploratory study examining explicit academic language instruction in science classrooms. The investigation documented how teachers' conceptualizations of academic language were implemented in their science instruction and to what effect. Over a 4-month period, the researchers interviewed teachers and observed instruction in seven Iowa classrooms. The data included in the case study was generated from a ninth-grade all-ELL science classroom. The study showed how a teacher's understanding of academic language affected her instruction and students' opportunities for learning. Through the analysis of classroom discourse, the researchers illustrated the "didactic tension" that existed between the teaching of science vocabulary and students' development of conceptual understanding in science. Richardson-Bruna et al. state that the teacher's emphasis on vocabulary obscured important semantic relationships among the phenomena taught in class; the teacher's pedagogical practices also ignored the linguistic resources needed to express those relationships. That is, the didactic tension withheld students from opportunities to not only to talk, but also think, like scientists. Research like the one implemented by Richardson-Bruna et al. may further support the efficacy of SFL to leverage already established science education frameworks. Thus while more research will be required to integrate SFL with existing science education frameworks, important work is already underway to build upon, and encouraging results are already being observed.

RECOMMENDATIONS AND FINAL THOUGHTS

Learning academic language involves linguistic and social processes that are not separated from particular social practices (Schleppegrell, 2004); rather, linguistic resources are used within those practices to construe and represent new knowledge (Halliday, 1978). SFL can synergistically complement the Instructional Congruence, ESTELL, and other science education frameworks toward these goals. In order to support this integration of science education and academic language education through integrating ideas from SFL into science education frameworks, however, we will need to make changes in terms of how teachers teach their students, including the linguistic supports we provide, and the training teachers receive. In closing, we now outline our thoughts in terms of both of these levels of granularity.

Linguistic Supports for Students

It is crucial that English language learners are provided with *access* to scientific discourse and the practices in which it is used. The process of learning of English within the context of science learning must be understood as learning discourse forms (or registers) intrinsically tied to learning the practices in which scientists engage while "doing science" (Lemke, 1990) by participating in scientific communities (i.e., classrooms, labs, etc.). Therefore, it is crucial for both, monolingual and ELL students, to have access to and engaged in scientific practices and use the scientific discourse through which scientists construct understandings, represent meanings, establish conventions, communicate procedures and inquiries to other scientists.

These experiences should be mediated through the integration of science instruction of the linguistic and cultural resources, as well as previous experiences, that students bring into the classroom, such that these resources can function as scaffolds for learning science. The Instructional Congruence, ESTELL, and other science education frameworks (e.g., Rosebery, Warren, & Conant, 1992; Warren, Ballenger, Ogonowski, Rosebery, & Hudicourt-Barnes, 2001) that focus on engaging diverse students in the inquiry and discourse of science provide excellent foundations for this aspect of the supports that students need.

But this foundation is not enough by itself. The notion of *cultural incongruence* has been extremely informative to scrutinize the low performance of many culturally and linguistically diverse students in U.S. schools, but it is not enough to help students identify linguistic mismatches between their home and school (Schleppegrell, 2004). English language learners need support to identify the configuration and challenges of the language expected at school. That is, ELL students need to know they are expected to use a particular "*kind of language.*" Thus, they need support to recognize what academic language entails and how it differs from other registers with which they might be familiar. This is where SFL can augment the foundation of the science education frameworks with explicit attention to the discipline-specific requirements and nuances of academic language.

Supports for Teachers Working With English language Learners

In order for teachers to support students in the ways pointed out above, science teacher preparation and development programs need to incorporate theoretical and conceptual views of language consistent with the research that supports instructional frameworks found in the literature for the teaching of science with culturally and linguistically diverse students. That body of research demonstrates the social and cultural nature of science as a *social practice* that requires the use of linguistic conventions to represent and create meanings and knowledge. As a result, it is necessary to provide teachers with a clear understanding of what "academic language" entails and how it is intrinsically tied to learning the content of academic disciplines and their specialized practices and language conventions. We believe that the view of language as represented in SFL framework and those found in sociocultural and sociolinguistic approaches to language learning are extremely useful to achieve this and at the same time those views of language depart from views of language exclusively grounded on psycholinguistic positions.

As part of this shift, teacher preparation and development programs need to adopt/develop pedagogical approaches to support English learners that not only integrate the students' primary languages and/or aspects of their cultural backgrounds, but also focus on the "*school language*" they are learning. To effectively assist ELL students identify the linguistics expectations of school, de Oliveira (2010) argues that there is a need to pay explicit attention to language in elementary science methods science, so that both teachers and students develop linguistic awareness of some typical discourse features of science. Teacher preparation and development programs also need to promote pedagogical approaches to science instruction that provide English learners with access to science discourse and the scientific practices in which it is used. Content-area teachers need to view learning science as learning the specialized practices, tools, and language that scientists use to "do science." Thus, it is crucial that teacher preparation programs provide pedagogical and instructional approaches that address such view in ways that integrate SFL with the frameworks for science education that highlight the importance of such practices, such as Instructional Congruence and ESTELL.

Final Thoughts

More research connecting SFL to science education frameworks needs to be conducted, particularly in terms of interventions with middle and high school students, who have generally been studied less frequently in terms of language and literacy development needs. Through this work, instructional models synergizing SFL with science education frameworks for diverse students may be developed. SFL provides a powerful potential tool to leverage the foundation created by the Instructional Congruence and ESTELL frameworks for science education in this regard. As part of this effort to synergize those frameworks, it is important to pay attention to Richardson-Bruna et al.'s (2007) proposal that recognizing the functionality of academic registers for construing knowledge, and the challenges that these registers pose for students unfamiliar with them, can lead to pedagogical interventions which make the language of schooling more accessible to all students. As Richardson-Bruna et al. explain,

> taking the call for integrated instruction seriously means taking what is known about quality science education and infusing into those goals of cognitive development corollary goals of language development. Just as science education is about meaningful inquiry into real-world problems and the opportunity to apply and generate conceptual knowledge in collaboration with students, teachers, and other members of the scientific community (Goldman, 1997; Krajcik, Blumenfeld, Marx, Bass, & Fredricks, 1998; Mercado, 1992; Merino & Hammond, 1998), it is also about the language and literacy upon which such activities of inquiry, application, generation, and collaboration rely. (p. 52)

REFERENCES

Amaral, O. M., Garrison, L., & Klentschy, M. (2002). Helping English learners increase achievement through inquiry-based science instruction. *Bilingual Research Journal, 26*(2), 213-239.

American Association for the Advancement of Science. (1989). *Science for all Americans.* New York, NY: Oxford University Press.

American Association for the Advancement of Science. (1993). *Benchmarks for sence literacy.* New York, NY: Oxford University Press.

American Council on the Teaching of Foreign Languages. (1996). *Standards for foreign language learning: Preparing for the 21st century.* Lawrence, KS: Allen Press.

Atwater, M.M. (1994). Research on cultural diversity in the classroom. In D. L. Gabel (Ed.), *Handbook of research on science teaching and learning* (pp. 558-576). New York, :NY: Macmillan.

August, D., & Hakuta, K. (Eds.). (1997). *Improving schooling for language-minority children: A research agenda.* Washington. DC: National Academy Press.

Bakhtin , M. (1981). *The dialogic imagination: Four essays.* Austin, TX: University of Texas Press.

Ballenger, C. (1997). Social identities, moral narratives, scientific argumentation: Science talk in a bilingual classroom. *Language and Education, 11*, 1-14.

Barba, R. H. (1993). A study of culturally syntonic variables in the bilingual/bicultural science classroom. *Journal of Research in Science Teaching, 30,* 1053-1071.

Bell, Y. R., & Clark, T. R. (1998). Culturally relevant reading material as related to comprehension and recall in African American children. *Journal of Black Psychology, 24,* 455-475.

Block, D. (2003). *The social turn in second language acquisition.* Edinburgh, Scotland: Edinburgh University Press.

Boquedano-López, P., Solis, J. L., & Kattan, S. (2005). Adaptation: The language of classroom learning. *Linguistics and Education, 6,* 1-26.

Brickhouse, N. (1994). Bringing in the Outsiders: reshaping the sciences of the future. *Journal of Curriculum Studies, 26*(4), 401-416.

Brickhouse, N. (1998). Feminism(s) and science education. In B. Fraser & K. Tobin (Eds.), *International handbook of science education: Part II* (pp. 1067-1081). Dordrecht, The Netherlands: Kluwer.

Buxton, C. (1999). Designing a model-based methodology for science instruction: Lessons from a bilingual classroom. *Bilingual Research Journal, 23*(2-3), 147-177.

Calabrese Barton, A. (1998). Margin and center: Intersections of urban, homeless children and a pedagogy of liberation. *Theory into Practice, 37*(4), 296-305.

Casteel, C. P., & Isom, B. A. (1994). Reciprocal processes in science and literacy learning. *The Reading Teacher. 47,* 538-545.

Cervetti, G.N., Pearson, P.D., Barber, J., Hiebert, E., & Bravo, M.A. (2007). Integrating literacy in science: The research we have, the research we need. In M. Pressley, A.K. Billman, K. Perry, K. Refitt & J. Reynolds (Eds.), *Shaping literacy achievement* (pp. 157-174). New York, NY. Gilford.

Chamot, A.U., & O'Malley, J. M. (1994). *The Calla handbook: Implementing the cognitive academic language learning approach.* White Plains, NY: Addison Wesley Longman.

Crawford, J. (2004). *Educating English learners: Language diversity in the classroom* (5th ed.). Trenton, NJ: Bilingual Education Services.

Cummins, J. (1981). The role of primary language development in promoting educational success for language minority students. In California State Department of Education (Ed.), *Schooling and language minority students: A theoretical framework* (pp. 3-49). Los Angeles, CA: National Dissemination and Assessment Center.

Cummins, J. (1984). *Bilingualism and special education: Issues in assessment and pedagogy.* Boston, MA: College-Hill Press.

Dalton, S. S. (1998). *Pedagogy matters: Standards for effective teaching practice.* Santa Cruz, CA: Center for Research on Education, Diversity & Excellence, University of California.

de Oliveira, L. C. (2010). Enhancing content instruction for ELLs: Learning about language in science. In D. Sunal, C. Sunal, M. Mantero, & E. Wright (Eds.), *Teaching science with Hispanic ELLs in K-16 classrooms* (pp. 135-150). Charlotte, NC: Information Age.

de Oliveira, L. C., & Dodds, K. N. (2010). Beyond general strategies for English Language Learners: Language dissection in science. *The Electronic Journal of Literacy Through Science, 9*(1), 1-14.

Deyhle, D. (1995). Navajo youth and Anglo racism: Cultural integrity and resistance. *Harvard Educational Review. 65*, 403-444.

Doherty, R. W., & Pinal, A. (2004). *Joint productive activity and cognitive strategy use.* TESOL.

Driver, R., Asoko, H., Leach, J., Mortimer, E., & Scott, P. (1994). Constructing scientific knowledge in the classroom. *Educational Researcher, 23*, 5-12.

Estrada, P., & Imhoff, B. D. (2001, Month). *Patterns of language arts instructional activity: Excellence, inclusion, fairness, and harmony in six first grade classrooms.* Paper presented at the annual meeting of the American Education Research Association, Seattle, WA.

Fradd, S. H., & Larringa-McGee, P. (1994). *Instructional assessment: An integrative approach to evaluating student performance.* Reading, MA: Addison-Wesley.

García, E. (1999). *Student cultural diversity: Understanding and meeting the challenge* (2nd ed.). Boston, MA: Houghton Mifflin.

Garcia, E., & Boquedano-López, P. (2007). Science instruction for all: An approach an approach to equity and Access in science education. *Language Magazine, 6*(6), 24-31.

Garrett, M. W. (1995). Between two worlds: Cultural discontinuity in the dropout of Native American youth. *School Counselor, 42*, 186-195.

Gay, G. (2000). Culturally responsive teaching: Theory, research, and practice. New York, NY: Teachers College Press.

Gee, J. P. (1996). *Social linguistics and literacies: Ideology in discourses.* London, England: Taylor & Francis.

Gee, J. P. (2008). *Social linguistics and literacies: Ideology in discourses* (3rd ed.). New York, NY: Routledge.

Gilbert, A., & Yerrick, R. (2001) Same school, separate worlds: A sociocultural study of identity, resistance, and negotiation in a rural, lower track science classroom. *Journal of Research in Science Teaching, 38*(5), 574-598.

Goldman, S. R. (1997). Learning from the text: Reflections on the past and suggestions for the future. *Discourse Processes, 23*, 357–398.

Gordon, E. W., & Yowell, C. (1992). *Educational reforms for students at risk: Cultural dissonance as a risk factor in the development of students.* East Lansing, MI: National Center for Research on Teacher Learning.

Hale, J. (2001). Culturally appropriate pedagogy. In W. Watkins, J. Lewis, & V. Chou (Eds.), *Race and education: The roles of history and society in educating African American students* (pp. 173–189). Boston, MA: Allyn & Bacon.

Halliday, M.A.K. (1973). *Explorations in the functions of language.* London, England: Edward Arnold.

Halliday, M. A. K. (1978). *Language as social semiotic.* London: Edward Arnold.

Halliday, M. A. K. (1980). Three aspects of children's language development: Learning language, learning through language, learning about language. In J. Webster (Ed.), *The language of early childhood* (Vol. 4, pp. 308–326). London, England: Continuum.

Halliday, M.A.K. (1994). *An introduction to functional grammar* (2nd ed.). London, England: Edward Arnold.

Harklau, L. (1994). "Jumping tracks": How language-minority students negotiate evaluations of ability. *Anthropology & Education Quarterly, 25*(3, Alternative Visions of Schooling: Success Stories in Minority Settings), 347-363.

Hart, J., & Lee, O. (2003). Teacher professional development to improve science and literacy achievement of English language learners. *Bilingual Research Journal, 27*(3), 475-501.

Hilberg, R. S., Tharp, R. G., & DeGeest, L. (2000). The efficacy of CREDE's standards-based instruction in American Indian mathematics classes. *Equity and Excellence in Education, 33*(2), 32-39.

Hollins, E., & Spencer, K. (1990). Restructuring schools for cultural inclusion: Changing the schooling process for African American youngsters. *Journal of Education, 172,* 89-100.

International Reading Association and the National Council of Teachers of English. (1994). *Standards for the assessment of reading and writing.* Newark, DE: International Reading Association (with National Council of Teachers of English).

Kelly, G., & Breton, T. (2001). Framing science as disciplinary inquiry in bilingual-classrooms. *Electronic Journal of Science and Literacy, 1*(1). Retrieved from http://www2.sjsu.edu/elementaryed/ejlts/

Krajcik, J., Blumenfeld, P. C., Marx, R. W., Bass, K. M., & Fredricks, J. (1998). Inquiry in project-based science classrooms: Initial attempts by middle school students. *Journal of the Learning Sciences, 7,* 313-350.

Krashen, S. (1981). *Second language acquisition and second language learning.* New York, NY: Pergamon Press.

Krashen, S. (1982). *Principles and practice in second language acquisition.* New York, NY: Pergamon Press.

Krashen, S. (1985). *The input hypothesis: Issues and implication.* New York, NY: Longman.

Ku, Y.M., Bravo, M., & Garcia, E. E. (2004). Science intruction for al. ABE *Journal of Research and Practice, 2*(1), 20-44.

Ku, Y. M., Garcia, E. E., & Corkins, J. (2005). *Impact of the instructional intervention on science achievement of culturally and linguistically diverse students.* Paper presented at the American Educational Research Association, Montreal, Canada.

Ladson-Billings, G. (1995). Toward a theory of culturally relevant pedagogy. *American Education Research Journal, 35,* 465-491.

Lee, O. (1999). Equity implications based on the conceptions of science achievement in major reform documents. *Review of Educational Research, 69*(1), 83-115

Lee, O. (2001). Culture and language in science education: What do we know and what do we need to know? *Journal of Research in Science Teaching, 38,* 499-501.

Lee, O. (2005). Science education and English language learners: Synthesis and research agenda. *Review of Educational Research, 75*(4), 491-530.

Lee, O., & Fradd, S. H. (1998). Science for all, including students from non-English language backgrounds. *Educational Researcher, 27*(4), 12-21.

Lee, O., & Fradd, S. H. (1999a). The water cycle: Promoting science inquiry for culturally and linguistically diverse students. (Unpublished instructional materials). Coral Gables, Florida, University of Miami.

Lee, O., & Fradd, S. H. (1999b). Weather: Promoting science inquiry for culturally and linguistically diverse students. (Unpublished instructional materials). Coral Gables, Florida, University of Miami.

Lee, O., & Fradd, S. H. (2001). Instructional congruence to promote science learning and literacy development for linguistically diverse students. In D. R. Lavoie & W.-M. Roth (Eds.), *Models for science teacher preparation: Bridging the gap between research and practice* (pp. 109-126). Dordrecht, The Netherlands: Kluwer.

Lee, O., & Luykx, A. (2004). *Science education and student diversity: Synthesis and research agenda.* A monograph supported by the Center for Research on Education Diversity, and Excellence (CREDE) at the University of California at Santa Cruz and the National Center for Improving Student Learning and Achievement (NCISLA) University of Wisconsin in Madison Press.

Lee, O., Deaktor, R., Hart, J. E., Cuevas, P., & Enders, C. (2005). An instructional intervention's impact on the science and literacy achievement of culturally and linguistically diverse elementary students. *Journal of Research in Science Teaching, 42*(8), 857-887.

Lee, O., Maerten-Rivera, J., Penfield, R., LeRoy, K., & Secada, W.G. (2008). Science achievement of English language learners in urban elementary schools: Results of a first year professional development intervention. *Journal of Research of Science Teaching, 45*(1), 31-52.

Lemke, J. (1990). *Talking science: Language, learning. and values.* Norwood, NJ: Ablex

Lemke, J. L. (2001). Articulating communities: Sociocultural perspectives on science education. *Journal of Research in Science Teaching, 38,* 296-316.

Lightbown, P. & Spada, N. (2006). *How languages are learned* (3rd ed.). Oxford, England: Oxford University Press.

Loving, C. C. (1997). From the summit of truth to its slippery slopes: Science education's journey through positivist-postmodem territory. *American Educational Research Journal, 31,* 421-452.

Martin, J. R. (1992). *English text: System and structure.* Philadelphia, PA: John Benjamins.

McLaughlin, M. W., Shepard, L. A., & O'Day, J. A. (1995). *Improving education through standards-based reform: A report by the National Academy of Education Panel on Standards-based Education Reform.* Stanford, CA: Stanford University, The National Academy of Education.

Miller, J. M. (2000). Language use, identity, and social interaction: Migrant students in Australia. *Research on Language & Social Interaction, 33*(1), 69-100.

Mercado, C. I. (1992). Researching research: A classroom-based student-teacher-researchers collaborative project. In A. N. Ambert & M. D. Alvarez (Eds.), *Puerto Rican children on the mainland: Interdisciplinary perspectives* (pp. 167-192). New York, NY: Garland.

Merino, B. J., & Hammond, L. (1998). Family gardens and solar ovens: Making science education accessible to culturally and linguistically diverse students. *Multicultural Education, 5,* 34-37.

Moll, L. C. (Ed.). (1990). Vygotsky and education: Instructional implications and applications of sociohistorical psychology. Cambridge, MA: Harvard University Press.

National Research Council. (1996). *National science education standards.* Washington, DC: National Academy Press.

Ndura, E. (2004). Teachers' discoveries of their cultural realms: Untangling the web of cultural identity. *Multicultural Perspectives, 6*(3), 10-16.

Nieto, S. (1999). *The light in their eyes: Creating multicultural learning communities.* New York, NY: Teachers College Press.

Olsen, L. (1996). *The unfinished journey: Restructuring schools in a diverse society.* San Francisco, CA: California Tomorrow.

Olsen, L. (1997). *Made in America: Immigrant students in our public schools.* New York: New Press.

O'Malley, M., & L. Valdez Pierce (1996). *Authentic assessment for English language learners.* New York, NY: Addison Wesley.

Palincsar, A. S., & Magnusson, S. J. (2001). The interplay of firsthand and text based investigations to model and support the development of scientific knowledge and reasoning. In S. Carver & D. Klahr (Eds.), *Cognition and instruction: Twenty five years of progress* (pp. 151-194). Mahwah, NJ: Lawrence Erlbaum.

Parsons, E. C. (2001). Using power and caring to mediate White male privilege, equality, and equity in an urban elementary classroom: Implications for teacher preparation. *Urban Review, 33*(4), 321-338.

Parsons, E. C. (2003). Culturalizing instruction: Creating a more inclusive learning context for African American students. *High School Journal, 86*(4), 23-30.

Parsons, E. C., Travis, C., & Simpson, J. S. (2005). The black cultural ethos, students' instructional context preferences, and student achievement: An examination of culturally congruent science instruction in the eighth grade classes of one African American and one Euro-American teacher. *The Negro Educational Review, 56*(2, 3), 183-203.

Portes, P. R. (2001). Social and psychological factors in the academic achievement of children of immigrants: A cultural history puzzle. *American Educational Research Journal, 38,* 461-492.

Ramirez-Marin, F. (2010). *Access to English: Mexican immigrant students' experiences in an Arizona high school.* Retrieved from http://www.uv.mx/bdh/documents/Ramirez_access_to_english.pdf

Richardson-Bruna, K., Vann, R., & Perales-Escudero, M. (2007). What's language got to do with it?: A case study of academic language instruction in a high school "English Learner Science" class. *Journal of English for Academic Purposes, 6,* 36-54

Rodriguez, I., & Bethel, L. J. (1983). An inquiry approach to science and language teaching. *Journal of Research in Science Teaching, 20*(4), 291-296.

Rogoff B. (1990). *Apprenticeship in thinking : Cognitive development in social context.* New York, NY: Oxford University Press.

Rogoff, B. (1991). Social interaction as apprenticeship in thinking: guided participation in spatial planning. In L. Resnick, J. Levine, & S. Teasley (Eds.), *Per-*

spectives on socially shared cognition (pp. 349-364). Hyattsville, MD: American Psychological Association.

Rogoff, B. (1995). Observing sociocultural activity on three planes: Participatory appropriation, guided participation, and apprenticeship. In J. V. Wertsch, P. del Rio, & A. Alvarez (Eds.), *Sociocultural studies of mind* (pp. 139-164). Cambridge, England: Cambridge University Press. (Reprinted (2008) in K. Hall & P. Murphy (Eds.), *Pedagogy and practice: Culture and identities*. London: SAGE).

Rogoff, B., & Wertsch, J. V. (Eds.). (1984). Children's learning in the "Zone of Proximal Development. San Francisco: Jossey-Bass Inc.

Rosebery, A. S., Warren, B., & Conant, F. R. (1992). Appropriating scientific discourse: Findings from language minority classrooms. *Journal of the Learning Sciences, 21,* 61-94.

Saunders, W., & Goldenberg, C. (1999a). *The effects of comprehensive Language Arts/ Transition Program on the literacy development of English learners* (Technical Report). Santa Cruz, CA: Center for Research, Diversity & Excellence, University of California.

Saunders, W., & Goldenberg, C. (1999b). The effects of instructional conversations and literature logs on limited and fluent English proficient students' story comprehension and thematic understanding. *The Elementary School Journal, 99,* 277-301.

Saunders, W., O'Brien, G., Lennon, D., & McLean, J. (1998). Making the transition to English literacy successful: Effective strategies for studying literature with transition students. In R. Gersten & R. Jimenez (Eds.), *Promoting learning for culturally and linguistically diverse students* (pp. 99-132). Monterey, CA: Brooks Cole.

Schleppegrell, M. J. (2001). Linguistic features of the language of schooling. Linguistics and Education, *12*(4), 431-459.

Schleppegrell, M. J. (2004). *The language of schooling: A functional linguistics perspective.* Mahwah, NJ: Lawrence Erlbaum Associates.

Snow, C. E. (1983). Age differences in second language acquisition: Research findings and folk psychology. In K. Bailey, M. Long, & S. Peck (Eds.). *Second language acquisition studies* (pp. 141-150). Rowley, MA: Newbury House.

Snow, C. E. (1987). Beyond conversation: Second language learners' acquisition of description and explanation. In J. Lantolf & A. Labarca (Eds.), *Research in second language learning: Focus on the classroom* (pp. 3-16). Norwood, NJ: Ablex.

Solano-Flores, G., & Nelson-Barber, S. (2001). On the cultural validity of science assessments. *Journal of Research in Science Teaching, 38*(5), 553-573.

Solis, J.L. (2005). Locating student classroom participation in science inquiry and literacy activities. In J. Cohen, K. McAlister, K. Rolstad, & J. MacSwan (Eds.), *ISB4: Proceedings of the 4th International Symposium on Bilingualism.* Somerville, MA. Cascadilla Press.

Stoddart, T. (1999). *Language Acquisition Through Science Inquiry.* Paper presented at the annual meeting of the American Educational Research Association, Montreal.

Stoddart, T. (2005). *Improving student achievement with the CREDE Five Standards Pedagogy.* Technical Report No. (J1). Santa Cruz, CA: University of California, Center for Research on Education, Diversity and Excellence

Stoddart, T, Abrams, R., Gasper, E., & Canaday, D. (2000) Concept maps as assessment in science inquiry learning—a report of methodology. *International Journal of Science Education, 22*(12), 1221-1246.

Stoddart, T., Pinal, A., Latzke, M., & Canaday, D. (2002). Integrating inquiry science and language development for English language learners. *Journal of Research in Science Teaching, 39*(8), 664-687.

Stoddart, T., Solis, J., Tolbert, S., & Bravo, M. (2010). A framework for the effective science teaching of English language learners in elementary schools. In D. Sunal, C. Sunal, & E. Wright (Eds.), Teaching science with Hispanic ELLs in K-16 Classrooms (pp. 151-181). Charlotte, NC: Information Age.

Sue, D. W., & Sue, D. (2003). *Counseling the culturally diverse: Theory and practice* (4th ed.). New York, NY: Houghton Mifflin.

Swain, M., & Lapkin, S. (1995). Problems in output and the cognitive processes they generate: A step towards second language learning. *Applied Linguistics 16,* 371-391.

Teachers of English to Speakers of Other Languages. (1997). *ESL standards for pre-K-12 students.* Alexandria, VA: Author.

Tharp, R. G. (1989). Psychocultural variables and constants: Effects on teaching and learning in schools. *American Psychologist, 44,* 349–359.

Tharp, R. G. (1997). *From at-risk to excellence: Research, theory, and principles for practice.* Santa Cruz, CA: Center for Research on Education, Diversity & Excellence.

Tharp, R. G., & Dalton, S. S. (2007). Orthodoxy, cultural compatibility, and universals in education. *Comparative Education, 43*(1), 53-70.

Tharp, R. G., & Gallimore, R. (1988). *Rousing minds to life: Teaching, learning, and schooling in social context.* New York, NY: Cambridge University Press.

Tharp, R. G., Estrada, P., Dalton, S. S., & Yamauchi, L.A. (2000). *Teaching transformed: Achieving excellence, fairness, inclusion and harmony.* Boulder, CO: Westview Press.

Tillman, L. C. (2002). Culturally sensitive research approaches: An African American perspective. *Educational Researcher, 31,* 3-12.

Tyler, K. M., Boykin, A. W., Miller, O. A., & Hurley, E. A. (2006). Cultural values in the home and school experiences of low-income African American students. *Social Psychology of Education, 9,* 363-380.

Tyler K. M., Uqdah, A. L., Dillihunt, M. L., Beatty-Hazelbaker, R., Conner, T., Gadson N, et al. (2008) Cultural discontinuity: Toward a quantitative investigation of a major hypothesis in education. *Educational Researcher 37*(5), 280-297.

U.S. Department of Education, National Center for Education Statistics. (2007). The condition of education: 2007. (NCES 2007-064). Washington, DC: U.S. Government Printing Office.

Valdés, G. (1999). Incipient bilingualism and the development of English language writing abilities in the secondary school. *So Much to Say: Adolescents, Bilingualism, and ESL in the Secondary School,* 138-175.

Valdés, G. (2001). *Learning and not learning English: Latino students in American schools.* London, England: Teachers College Press.

Vega, W. A., Khoury, E. L., Zimmerman, R. S., Gil, A. G., & Warheit, G. J. (1995). Cultural conflicts and problem behaviors of Latino adolescents in home and school environments. *Journal of Community Psychology, 23,* 167-179.

Vygotsky, L. S. (1978). *Mind in Society.* Cambridge, MA: Harvard University Press.

Warren, B., Ballenger, C., Ogonowski, M., Rosebery, A., & Hudicourt-Barnes, J. (2001). Rethinking diversity in learning science: The logic of everyday language. *Journal of Research in Science Teaching, 38*(5), 529-552.

Webb-Johnson, G. C. (2003). Behaving while Black: A hazardous reality for African American learners. *Beyond Behavior, 12*(2), 3-7.

Wellington, J., & Osborne, J. (2001). *Language and literacy in science education.* Philadelphia, PA: Open University Press.

Wertsch, J. V. (1985). Culture, communication and cognition: Vygotskian perspectives. Cambridge, England: Cambridge University Press.

Wertsch, J. V. (1991). *Voices of the mind: A sociocultural approach to mediated action.* Cambridge, MA: Harvard University Press

Wong-Fillmore, L., & Snow, C. (2002). *What teachers need to know about language.* Washington DC: Center for Applied Linguistics.

CHAPTER 9

ENGLISH LANGUAGE LEARNING AND LEARNING ACADEMIC LANGUAGE IN MATHEMATICS

James A. Middleton,
Silvia Llamas-Flores, and Paula Patricia Guerra-Lombardi

INTRODUCTION

We are at a precarious moment in the history of our education system. The ubiquity of technology insures that more people have more access to more information than ever before. The world's economy is becoming more pluralistic, engaging workers and corporations in ever more complex forms of organization and distribution. But the nature of that access, the nature of the organization is still in question for many. Approximately 2.7 billion people in the world live on less than $3 per day. In Mexico and Central America, the World Bank estimates that between 14 and 16% of the population earns less than $3 per day (http://web.worldbank.org, 2006). Many of these workers emigrate, moving ever northward in hopes of improving fortunes for themselves and their families. In 2005, over 5 million students in the United States were classified as English language learners (ELLs) (around 10.5% and rising). Of these around 80% speak

Academic Language in Second Language Learning, pp. 201–224
Copyright © 2013 by Information Age Publishing
All rights of reproduction in any form reserved.

Spanish as their native tongue, and 60% (2.5 million) of these live in just *six* states: Arizona, California, Florida, Texas, and New York (Payan & Nettles, 2008).

Problems have arisen in conjunction with these increased populations of ELLs because the education system does not have adequate numbers of bilingual teachers, materials and supplies that accommodate English learners, or most importantly, norms and routines for handling cultural, economic, and linguistic differences.[1] The result of this lack of facility and resources is that students whose language of origin is not English tend to achieve at a much lower level than language-majority learners. On the 2005 National Assessment of Educational Progress about half to three-quarters of ELL students in the nation scored below basic proficiency in mathematics. In Arizona, about 85% of White test-takers and 60% of non-White Hispanics were above proficiency compared to ELL students, among whom only 40% were scored above proficiency (Fry, 2007).

These disparities are serious business. Again, to use our home state, Arizona, as an example, policies—laws—have been enacted forcing teachers to limit the use of ELL's first language in the classroom, and to seriously curtail bilingual programs and other approaches to instruction (Arizona Proposition 203, 2006). When it comes to developing reading proficiency, the difficulties and sometimes advantages associated with second language learning are well documented (Lesaux & Siegel, 2003); including overrepresentation of ELL populations in special education (Artiles, Rueda, Salazar, & Higareda, 2005; Klingner, Hoover, & Baca, 2008).

When the first author of this chapter was approached by the editors to provide an analysis of the research on learning the academic language of mathematics, he was somewhat perplexed. His expertise is more suited to cognitive development and classroom research than linguistics. A few years ago, he had done some linguistic analysis of teacher questioning in ELL classrooms (Middleton, Poynor, Toluk, Wolfe, & Bote, 1999), but he felt that his knowledge-base of the broader linguistic field was limited. Moreover, it seemed that for this topic, which is so tied up with race and class ideologies, the perspective of colleagues with first-hand experience learning mathematics as a second academic language, and with teaching mathematics to second language learners, would provide an important gut-check on the implications of the research base. The coauthors are both ELLs studying language acquisition and learning in mathematics from a linguistic perspective and from a critical perspective. This chapter represents a unique melding of our experiences and expertise in an attempt to describe the research findings in the field, and to explain how those findings interrelate in the lives of ELL students.

While this chapter is ostensibly about the implications of research for helping ELL students learn more and better mathematics, its subtext is about developing a more cogent argument for adopting practices that better serve the needs of ELL populations. To do *this* requires that we digress slightly to examine the purposes language serves in our society, and to project that the problems we are facing today have as much to do with language as a means for *belonging* than it does with language as a means for communication of *information*.

Following this digression, we jump into the research on ELLs, language acquisition, and their implications for learning the academic language of mathematics. On occasion we will distinguish "school mathematics," a rather constrained subset, from the larger discourse community of mathematicians and mathematically-proficient individuals. We do this because we see school in the United States as having its own norms related to mathematics that define only certain practices that would be considered legitimate by mathematicians as being "legitimate" in the school context. Because immigrants and students who come from educational backgrounds and family contexts may bring different forms of representation, symbols and procedures that are perfectly correct and accepted in their culture of origin, these may not be accorded legitimacy in the eyes of the teacher or the testing system in the United States.

Last, like other authors in this volume, we include gesture, writing, use of technology and other forms of knowledge representation and communication in our discussion of "language" because these forms of expression have specific manifestations in mathematical discourse, and our goal is for students to develop coordinated systems of knowing, speaking and behaving that serve them well in their quest for happiness and prosperity.

On the Evolution and Purpose of Language

If we are to understand the reasons we have difficulty developing an equitable and effective means for dealing with differences in language of origin and formal mathematical language, we must examine the function that language has served evolutionarily, as both a physiological (i.e., genetic) adaptation which we hold common among members of our species, and as a culturally-determined variable that differs across human social groups. While we are less concerned with the biological bases for complex social behavior, it is important to understand that gesture, language, writing and other forms of communication have their origins in our evolutionary heritage, and therefore, there must have been some time when our ancestors did *not* have these capacities. What *did* we have at this stage in our development as a species that led to the capacity for speech and writing?

Writing is easier to contemplate in this manner than spoken language, as we have a much clearer history of its beginnings and evolution, at least as a system of notation dependent upon earlier innovations of language and gesture. Writing, can be seen as having evolved through a series of *preadaptations*, including but not limited to the brain's development of the capacity to use symbols to stand for physical objects and actions, and gracialization allowing for fine motor coordination. For spoken language detachment of the hyoid bone created the preconditions for complex verbalizations. But even earlier than these, the very fact that humans are social animals is itself a preadaptation. Our social nature allows us to imitate complex actions, to follow the gaze or gesture of another, and to coordinate these actions towards a collective goal (Christiansen & Kirby, 2003).

Sociobiologists assert that language evolved as a means for establishing and maintaining social ties, serving much the same role that social grooming does for our nearest primate cousins. Basic rules of sociobiology, therefore, would predict that as social groups get larger—as the genetic ties between group members—becomes more diffuse, *either* small groups must break off to maintain the capacity to discern whose genes are whose and therefore whom to defend and who to fight, *or* some alternative method of maintaining group affiliation (like language) must be established for the survival benefits of the collective.

On the other hand, language capacity is not solely a function of biology (Kirby, Dowman, & Griffiths, 2007). Cultural transmission heavily determines both the capacity of any individual to engage in a particular language, but also in part cultural transmission determines the larger history of how the capacity for language has "evolved" over the millennia since our preadaptations predisposed us towards verbal communication. George Kelly (1955), in developing his theory of construct development, suggested that individuals choose ideas and behaviors from a given repertoire, because of their capacity to increase the utility of a person's way of seeing and acting in the world—to increase the adaptivity of the person's system of constructs. Here we use the word "evolved" in its nonbiological sense. Languages change over time because of their capacity to "evolve" new lexical, grammatical, and syntactic structures that are more useful for generating and conveying ideas. This meaning of "evolution" is NOT closely tied to natural selection, and in fact may reduce selection pressure on biological mechanisms, in essence switching over the selective function from *genes* to *thoughts*.

Lackoff and Johnson (1999) and Lackoff and Nuñez (2001) have illustrated that there appear to be some universals that form in our earliest interactions with our mothers and fathers, that constitute the basic units of our cognitive-linguistic system. The notion that *up is good*, for example, appears to be universal across cultures because our first notion of *goodness* can be traced to the time when we were infants and needed to be cared for by being picked *up*. *Up*, therefore is a basic metaphor for goodness. It is also closely associated with other metaphors of affiliation such as *love is warm*. Conflation, a concept developed by Johnson (1999), predicts that associations are formed between sensorimotor experiences and conceptual experiences early on in infancy, melding the two in such a manner that the most basic social experiences become instantiated as basic metaphors (i.e., thoughts that associate all higher-level understanding with basic feelings and emotions).

The key here is that these basic metaphors appear to be universal across cultures and languages. They even appear to be universal across our ape cousins the chimps, bonobos, gorillas, and orangutans, whose verbal prowess is limited due to lack of our preadaptations. Our first exposure to spoken language when we emerge from the womb is initiated by vocalizations from a caregiver. Even neonates' body movement quickly becomes synchronized to the patterns of speech of adults, and they become attuned to their first language in this participation in a form of social organization between adult and child (Condon & Sander, 1974). Much later, the infant develops the capacity to encode and transmit packets of information through speech.

We can postulate therefore that language serves two primary purposes for the individual within a social group: (1) affiliations or closeness; and (2) coordinated action; *in that order*. We first must be members *of* a group before we can act *as* a group.[2] Academic language also serves these two functions. As a means to affiliation, the use of academic language determines who gets to play the academic game and who is excluded. Fluent speakers of mathematics are familiar with the norms of interaction expected of members of the mathematics community. They are able to spot individuals who are not members by their halting and incorrect usage, and they can gravitate towards individuals whose usage is near their own level or better in order to develop their skills. This academic language therefore, serves an exclusionary purpose as much as its inclusionary purpose.

Like everyday language, individuals feel comfortable with academic language they are used to. The first author of this chapter recently had an argument with a graduate student over the definition and use of the word, "matrix." Matrices are an important structure in algebra. They can be used to denote systems of related variables in multiple dimensions. For this reason, they are also useful for organizing and operating on data in statistical applications, or to determine the location and orientation of points in space in geometrical applications. On these tenets we had no quarrel. However, on the proper representation of matrices, we disagreed vehemently: Amy holding a stricter, more orthodox perspective, asserted that a *matrix* has a specific symbolic form, while Middleton accepting "invented spelling" as it were, allowed almost any tabular representation of an algebraic system to be considered a matrix. These stances were derived from our different mathematical backgrounds and as such, represented different communal traditions regarding the use of the term "matrix" and its subtle meanings. In essence the different uses of "matrix" identified us as members of different communities within mathematics—in effect drawing an exclusionary boundary of a certain type.

These boundaries, important though they are from an evolutionary perspective, are difficult to transcend in a teaching and learning community. Learners coming from a slightly different tradition will use symbols, terms, and procedures in irritatingly different ways—in ways not recognized by the teacher or other learners in the classroom—demarcating "us" versus "them." In terms of the larger community of mathematicians, these traditions may not be incorrect, but in the local context of the classroom, they may be misinterpreted as such. The extent to which a teacher or student in the mathematics classroom can identify a *different* tradition as *correct* or *useful* may determine the extent to which children educated in another culture can begin to incorporate their prior academic knowledge into the routines and discourse of the classroom.

Academic disciplines, as communities of practice, evolve specialized forms of recording and communicating that have specific uses and meanings for each discipline. Disciplinary discourse is carried largely by its forms of representation, some of which are speech, others of which are graphical or symbolic. Verbalizations may structure a conversation, but gestural, graphical, and manipulative "inscriptions" make up the bulk of the conversation, and provide the explicit focus of practice around which conversations evolve (Roth & McGinn, 1998). In mathematics, these signs, symbols, and forms have evolved to such a degree that a great deal of meaning can be conveyed with only a few marks on paper, or in more contemporary times, a spreadsheet, graph or table of values.

Typically, it is only in closely related disciplines (e.g., theoretical physics and astronomy) that these forms are recognizable and understandable across communities. Mathematics, however, at least in its symbolic and representational forms, has been appropriated by the sciences, economics and other business fields, geography and the social sciences, art and engineering, as a set of conceptual tools by which phenomena of interest to these communities can be modeled and better understood. So, mathematics is a special case: One in which the forms of representing and communicating ideas which have evolved *within* the discipline are being utilized extensively *outside* the discipline.

Moreover, these forms of inscription have a global universality. For the most part, the uses of mathematical notation and other forms of inscription are common across modern cultures although there are some notable exceptions (like the use of ÷ to indicate division in the United States, instead of : which is commonly used in countries around the world). This universality should be an enabling feature of the mathematics curriculum for engaging second-language learners. Instead, it often functions as a barrier for a variety of reasons.

Often times, it is assumed that students (in English-speaking countries) do not need proficiency in English to perform well in mathematics (Lee & Jung, 2004). Contrary to this pervasive myth we now know that language is used to facilitate mathematical thinking, and it is through the use of the language of mathematics that students communicate and reason mathematically (Dale & Cuevas, 1992). However, we must recognize that mathematics, its conventions and traditions are intricately connected to the linguistic context that surrounds it. School mathematics in particular is dependent upon this context, as the mathematical symbols and conventions are not yet learned well enough to be understood without the support of the common language. "Part of the reason English learners struggle in mathematics is that rather than being language free, mathematics uses language that is a highly compressed form of communication where each word or symbol often represents an entire concept or idea" (Garrison, Amaral, & Ponce 2006, p. 14). To conceptually learn mathematics, therefore, students must use a variety of linguistic skills in the language of instruction that ELLs may not have yet mastered (Cuevas, 1984).

For example, Spelke and Tsvikin (2001) showed language-specific advantages for Russian-English bilingual adults when they were trained in advanced arithmetic procedures including estimation of logarithms and cube-roots. Interestingly, for tasks that required an exact answer, the intervention showed benefits only in the language of training, while for approximation, both trained and untrained languages showed benefits, indicating generalization from language of instruction to second language *regardless of which language was used for instruction*. These results reinforce general findings that bilingual adults create common representations of complex ideas that can be accessed by *either* or *both* languages.

Research on Asian languages, where the base-10 place value structure is made explicit (as opposed to English and other Western languages that use archaic phrases like "Twelve"—which means literally "the second eleven") shows that differences in the structure of number words in the sequence both affects the emergence of number sense, and also conceptual understanding of quantity (Miura, 1987; Miura & Okamoto, 2003;

Miller, Kelly, & Zhou, 2005). Put together these findings suggest that there are certain advantages to learning mathematics in two languages, and that the primary language of instruction has significant impact on the kinds of initial representations formed in children, and their development over time.

Referring to the affiliational purpose of language in society, lack of proficiency not only prevents ELLs from playing the school mathematics game, but this also marks them as not being part of the North American mathematical community, contributing to the myth that ELL status *causes* mathematical deficiency as opposed to being the target of bias inherent in English-only education policy (Secada, 1990). So, not only may students' first language cause them to think slightly differently about mathematical concepts, but lack of recognition by teachers and peers that these differences have advantage may prevent them from exercising these advantages in class.

It must also be noted that much of the ELL problem in the United States is centered around race and class conflict. Language differences have not proven to be particularly problematic in regions, like the BeNeLux countries, where open borders and expectations of multilingualism are the norm, *and* where there historically existed only subtle racial differences.

Again, the affiliational purpose of language works both to identify members of a community, in this case school mathematics, and to identify non-members. By controlling language, a dominant culture can assert its superiority over newcomers. Language facility, then, can serve as a mechanism for maintaining social and economic status, by first subordinating the less facile, and then institutionalizing policies that prevent equitable access to education, eliminating the capacity for subordinated groups to become more facile. This process is not carried out overtly, and may not be noticeable or even cognitively palatable to the dominant culture, but is a complex system of policies, norms, practices and basic economic presses that play out as inequitable on the whole (Freire, 1970, 1998, 2000, 1994; Freire & Faundez, 1992).

Mathematics as a Language

The process of learning mathematics while learning a second language can be particularly difficult for ELLs because of the specialized technical vocabulary used to represent concepts and describe operations (Cuevas, 1984; Chamot & O'Malley, 1994). This technical vocabulary becomes increasingly abstract and complex as students progress through the grade-bands. But more than vocabulary, the symbols, syntax, and mathematical ideas themselves build on each other in an array of practices and norms that are bewildering to many native English speakers, let alone ones not yet conversant in the language of instruction (Barnett-Clarke and Ramirez 2004; Mora, 2008). For students to read, write, and engage in substantive conversations about mathematics, they must be able to manipulate the academic language of mathematics. That is, when faced with a mathematics problem, students must be able to represent the situation, solve the problem, interpret the solution, and be able to communicate their reasoning behind the solution in a language that the teacher and society-at-large recognizes and values.

The Mathematics Register

Similar to any language register, which refers to the meanings that serve a particular function in the language, together with the words and structures that communicate those meanings, the mathematics register includes specialized mathematical vocabulary, syntax, and other features that represent mathematical concepts (Kang & Pham, 1995). Fillmore (2007) states that while possessing familiarity with words used in discussing mathematics, the register of mathematics goes beyond this familiarity with words to "include familiarity with distinctive grammatical structures and rhetorical devices" (p. 3). Thus, mathematics is a language with a register of words, expressions, and meanings that differ from those of everyday language (Secada, 1991). In addition to the particularized mathematics vocabulary, "a mathematics register also includes styles of meaning and ways of presenting arguments within the context of mathematics" (Cuevas, 1984, p. 136).

As mentioned earlier, Miura and her colleagues (Miura, 1987; Miura, Chungsoon, Kim, Chang, & Okamoto, 1988; see also Wang & Lin, 2005, and especially Miller, Kelly, & Zhou, 2005, for discussions of these issues in the context of our different educational systems and cultures), studied the relationship between language of origin and the development of the concept of number and place value in kindergarten and first graders. They found that students whose home language is Asian, which have a consistent, explicit order and sequence for expressing place value, tend to have a more advanced conception of number and place value than students whose home language is English. Asian elementary students tended to utilize representations of groupings by 10s and 1s early on compared to English speaking students who tended to group primarily by 1s. So there is a relationship between a student's first language and the way in which it expresses mathematical concepts and relationships, and their ability to learn and understand those concepts.

Developing linguistic competencies in the four language domains— reading, writing, speaking, and listening—are essential to the development of academic language. While social English also requires the linguistic competencies in the four domains, academic language is more cognitively demanding and must be learned without the density of contextual clues available for conversational language. In mathematics this means learning (1) semantic features, such as specialized mathematical language, everyday words that take on new meaning in mathematics, and word-symbol correspondence, and (2) syntactic features, such as comparatives, prepositions, lack of one-to-one correspondence between mathematical symbols and the words they represent, and syntactic variation on a single semantic notion (Scarcella & Rumberger, 2000).

Semantics. Mathematical discourse includes words that have specific meanings and serve a particular function in the context of mathematics. Words like "algebraic," "monomial," and "numerator" are used in mathematics to clearly represent a mathematical concept or related set of ideas. While some words are exclusive to mathematics, others take on special meanings in the context of mathematics. Polysemous words, those with multiple meanings, such as "power," "table," "rational," and "odd," can present potential challenges and difficulties for ELLs since there is ambiguity and lack of specificity in the form in which the words can be interpreted given multiple contexts. For instance, in everyday English, the word "odd" may refer to a strange or unusual circumstance, whereas in the context of mathematics, "odd" refers to an integer of the form $n = 2k + 1$, where k is an integer. Similarly, the word "rational" can refer to sensible or reasonable behavior, whereas in mathematics it refers to a number that can be in the form p/q where p and q are integers and q is not equal to zero. As a telling example, for Spanish speakers, the word "mas" has two connotations: More, and "added to." Evidence shows that for very young learners, this polysemy in their first language is related to errors on problems where a direct translation of the English words "How many more" (¿cuántas más hay?) is misconstrued as addition versus subtraction (Moschkovich, 2002).

The ability to interpret, differentiate, and manipulate the meaning(s) of words and symbols, as well as connect them with mathematical ideas and concepts is a critical aspect of developing the academic language necessary to be considered effective learners of mathematics. Developing this level of fluency involves complex language skills and cognitively demanding tasks that require students to communicate the reasoning behind mathematical solutions (Garrison, Amaral, & Ponce, 2006). However, for some students, particularly ELLs, learning and manipulating the register of mathematics in a way that allows them to reason mathematically can present its challenges.

A particular source of ELLs' reading difficulties relates to their limitations in academic vocabulary—the words necessary to learn and talk about academic subjects. This academic vocabulary is central to text and its comprehension, and plays an especially prominent role in the upper elementary, middle, and high school years as students read to learn about concepts, ideas, and facts in content-area classrooms such as math, science, and social studies. In doing so, ELLs encounter many words that are not part of everyday classroom conversation. These types of words, including analyze, therefore, and sustain, are more likely to be encountered in print than orally, and are key to comprehension and acquisition of knowledge. (Francis, Rivera, Lesaux, Kieffer, & Rivera, 2006, p. 8)

While the different uses of vocabulary, symbols, and syntax in everyday English and mathematics can cause confusion for ELLs, it is important to examine the level of complexity involved in learning the academic language of the mathematics classroom more specifically. Barnett-Clarke and Ramirez (2004) contend that,

These students not only have to understand the meaning of a word like *table* in everyday English, but they also must refer back to their primary language for its meaning, gain fluency in using the word, and then repeat the whole process again when they learn the word in mathematics. (p. 57)

In other words, for polysemous words, ELL students must learn the words in one context, make sense of the words in a language that is familiar to them, understand the use and function of the words in that context, and then relearn the words in the context of mathematics. Cuevas (1984) explains that to deal with the range of linguistic nuances implied by polysemy, cognates among home versus school languages, their representations and norms of usage, students must posses considerable proficiency in *both* their primary language (L1) *and* their second language (L2).

The use of synonyms, homophones, and near homonyms in mathematics poses an additional challenge for ELLs. For example, the concept of addition can be expressed using a variety of terms. The synonyms "add," "plus," "combine," and "sum" can all refer to the same operation, but may cause confusion for ELL students since they have to make the connection between the L1 term and the mathematically correct equivalent in English (Olivares, 1996; Thompson & Rubenstein, 2000). Similarly, the homophones "sum/some" and "whole/hole" are examples of words that can also present challenges for ELL students who are still in the process of learning mathematics in a second language. The use of near homonyms in mathematics can also be an added source of difficulty for ELL students, particularly when trying to make sense of oral mathematical discussions. For example, the terms "third and thirds" can cause confusion among students, as it is difficult to hear the subtle difference between the two terms, yet they represent two different mathematical ideas. The mathematics register is rather intimidating when new, complicated meanings are being developed, particularly when spoken words can easily be confused or interchanged because of unclear pronunciation or inability to hear subtle differences in pronunciation (Khisty, 1993). Table 9.1 demonstrates examples of some of these potential difficulties that ELL students encounter in the process of learning the register of mathematics. To overcome such confusion, Khisty (1995) recommends two strategies: (1) recasting mathematical ideas, using alternative ways of saying and/or representing them; and (2) using a variety of techniques such as varying tone and volume to emphasize the meanings of words. Of course, awareness of these difficulties can attune the teacher to potentially confusing situations, where s/he can check for comprehension and make the differences between third and thirds explicit for the struggling student.

Mathematical symbols and representations. In addition to specialized mathematical vocabulary and syntax, the register of mathematics also includes the ability to decode mathematical symbolism and notation, connect them to broader mathematical ideas, and produce new ideas using the symbolism. Like the textual features of the register, mathematical symbolism and notation also presents unique challenges for students learning a second language. Analogous to our discussion on the ways in which everyday words take on specific meaning in mathematics, symbols are used in different ways: The same symbols used in everyday text are used with different meanings in mathematics, and mathematically-specific symbols are used in different ways within mathematics. Both situations are sources of confusion. For example, the symbol "-" is used to represent *subtraction*, but it also can represent a similar concept, *range* in statistical applications. It can also be interpreted as a hyphen in everyday English. Similarly, while the symbol ":" can be used to represent a ratio or the division operation in mathematics, it can also be used to denote logical analogy. In English grammar,: is used as a colon to represent a logically incomplete clause.

Table 9.1. Words Presenting Difficulties in the Register Of Mathematics

Classes of Words Presenting Difficulties	*Examples*
• Math-specific words	additive, monomial, denominator
• Everyday vocabulary that has special meaning in mathematics	square, power, odd, table, rational
• Synonyms	add, plus, combine, sum
• Homophones	sum/some, whole/hole
• Near Homonyms (close "confusers")	fourths/fours, thirteen/thirty

Digging deeper into the field-specific use of symbols in mathematics, we see that, like in conversation or text, symbols take on specific meanings from the context in which they are used. The letter x, for example, can be used to represent a variety of situations, such as a variable, the multiplication operation or as a label for an axis (which in turn represents a variable quantity). On the same note, there are typically a multitude of ways to represent any mathematical idea. For instance, one can represent multiplication by using any of the following symbols: x, ( ), *, ˙, or ab. Thus, in order to effectively decode and interpret the language of mathematics, ELL students must interpret and make sense of the textual and symbolic features in context, meaning that they must understand the relationship(s) between symbol and text, discern the norms of usage in the particular mathematical context within which they are situated, and coordinate these two understandings into some productive, generative behavior. Barton and Heidema (2002) explain,

> In reading mathematics text one must decode and comprehend not only words, but also signs and symbols, which involve different skills. Decoding words entails connecting sounds to the alphabetic symbols, or letters….In contrast, mathematics signs and symbols may be pictorial, or they may refer to an operation, or to an expression. Consequently, students need to learn the meaning of each symbol much like they learn "sight" words in the English language. In addition they need to connect each symbol, the idea it represents, and the written or spoken term that corresponds to the idea. (p. 15)

Syntax. Learning the syntax of mathematics can be overwhelming for ELL students. In everyday language, students must learn the formation of sentences and how words are combined to units larger than words. In mathematics, this means that students must unpack and interpret the mathematical language, which includes the mathematical symbolism and notation, as it is used in textbooks and word problems, and understand that in mathematical speech, these rules are sometimes relaxed to facilitate conversation. According to Fillmore (1982), unpacking and interpreting the language of textbooks requires comfort with words, patterns of grammar, argumentation style and relation between text, figures and tables that are "wholly alien to ordinary informal talk" (p. 6). These syntactic features can include comparatives such as "greater than/less than," or "x times as much," as well as prepositions such as "maps onto." Lack of one-to-one correspondence between such terms, the syntactic variation that can be used to express a single mathematical idea, and the fact that a small number of terms can be used to express a variety of ideas constitutes much of the power of the mathematical language (Roe, Stroodt, & Burns, 1987). But for neophytes to that language, who are struggling to understand conventional uses for many of the same terms and symbols, and who have the additional burden of keeping up in age-cohort defined by the linguistic majority, the difficulties are often impossible to overcome under conventional practices which ignore the L1 capital they bring to the classroom.

The use of prepositions in mathematics is a particular cause for difficulty in understanding tasks (McGregor, 1991). For example, take one fourth *of* the sale price ... increase the sale price *by* one fourth ... increase the sale price *to* one fourth. Depending on the specific function of the prepositions, the mathematical tasks change, giving a different solution to the mathematical problem. Similarly, the lack of one-to-one correspondence between mathematical symbols and the words they represent is a syntactical structure that may cause students to incorrectly interpret the meaning of mathematical statements. Consider the following example: *The number x is three less than the number y.* Reading this sentence and translating the words into symbols, many students incorrectly interpret this statement as $x = 3 - y$, rather than $x = y - 3$. If students do not have a coherent understanding of the mathematical relationship between the two variables and the syntactic structures that describe this relationship, students will incorrectly interpret the statement. This applies for L1 learners of mathematics as well as ELL students. The additional burden placed on ELLs is located in their as-of-yet lack of proficiency in discerning the object of the preposition, and reconciling that with the order in which the variables are presented.

Understanding the syntactic variation of a single mathematical idea can also pose challenges for students. There are multiple ways in which one can describe and express a mathematical task or idea. For instance: How many pencils are there in all? How many pencils are there? How many more pencils are there? Table 9.2, below, details additional syntactic structures in mathematics that can potentially cause difficulty for students, particularly ELL students.

The Relationship Between First Language, Second Language, and Academic Language

Young children in elementary school, face a double challenge in mathematics: not only is the learning of the new concepts a lot of work in itself,

Table 9.2.   Examples oF Difficult Syntax in Mathematical Language

Difficulty	Examples
• Mathematically-specific expressions	If ... then, If and only if...., given that, ...
• Conditional clauses	Assuming x is true, then y...
• Comparative constructions	If Maria is taller than Juan, and Juan is taller than Isabel, then Maria must be taller than Isabel.

but as we have shown, it is also a chore to manipulate the new system of symbols, and the academic language associated with mathematics learning. As a "highly compressed form of communication" (Roe, Stroodt, & Burns, 1987, p. 36), the academic language of school mathematics can be considered problematic for being terse—utilizing predistilled terms that, to mathematicians, connote deep, highly interconnected networks of associations among mathematical objects. Communication in this terse system relies heavily on linguistic cues, deciphered in context-embedded communication, where because of being face-to-face, the particular meanings of utterances or inscriptions can be negotiated (Collier, 1987).

Part of our argument in this chapter has been that learning mathematics with understanding is hard no matter what language students bring to the learning environment. The difficulties we reviewed in the previous sections are not peculiar to ELLs. But when the language of instruction is different from the language of origin, then those problematic situations reach a different level of difficulty. How *can* ELL students use their native language (L1) to develop the academic language needed for learning mathematics? Because this academic language is couched in the predominant language of instruction (L2), we will refer to it as AL2, *Academic Second Language*. The burden placed on ELL students, then can be seen as having the additional requirement of learning L1, simultaneously becoming conversant in L2, all the while reserving cognitive and linguistic resources for the special case of learning mathematical content in AL2. What are the relationships between L1 and AL2? L2 and AL2? How does academic language in the mother tongue (AL1) influence the development of AL2? Those are the questions this section addresses.

ELL students arriving at school encounter the difficulty of having to communicate in a language other than their own, learning new cultural norms and practices. Young children have demonstrated though, that they don't need to learn a new language to be able to interact with other children with whom they do not share native language (Saville-Troike, 1984). Interactions necessarily occur in informal ways among peers. They do not require that individuals share the same language for many aspects of everyday communication Weitzman (2008). However this changes when the purpose of communication becomes more formal and one considers the interactions needed to engage during the processes of teaching and learning.

For all the reasons cited earlier, we know that learning AL2 is made more difficult when the major emphasis of instruction is placed on learning the technical language of textbooks and classrooms first, over basic communication in L2 (Cuevas, 1984). In such a model, L1 resources such as textbook translations may be used as important conceptual supports.

But, the language of textbooks requires that students have a familiarity with AL2 in general that ELL students don't yet have.

For terms of comparison, native speakers of the academic language of mathematics do not wait for ELLs to catch up. They are busy improving their academic language, even as their second-language peers are struggling with the burden of learning and translating among L1, L2, AL1 and AL2 simultaneously. So when non-native speakers receive the "same" instruction and evaluation as native speakers, they are really shooting at a moving target, and this moving target accelerates as mathematical content becomes more abstract and formal in the middle and high school years (Collier, 1995). Even in the case of ELL adolescents with good cognitive development in L1, who show they are able to achieve good basic skills in two years, they often fail to progress in technical content areas (Collier, 1989). These students are losing up to 2 years of academic progress.

This puts them at a clear disadvantage as mathematical requirements become more stringent. In Arizona, for example, all students must take the equivalent of Algebra I by the end of the eighth grade, 4 years of high school mathematics of which one year must be post Algebra II (e.g., pre-Calculus). It is unclear how these policies which are mathematically reasonable for the English-speaking majority will affect the ELL population without significant investment and attention to providing AL2 support.

Moschkovich (1999) pointed out like Collier, that being overall proficient in one language does not mean that one can understand the mathematical discourse in that language. Basic interpersonal communication skills (BICS) are context bound, face to face communication type of language, while cognitive academic language proficiency (CALP) refers to a decontextualized type of language, that is highly abstract and that takes place in the classrooms (Weitzman, 2008). When considering the differences between the types of languages required, it is not hard to imagine why they reached that conclusion. Saville-Troike (1984), for example, found that students who achieved at high levels, were not necessarily those that were more talkative, and that some of the students who were using English in social settings not related to school/academics, were among the poorest in their achievement tests. This reminds us that the relationships among L1, L2, AL1 and AL2 are not simple or linear.

In cases where AL1 is well developed in the domain, the conceptual understanding indexed in AL1 can serve as a support for learning mathematics in AL2. In short, students can rely on what they know in their native language to provide meanings and even procedures for use in the AL2 environment. Research shows that adult bilinguals go back to their native language to perform tasks like computations, or retrieving arithmetical facts (Spelke & Tsvikin, 2001; Moschkovich, 2006). This raises the question of whether there are certain concepts that having been learned in AL1, are more difficult to access in AL2.

The native conversational language of children has an undeniable influence in the development of L2 and AL2, and generally competence in L1 and development of L2 appears to be positively-related (Saville-Troike, 1984). According to Cummins (1981) in Collier (1987):

> To the extent that instruction in L*x* is effective in promoting proficiency in L*x*, the transfer of this proficiency to L*y* will occur provided there is adequate exposure to L*y* (either in school or environment) and adequate motivation to learn L*y*. (p. 632)

So does schooling in L1 tend to help or interfere with AL2? Table 9.3 below provides a simple analytic framework for conceptualizing the general patterns of language development across AL1 and AL2 depending on the knowledge of mathematics students bring with them to the school context.

Collier's (1987, 1989) work has provoked attention on different sides of the debate. In particular she suggests that a minimum of 2 years of schooling in the L1 helps the progress of schooling in L2. Likewise, Cummins (1979) claimed that a cognitively and academically beneficial bilingualism can only be achieved if L1 is well developed as well. The ideal scenario has students being introduced to L2 early, but that students continue developing L1 at least till they are somewhere in the middle school years (Collier, 1989). The transfer that happens from L1 to L2 is promising when working with ELL students, as L1 appears to be a useful tool in this process. Again, AL1 and AL2 being added to the mix makes the job

Table 9.3.   General Patterns of Development Across AL1 and AL2 and Prior Mathematics Understanding

		Language of Instruction (AL)	
		AL1	*AL2*
Understanding of conceptual domain (usually developed in AL1)	**Deep, Rich**	Mastery in both AL1 and mathematics	Primarily language development, mathematics secondary, but positive
	Poor, Shallow	Primarily conceptual development of mathematics in AL1, AL2 Not developed	Limited learning opportunities as students spend most time learning L2. AL2 lags as does mathematical learning

of the ELL student more complicated. Nevertheless, as we have continually seen, because the development of competence in a second language is partially a function of the type of competence already developed in the first language, the general idea of continued emphasis on academic competence in both appears to be an ideal goal for a pluralistic society, pragmatic and political reality notwithstanding.

Asking students to use AL2 to the exclusion of (A)L1 prevents them from accessing many of the key metaphors and conceptual substrata initially developed in their mother tongue, in essence forcing students to work at a cognitive level below their age and level of knowledge (Collier, 1995). The discontinuation of L1 cognitive development during second language acquisition, may not have the desired effect of improvement in L2 development, but quite the contrary. In fact, extinguishing the use of L1 and AL1 may actually lower students' academic performance in AL2. Moreover, there is some evidence that certain restrictive practices around (A)L1 may also signify a loss of identity, culture and connection to the student's community of origin (Weitzman, 2008).

CONCLUSIONS

And so, here we are back at affiliation. Cognitively it appears that, though difficult, thinking of students' AL1 as an asset may allow us to create appropriate educational experiences that allow ELLs to access their rich conceptual knowledge, codified in their home language, and to use that knowledge as a support for more rapidly acquiring English or whatever the formal language of instruction may be. Paying attention to the pitfalls of second language development in mathematics may be able to empower teachers to see where students are making critical errors, not because the material is difficult or because they are less able than their English-speaking peers, but because their ear isn't yet attuned to AL2 or because particular mathematical idioms or symbolic conventions are not yet familiar to them. All of this is tractable within our current public school structure and curriculum. But the problem of language and affiliation keeps rearing its head in American educational policy, creating counterproductive educational experiences for our nation's ELL children.

In our experience, teachers often tell young students to explain their thinking using "their own language." By this they mean children do not need to use the technical language of textbooks. The same reasoning applies for the use of L1 in the acquisition of a mathematical AL2. Allowing students to rely on their natural language as they learn both mathematics and English, will help them map important basic metaphors and ideas of quantity and space successfully onto L1. Just as important, they will also receive the same respect for their culture as native (English) speakers do, and realize that their knowledge of mathematics that is accessed and explained in Spanish (or whatever the native language is), is valuable.

The language of mathematics is a fundamental tool for student learning. As this chapter has illustrated, if ELL students are to make significant gains in mathematics, and engage in substantive conversations about mathematics, then it is imperative that teachers provide opportunities for students to actively engage with, and become fluent with, the symbolic, semantic, and syntactic structures embedded within the language of mathematics. However, for this participatory dialogue to occur, teachers must first identify any potential linguistic and cultural pitfalls to effectively address the specific needs of ELL students, as well as provide instructional support that focuses on developing proficiency in mathematics, as well as linguistic competencies in the four language domains (L1, L2, AL1, and AL2).

Equally important to identifying potential linguistic and cultural pitfalls is the identification of students' resources, such as students' first language, experience with AL1, and cultural experiences. To be most effective, teachers should legitimize these experiences and knowledge as valuable resources, build new mathematical ideas around them, and provide contextual support in the process.

Recommendations for Practice

To interpret, make sense, and be able to articulate the relationships between abstract mathematical ideas, ELL students must be given ample opportunities to use and practice the language of mathematics. One way to do this is to provide instructional contexts that are language rich, yet provide linguistic and contextual cues, so that students are actively engaged in utilizing mathematical terms and ideas in multiple ways over extended periods of time (Blachowicz & Fisher, 2000; Pressley, 2000). According to Moschkovich (2006), one of the goals of mathematics instruction for ELL students should be to support all students, regardless of their proficiency in English, in becoming active participants in discussions that focus on the important mathematical ideas, rather than on vocabulary, pronunciation, and cognitively undemanding skills. Similarly, Gutierrez (2002), argues that teachers need to engage students in "language experimentation" so that the language of mathematics and its interconnected mathematical concepts are more accessible to students.

Providing contextual and linguistic cues, such as using gestures and objects to clarify meanings is a way in which teachers can help support ELL students in learning English while developing mathematical discourse. Developing mathematical discourse entails not only "doing" mathematics, but also "talking" mathematics, both of which involve an understanding of the mathematics register. While the mathematics register is shaped by the teacher, it is not always made explicit for ELL students (Solomon & Rhodes, 1995). Khisty (1995) makes a case for the importance of "talking" mathematics to develop mathematical discourse. In Guerrero (2004), Khisty maintains that ELL students can develop mathematical discourse

> by having ample opportunities to talk about mathematics, to ask questions that test their understandings, to engage in debates about various mathematical processes, and in general, to participate in the higher cognitive levels of the subject that accompany active dialogue (p. 290)

It is important to note that while developing mathematical competence involves having an understanding of the register of mathematics, it is not limited to merely learning vocabulary. Using the language of mathematics to communicate mathematically means more than simply distinguishing between everyday and the mathematics register. In fact, ELL students participate in mathematical discourse by using their first language, gestures, and objects- resources and practices that may not necessarily be valued by the discipline—to make mathematical claims, representations, hypothesizes, and predictions—(Moschkovich, 2002). By using a perspective that focuses on legitimizing students' resources, teachers shift away from viewing ELL students' language as deficient to viewing it as valuable resource from which to build new mathematical knowledge.

NOTES

1. Of course, this discussion is not limited to Spanish-speaking immigrants. Many US citizens are English Language Learners regardless of home language, and many immigrants do not speak Spanish. Nevertheless, current policy and political rhetoric revolves around Latin American immigrants and Spanish speakers. Our discussion of language as serving both an inclusionary and an exclusionary purpose is motivated in part by these issues.
2. Of course, when we say "group," we do not refer to geographic proximity, but of some common set of norms and practices that define membership (and by extension, *non*membership).

REFERENCES

Arizona Proposition 203 (2006). English Language Education for Children in Public Schools. Arizona Department of Education. Ballot Proposition Retrieved from http://www.ade.state.az.us/oelas/proposition203.pdf

Artiles, A. J., Rueda, R., Salazar, J. J., & Higareda, I. (2005). Within-group diversity in minority disproportionate representation: English language learners in urban school districts. *Exceptional Children, 71*(3), 283.

Barnett-Clarke, C., & Ramirez, A. (2004). Language pitfalls and pathways to mathematics. In R. N. Rubenstein (Ed.), *Perspectives on the teaching of mathematics* (pp. 56-66). Reston, VA: National Council of Teachers of Mathematics.

Barton, M. L., & Heidema, C. (2002). *Teaching Reading in Mathematics* (2nd ed.). Aurora, CO: Mid-continent Research for Education and Learning.

Blachowicz, C., & Fisher, P. (2000). Vocabulary instruction. In M. Kamil, P. Mosenthal, P. D. Pearson, R. Barr (Eds.), *Handbook of reading research* (Vol. III, pp. 503-523). Mahwah, NJ: Lawrence Erlbaum Associates.

Chamot, A. U., & O'Malley, J. M. (1994). *The CALLA handbook: How to implement the Cognitive Academic Language Learning Approach.* Reading, MA: Addison-Wesley.

Christiansen, M. H., & Kirby, S. (2003). Language evolution: consensus and controversies. *Trends in Cognitive Sciences, 7*(7), 300-307.

Collier, V. P. (1987). Age and rate of acquisition of second language for academic purposes. *Teachers of English to Speakers of Other Languages, 21*(4), 617-641.

Collier, V. P. (1995). Acquiring a second language for school. *Directions in Language & Education National Clearinghouse for Bilingual Education, 1*(4), 2-10.

Collier, V. P. (1989). How long? A synthesis of research on academic achievement in second language. *Teachers of English to Speakers of Other Languages, 23*, 509-531.

Condon, W. S., & Sander, L. W. (1974). Synchrony demonstrated between movements of the neonate and adult speech, *Child Development, 45*, 456-462.

Cuevas, G. J. (1984). Mathematics learning in English as a second language. *Journal for Research in Mathematics Education, 15*(2), 134-144.

Cummins, J. (1979). Linguistic interdependence and the educational development of bilingual children. *Review of Educational Research, 49*(2), 222-251.

Cummins, J. (1981). The role of primary language development in promoting educational success for language minority students. In *Schooling and language minority students: A theoretical framework* (pp. 3-49). Los Angeles, CA: California State University, National Evaluation, Dissemination and Assessment Center

Dale, T., & Cuevas, G. (1992). Integrating mathematics and language learning. In P. Richard-Amato & M. Snow (Eds.), *The multicultural classroom* (pp. 330-348). White Plains, NY: Longman.

Fillmore, L. (2007). English learners and Mathematics learning: Language issues to consider. In A. H. Schoenfeld (Ed.), *Assessing mathematical proficiency.* Cambridge, England: Cambridge University Press.

Fillmore, L. W. (1982, April). *The development of second language literacy skills.* Paper presented to the National Commission on Excellence in Education, Houston, TX.

Francis, D. J., Rivera, M., Lesaux, N., Kieffer, M., & Rivera, H. (2006). *Practical Guidelines for the Education of English Language Learners: Research-based Recommendations for Instruction and Academic Interventions.* Houston, Texas: Center on Instruction.

Freire, P. (1970). *Pedagogy of the oppressed* (M. B. Ramos, Trans.). New York, NY: Continuum.

Freire, P. (1998). *Pedagogy of the oppressed.* (M. B. Ramos, Trans.). New York, NY: Continuum

Freire, P. (2000). *Pedagogy of the oppressed* (M. B. Ramos, Trans.). New York, NY: Continuum

Freire, P. (1994). *Pedagogy of hope: Reliving* Pedagogy of the Oppressed (R. R. Barr, Trans.). New York, NY: Continuum.

Freire, P., & Faundez, A. (1992). *Learning to question: A pedagogy of liberation.* New York, NY: Continuum.

Fry, R. (2007). *How Far behind in math and reading are English language learners?* Washington, DC: Pew Hispanic Center.

Garrison, L., Amaral, O., & Ponce, G. (2006). UnLATCHing mathematics instruction for English learners. *NCSM Journal of Mathematics Education Leadership, 9*(1), 14-24.

Guerrero, M. D. (2004). Acquiring academic English in 1 year: An unlikely proposition for English language learners. *Urban Education, 39,* 172-199.

Gutierrez, R. (2002). Beyond essentialism: The complexity of language in teaching mathematics to Latina/o students. *American Educational Research Journal, 39*(4), 1047-1088.

Johnson, C. (1999). Metaphor vs. conflation: The case of SEE. *Amsterdam Studies in the Theory ad History of Linguistic Science Series 4, 4*(152), 155-170.

Kang, H. W., & Pham, K. T. (1995, March-April). *From 1 to Z: Integrating math and language learning.* Paper presented at the annual meeting of the Teachers of English to Speakers of Other Languages, Long Beach, CA.

Kelly, G. A. (1955). *The psychology of personal constructs: A theory of personality* (Vol. 1). New York, NY: W. W. Norton.

Khisty, L. (1993). A naturalistic look at language factors in mathematics teaching in bilingual classrooms. In *Proceedings of the Third National Research Symposium on Limited English Proficient Student Issues: Focus on middle and high school issues: Vol. 2.* (633-654). Washington, DC: US Department of Education.

Khisty, L. (1995). Making inequality: Issues of language and meanings in Mathematics teaching with Hispanics students. In W. G. Secada, E. Fennema, & L. B. Adajian (Eds.), *New directions for equity in mathematics education* (pp. 279-297). Cambridge, England: Cambridge University Press.

Kirby, S., Dowman, M., & Griffiths, T. L. (2007). Innateness and culture in the evolution of language. *Proceedings of the National Academy of Sciences, 104,* 5241-5245.

Klingner, J. K., Hoover, J. J., & Baca, L. M. (2008). Why do English language learners struggle with reading?: Distinguishing language acquisition from learning disabilities. Thousand Oaks, CA: Corwin Press.

Lackoff, G., & Johnson, M. (1999). *Philosophy in the flesh: The embodied mind and its challenge to Western thought.* New York, NY: Basic Books.

Lakoff, G., & Nuñez, R. (2001). *Where mathematics comes from: How the embodied mind brings mathematics into being*. New York, NY: Basic Books.

Lee H., & Jung, W. S. (2004). Limited-English-Proficient (LEP) students and mathematical understanding. *Mathematics Teaching in the Middle School, 9*(5), 269-272.

Lesaux, N. K., & Siegel, L. S. (2003). The development of reading in children who speak English as a second language. *Developmental Psychology, 39*(6), 1005-1019.

McGregor, M., (1991). Language, culture and mathematics learning, in M. McGregor & R. Moore (Eds.), *Teaching mathematics in the multicultural classroom: A resource for teachers and teacher educators* (pp. 5-25). Melbourne, Australia: University of Melbourne, School of Mathematics and Science Education, Melbourne.

Middleton, J. A., Poynor, L., Wolfe, P., Toluk, Z., & Bote, L. A. (1999, April). *A sociolinguistic perspective on teacher questioning in a cognitively guided instruction classroom*. Paper presented at the annual meeting of the American Educational Research Association, Montreal, Canada.

Miller, K. F., Kelly, M., & Zhou, X. (2005). Learning mathematics in China and the United States. Crosscultural insights into the nature and course of preschool mathematical development. In J. I. D Campbell (Ed.), *Handbook of mathematical cognition* (pp. 163-178). New York, NY: Psychology Press.

Miura, I. T. (1987). Mathematics achievement as a function of language. *Journal of Educational Psychology, 79*(1), 79-82.

Miura, I. T., & Okamoto, Y. (2003). Language supports for mathematics understanding and performance. In A. Baroody & A. Dowker, (Eds.), *The development of arithmetical concepts* (pp. 229–242). Mahwah, NJ: Lawrence Erlbaum Associates.

Miura, I. T., Chungsoon C. K., Chang, C., & Okamoto, Y. (1988). Effects of Language Characteristics on Children's Cognitive Representation of Number: Cross-National Comparisons. *Child Development, 59*(6), 1445-1450.

Mora, J. (2008). Vocabulary development for English language learners: The language-concept connection. *Ideas for English Language Educators* [Newsletter].

Moschkovich, J. (1999). Supporting the participation of English language learners in mathematical discussions. *For the Learning of Mathematics 19*(1), 11-19.

Moschkovich, J. (2002). A situated and sociocultural perspective on bilingual mathematics learners. *Mathematical Thinking and Learning, 4*(2&3), 189-212.

Moschkovich, J. (2006). Statement for the National Mathematics Panel. Representing TODOS: Mathematics for All.

Olivares, R. (1996). Communication in mathematics for students with limited English proficiency. In P. C. Elliott (Ed.), *Communication in mathematics, K–12 and beyond: Yearbook of the national council of teachers of mathematics* (pp. 219-230). Reston, VA: National Council of Teachers of Mathematics.

Payan, R., & Nettle, M. (2008). Current state of English-language learners in the U.S. k-12 student population. *ETS 2008 English Language-Learner Symposium*. Princeton, NJ: Educational Testing Service.

Pressley, M. (2000). What should comprehension instruction be the instruction of? In M. Kamil, P. Mosenthal, P. D. Pearson, R. Barr (Eds.), *Handbook of reading research* (Vol. III, pp. 545-561). Mahwah, NJ: Lawrence Erlbaum Associates.

Roe, B., Stoodt, B., & Burns, P. (1987). *Secondary school reading instruction: The content areas.* Boston, MA: Houghton Mifflin.

Roth, W., & McGinn, M. K. (1998). Inscriptions: Toward a theory of representing as social practice. *Review of Educational Research, 68*(1), 35-59.

Saville-Troike, M. (1984). What really matters in second language learning for academic achievement? *Teachers of English to Speakers of Other Languages, 18*(2), 199-219.

Scarcella, R., & Rumberger, R. W. (2000). Academic English key to long term success in school. *UC Linguistic Minority Research Institute Newsletter, 9,* 1-2.

Secada, W. G. (1990). Research, politics, and bilingual education. *The ANNALS of the American Academy of Political and Social Sciences, 508,* 81-106.

Secada, W. G. (1991). Degree of bilingualism and arithmetic problem solving in Hispanic first graders. *Elementary School Journal, 92*(2), 211-229.

Solomon, J., & Rhodes, N. (1995). *Conceptualizing academic language.* Wahsington, DC: Center for Applied Linguistics, National Center for Research on Cultural Diversity and Second Language Learning.

Spelke, E. S., & Tsivkin, S. (2001). Language and number: a bilingual training study. *Cognition, 78*(1), 45-88.

Thompson, D. R., & Rubenstein, R. N. (2000). Learning mathematics vocabulary: Potential Pitfalls And Instructional Strategies. *Mathematics Teacher, 93*(7), 568-373.

Wang, J., & Lin, E. (2005). Comparative studies on U.S. and Chinese mathematics learning and the Implications for Standards-Based Mathematics Teaching Reform. *Educational Researcher, 34*(5), 3-13.

Weitzman, E. (2008). One language or two? Home language or not? Some answers to questions about bilingualism in language-delayed children [The Wig Wag Newsletter issue].

AFTERWORD

Karen E. Lillie

Learning a language is difficult. While much has been debated about or blindly accepted as truth regarding the "cognitive demands" of learning an academic language (e.g., the BICS/CALP dichotomy), there should be no question that language learning is no easy task. Regardless of where one falls on the spectrum of the BICS/CALP distinction, it is still imperative to make sure that *all* language learners—whether English learners (ELs), heritage language learners, or others who speak a "nonstandard" dialect of English, such as African American Vernacular English (AAVE)—are being supported in their language and learning in academic settings. Of course, how to do this effectively and successfully has been a question in studies on language teaching for quite some time. The chapters presented in this book have helped to address this by arguing the case for why academic language is necessary not just in classrooms for students' benefits but also in teacher knowledge and practice. This text will assist us as researchers, scholars, and practitioners in the ways of thinking about this matter.

Defining and Understanding Academic Language

Defining the term and concept of *academic language* (AL) is still disputed, and dialogue about it continues regarding how best to teach our children (Schleppegrell, 2004; Valdés, 2004; Zwiers, 2008). It comes as no surprise that AL is hotly contested, which speaks to the underlying social,

Academic Language in Second Language Learning, pp. 225–234
Copyright © 2013 by Information Age Publishing
All rights of reproduction in any form reserved.

political, and economic ideologies which invade our education system in regard to language learners. The discussion of language, especially that of AL, is informed by and discussed from one's ideological stance and positioning on standard language and bi- or multilingualism more generally (Lippi-Green, 2012; Valdés, 2004). Language cannot and should not be taught in a vacuum and yet many still believe that the best way to teach ELs is to force feed them prescriptive type curricula in order to help them learn English so they can "succeed" in mainstream classrooms. It is typically agreed, as well, that language should not be decontextualized and that incorporating the ability to recognize and use students' *funds of knowledge* is imperative to academic success (González, Moll, & Amanti, 2005; Moll, Amanti, Neff, & González, 1992). In short, AL is important for all students to know and learn, especially in today's world full of standardization.

One of the larger questions in the discussion of AL is the idea of whether or not "academic language" is really more *cognitively* demanding then nonacademic language. Faltis (Chapter 1, this volume) articulates this discussion very clearly and presents valid and sound arguments against this belief. The fact that many people continue to impart to teacher candidates (TCs) of English as a Second Language (ESL) or English as a Foreign Language (EFL) disciplines that there is a separation between a "less demanding" social language and a higher-order thinking academic language shows that this remains a relevant discussion in the applied linguistics field. What is interesting is that the strict BICS/CALP dichotomy created over thirty years ago by Cummins (1981) has even been adapted by Cummins himself. Though it appears that today most researchers of language acquisition and second language teaching recognize that all language is demanding, it is important to stress that social language is just as cognitively challenging in some cases as it is in academic settings. This is especially the case when one looks at language acquisition from a sociocultural or sociolinguistic theoretical perspective (SCT and SLT respectively).

Seeing the Bigger Picture

Faltis (Chapter 1, this volume) is right on the mark when he argues that current approaches to teaching AL must focus on and not ignore the broader social contexts at play when trying to make schooling more accessible for language minority (LM) students. Many of the chapters in this text (Faltis, Chapter 1, this volume; Fitts & Bowers, Chapter 2, this volume; Lucero, Chapter 3, this volume; Ramírez-Marín & Clark, Chapter 8, this volume) discuss the significance of situating language learning in a wider social/political realm. Multiple varieties of English are present in today's classrooms, and by focusing on the larger picture of sociocultural and sociolinguistic factors at work helps take the burden off the students' shoulders and puts it more squarely where it should be: on us as educators. Faltis's point that everyone must look at whose language (and which language varieties count) is especially important as we move forward in a more digitally-connected, globalized world. Lucero's remark that not only is language dependent on contextual factors, but that much is dependent on *how* students are allowed to communicate and participate is a theme that other chapters (Faltis, Chapter 1, this volume; Galaguera, Chapter 5, this volume; Ramírez-Marín & Clark, Chapter 8, this volume) echo as well. This goes back to the idea of the value we place on certain people, places, and registers and whether or not they have been silenced.

Fitts and Bowers (Chapter 2, this volume) stress that the attention to AL cannot take away from the importance of continually developing ELs' linguistic abilities so that students have cross-cultural competence. Embracing students' funds of knowledge in order to help build cultural and communicative competence is something all teachers should strive to do. In the science, social studies, and math classrooms, it is imperative that we remember to tap into students' previous understandings and schema while addressing their grasp of academic language. In courses like social studies, many topics are presented from the Westernized, White, colonizer, male view of how major historical events have occurred. As de Oliveira (Chapter 7, this volume) mentions, history texts that ELs are responsible for knowing and learning are, by nature of the topic, interpretations and explanations of things that happened. By instructing students on how to recognize the interpretive nature of historical texts and thus the specific discourse used, students can become more critical in their understanding of the social sciences and more expert in the language used within this discipline. It is important to keep social studies as culturally-relevant as possible and to critically examine how we talk about this subject, including what language is used in those discussions. Additionally, Ramírez-Marín and Clark (Chapter 8, this volume) make the point of reminding us not to leave a students' prior knowledge about how the world works at the classroom door, since science is also taught from a primarily Westernized perspective. Middleton, Llamas-Flores, and Guerra-Lombardi (Chapter 9, this volume) concur in the sense that they recognize how all students and their understanding of math and mathematical concepts must be embraced in order to create strong *communities of practice* within the classroom so that students can wholly participate in and be active members of a math group. Using what our students know while teaching them how to master AL is essential to helping students succeed on a larger scale outside of the four classroom walls.

Preparing Teachers: Doing, Knowing, and Using AL in the Classroom

In order for students to be able to recognize and learn AL, many of the chapters here have expressed the need for teachers not only to learn about and be able to articulate specifics of AL as related to their own discipline, but also to do so while not fundamentally leaving the core content of their discipline behind (e.g., Chapters 4-9, this volume). Teachers must become masters themselves of their own discipline's discourse and be able to recognize when AL is present in their course texts, lesson design, and delivery. Curricula cannot be watered down in the attempt to make sure that students are being taught AL. To do this would be a disservice to the students and potentially posit them for future failure on the numerous standardized tests we require of them, as well as preclude them from succeeding more fully in their future K-12 schooling and college/career.

Part of the answer is to make sure that all teachers are trained in better using and developing AL within their own daily practice. In order to do so, we must begin to look more closely at the types of instruction provided in a classroom as suggested by many of the chapters (e.g., Chapter 3, this volume. In other words, what repertoire of approaches and methods do teachers have to bring to the classroom so that they are successful in developing students' AL? This discussion is similar to that in Chapter 2 (Fitts & Bowers, this volume) and others (Athanases & Michelsen Wahleithner, Chapter 6, this volume) in that students must be in environments where they are producing and using the language, while being provided scaffolded instruction and direct, explicit models when needed. Viewing the chapters as a whole, there seem to be five key elements to successful AL instruction in the classroom, much of which has been argued as solid pedagogy and practice in the teaching and working with ELs in one way or another (Baker, 2011; Chamot & O'Malley, 1994; de Jong & Harper, 2005; Echevarria, Vogt, & Short, 2004; Wright, 2010). However, the specific skills and techniques that teachers must use when teaching AL, showcase how understanding and teaching AL actually strengthens good pedagogy (see, e.g., Chapter 2, this volume; Chapter 3, this volume). The five aspects presented as integral to assisting in promoting AL in a classroom are (1) the simultaneous teaching of both language and content, and the understanding that these elements should not be separated; (2) instruction of ELs must be scaffolded both in terms of content knowledge and language, such as having ELs working directly with non-ELs; (3) providing opportunities to practice and literally use the language via "dialogic interactions"; (4) varying the amount of context so that students learn to understand language when it is presented both contextually and in a decontextualized manner; and (5) the use, at times, of explicit instruction such as when working with developing students' meta-linguistic awareness and helping them recognize the different registers used in certain settings. While doing all of this, however, it is imperative to make sure that these elements do not become discrete skills but are situated to be culturally-relevant to the students and presented in and derived from the wider social and political framework.

In addition to valuing students' funds of knowledge, it is necessary to help students access the discipline-specific language used in academic settings. Teachers need to be equipped to do so by thus preparing themselves to be cognizant of their own understanding of language and how language works, especially in their particular discipline. Many of the chapters in this text have outlined this need (e.g., Chapters 3- 8, this volume). Merino, Pomeroy, Mendle, and Gomez (Chapter 4, this volume) address the important point of what can academia do in better addressing AL in future teachers' instruction and practice. One way is to prepare teachers so that they are "teaching linguistically" (Bailey, Burkett, & Freeman, 2008, p. 614). This, however, can sometimes be regarded as "just good teaching" (JGT), which is problematic since having teachers master a core knowledge of how language works within specific subjects and thus learning environments is central to helping students master AL (Bailey et al., 2008; de Jong & Harper, 2005; Wong Fillmore & Snow, 2000). When teaching ELs and other LM students we must move past JGT (de Jong & Harper, 2005). Developing teachers to become linguistically aware will be evidenced in their ways of thinking, of designing and implementing lessons, and in their daily practice. As Chapters 5-9 (this volume) articulate, teachers must have critical language awareness and be able to participate in their own discipline's pedagogical language.

The Common Core and AL

The Common Core Standards have been adopted in all but five states (http://www.corestandards.org/in-the-states). This is highly significant in relation to AL because of the importance that is being emphasized on the standardization of education in general. Chapters 1, 2, and 5 mention the significance of the Common Core (or standards in general) as it relates to AL. Within the Common Core, there is also an emphasis on "conventions of standard English" as well as knowledge of how English functions in various situational arenas. The adoption of the Common Core may be beneficial to the creation of consistency within and between states and the fundamental aspect of improving education for all. There is still room, however, for wide variation in practice depending upon in which state and by whom ELs are being taught.

The implications within the design of the Common Core seem to indicate that all students of the future must be taught in a linear, "staircase" manner—particularly in regard to "complex texts"—while at the same time arguing that a students' "ability to read complex text does not always develop in a linear fashion" (National Governors Association Center for Best Practices & Council of Chief State School Officers [NGACBP & CCSSO], 2010c, p. 9). For example, when one looks at the presentation of the Common Core English Language Arts standards, especially Standard 10, the running theme is that the four key language skills (reading, writing, speaking and listening, or RWSL) should be taught in an increasingly more complex manner. This suggests that the perception of language becoming more and more cognitively demanding and complex as one progresses is embedded in the Common Core. However, the point is made that these skills are not discrete from one another, nor does the Common Core demand a prescriptivist approach to how these skills are to be taught or developed when designing curricula. Teachers still have the power to determine how best to teach the material, as long as the standards are met. The Common Core also highlights how teaching our students is a whole-school concern, stating that these skills of RWSL are a "shared responsibility" (NGACBP & CCSSO, 2010b, p. 4). Making sure that every school personnel is involved in the process of educating our ELs, and for that matter every student, is something that was reiterated in many of the chapters presented in this text.

It is promising that the information presented from the NGACBP and CCSSO about applying the standards to ELs' learning seems to be from a more holistic understanding of language as opposed to a deficit perspective. The Common Core notes that ELs are a heterogeneous group and mention how these students come equipped with their own funds of knowledge to the classroom. Teachers are even encouraged to take advantage of ELs' wealth of cultural knowledge and literacy skills that they may bring with them to the classroom, as well as to recognize that ELs can "achieve the standards ... without manifesting native-like control of conventions and vocabulary" (NGACBP & CCSSO, 2010a, p. 1). This echoes this book in that capturing an ELs' strengths from their primary language and culture is vital in maintaining their sense of self while at the same time preventing cultural discontinuity (see, esp., Chapter 8, this volume).

The Common Core specifically addresses academic language in the brief about ELs and math, stating "mathematics instruction for ELLs should address mathematical discourse and academic language" (NGACBP/CCSSO, 2010a, p. 2). It is recognized that it is not just enough to know mathematical vocabulary, but that it is "critical" that ELs become proficient users in the discourse of mathematics so that they may succeed in the discipline. All of this is mentioned, as well as the acknowledgement that many ELs come to U.S. math courses with their own previous knowledge of mathematical concepts and methods. This agrees with the discussion on legitimizing students presented in Chapter 9 of this volume.

Literacy skills as supportive of the other disciplines of science, social studies, and technology are also accentuated as students will be competing in a global market. Increasing complexity in reading is the Common Core's key requirement for the reading standard because of an analysis of research relating to the college-preparedness of all students on which the Common Core is justified. The Common Core cites the ACT's 2006 publication, *Reading Between the Lines,* which found that students were not meeting benchmarks because they were unable to answer questions related to complex texts (NGACBP & CCSSO, 2010c, p. 2). The NGACBP and CCSSO remark that K-12 schooling has had a decline in the complexity of texts that students are required to read. This understanding of complexity seems to mirror the discussion of AL in this text.

The NGACBP and CCSSO highlight also that the Common Core literacy standards must be complementary to and in conjunction with the content standards, so teachers must be prepared to deliver and be experts in not just their content knowledge but also be able to use the literacy standards in supporting the content standards (NGACBP & CCSSO, 2010b). This is similar to the discussions in this book, which look closely at how important it is for teachers to have a strong grasp on not just their own content expertise, but also on how to relay this information so that students are presented with the language they need to have access to the core content.

Implications for the Future of AL and Concluding Remarks

In continuing discussion about academic language for LM students, one must always remember to account for the social conventions in and by which much language policy, planning, and schooling is thus situated and dictated. Linguistically speaking, grammar is rule-governed structure of language. It is not, contrary to the mainstream popular belief, ungrammatical to say something like "You know Vicky be working after school" (Lippi-Green, 2012, p. 11; see also Adger, Wolfram, & Christian, 2007). However, to a nonlinguist socially driven ideological beliefs about language and how it should be (hence the idea of "Standard English") are forced on our children with potentially detrimental outcomes, such as a denial of one's home language and culture as being worthy. The key should be to not take language from a child, especially spoken language, but to perhaps teach children the "proper" registers by which much of society will demand of them in their schooling and future. The caution to adopting and emphasizing AL in the classroom is to make sure we do not ignore a students' prior knowledge, and that the primary value should not be only on producing and showcasing information quickly and error-free. The idea of trying to determine what constitutes effective instruction for academic language development goes back to the asking ourselves who and which languages are valued and therefore, which related knowledge is important? Typically, the responses to that tell you which types of instruction are deemed "effective". Politicians and lawmakers will remark that it is the tests that matter, whereas as educators we know it is so much more than a test, particularly when talking about ELs and their learning. The adoption of the Common Core in conjunction with No Child Left Behind may make the idea of "effective" EL instruction much worse if we are not careful to remember to look at the education of ELs in the broader, more global context.

Teachers need more preparation in theoretical and practical knowledge about AL so that teachers know what AL is, how to use it, and then how to actually go about implementing this in the classroom with students. This would mean, then, that in teacher preparation programs all TCs must be better informed about L1 and L2 language acquisition. Further, if we are coaching TCs to become cognizant about more recent second language acquisition theories (e.g., SLT, SCT) in order to help guide their teaching practices, in addition to truly learning how to teach AL, is the BICS/CALP dichotomy as initially explained by Cummins (1981), even important to teach anymore? Perhaps the lessons from this text inform us that the larger concern should be how to instruct LM students in academic language while maintaining a clearer picture of the sociocultural and sociopolitical forces behind education.

The arguments made in this text that all teacher prep programs need to show TCs which pedagogical practices can help in developing students' AL is significant. However, if people in our field have a difficult time in even defining what AL is, then it may be hard to address this need in teacher prep programs. Looking to training teachers to be critically aware of language, particularly in regard to their own content area, may begin to help teachers to start developing sound practices in teaching AL. We need to make sure that we do not have TCs lose sight of their foundational understanding of their own discipline while also teaching TCs linguistics.

All teachers and educational professionals must be responsible for teaching our students. In states where language policy still allows for ESL students to be pushed in to the core content classes, having non-ESL teachers trained in AL can help so that ELs in those classes are not left to sink or swim. Providing TCs with the knowledge about the truly complex nature of language may remove some of the deficit perspectives that still exist about those who are learning English. Instead of seeing the learner or the language as the problem, the focus is shifted to how to best teach the core discipline so that all students can succeed. As Valdés (2004) points out, "Academic English is central to the school achievement of all learners in the U.S." (p. 28). The challenge now is to begin thinking about how we may re-envision teacher prep and continued professional development so that it is not a top-down experience. We must start thinking seriously about how the Common Core is going to impact not just our classrooms, but how the standards are going to impact teaching AL in schools. This is not a job for one person, but for all of us. All children must be prepared to be global citizens, and the starting point may be in preparing all students and TCs to be critical thinkers and users of language.

REFERENCES

Adger, C. T., Wolfram, W., & Christian, D. (2007). *Dialects in schools and communities* (2nd ed.). Mahwah, NJ: Lawrence Erlbaum Associates.

Bailey, F., Burkett, B., & Freeman, D. (2008). The mediating role of language in teaching and learning: A classroom perspective. In B. Spolsky & F. M. Hult (Eds.), *The handbook of educational linguistics* (pp. 606-625). Malden, MA: Blackwell.

Baker, C. (2011). *Foundations of bilingual education and bilingualism* (5th ed.). Bristol, England: Multilingual Matters.

Chamot, A., & O'Malley, J. (1994). *The CALLA handbook: Implementing the cognitive academic language learning approach.* New York, NY: Addison-Wesley.

Cummins, J. (1981). The role of primary language development in promoting educational success for language minority students. In California State Department of Education (Ed.), *Schooling and language minority students: A theoretical framework* (pp. 3-49). Los Angeles, CA: California State Department of Education.

de Jong, E. J., & Harper, C. A. (2005). Preparing mainstream teachers for English-language learners: Is being a good teacher good enough? *Teacher Education Quarterly, 32*(2), 101-124.

Echevarria, J., Vogt, M., & Short, D. (2004). *Making content comprehensible for English language learners: The SIOP model* (2nd ed.). Boston, MA: Allyn & Bacon.

González, N., Moll, L.C., & Amanti, C. (Eds.). (2005). *Funds of knowledge: Theorizing practice in households, communities, and classrooms.* Mahwah, NJ: Lawrence Erlbaum Associates.

Lippi-Green, R. (2012). *English with an accent: Language, ideology and discrimination in the United States* (2nd ed.). Abingdon, Oxon, England: Routledge.

Moll, L., Amanti, C., Neff, D., & González, N. (1992). Funds of knowledge for teaching: Using a qualitative approach to connecting homes and classrooms. *Theory into Practice, 31*(2), 132-141.

National Governors Association Center for Best Practices & Council of Chief State School Officers. (2010a). *Common core state standards: Application of common core state standards for English language learners.* Washington, DC: National Governors

Association Center for Best Practices, Council of Chief State School Officers. Retrieved from http://www.corestandards.org/assets/application-for-english-learners.pdf

National Governors Association Center for Best Practices & Council of Chief State School Officers. (2010b). *Common core state standards for English language arts & literacy in history/social studies, science, and technical subjects*. Washington, DC: National Governors Association Center for Best Practices, Council of Chief State School Officers. Retrieved from http://www.corestandards.org/assets/CCSSI_ELA%20Standards.pdf

National Governors Association Center for Best Practices & Council of Chief State School Officers. (2010c). *Common core state standards for English language arts & literacy inhistory/social studies, science, and technical subjects: Research supporting key elements of the standards*. Washington, DC: National Governors Association Center for Best Practices, Council of Chief State School Officers. Retrieved from http://www.corestandards.org/assets/Appendix_A.pdf

Schleppegrell, M. J. (2004). *The language of schooling: A functional linguistics perspective*. Mahwah, NJ: Lawrence Erlbaum Associates.

Valdés, G. (2004). Between support and marginalization: The development of academic language in linguistic minority children. In J. Brutt-Griffler & M. Varghese (Eds.), *Bilingualism and language pedagogy* (pp. 10-40). Clevedon, England: Multilingual Matters.

Wong Fillmore, L., & Snow, C. E. (2000). *What teachers need to know about language*. Washington, DC: ERIC Clearinghouse on Languages and Linguistics.

Wright, W. E. (2010). *Foundations for teaching English language learners: Research, theory, policy, and practice*. Philadelphia, PA: Caslon.

Zwiers, J. (2008). *Building academic language: Essential practices for content classrooms*. San Francisco, CA: Jossey-Bass.

ABOUT THE CONTRIBUTORS

M. Beatriz Arias (PhD Stanford University) is associate professor in the College of Liberal Arts and Sciences at Arizona State University. For 2012-2013 she will be on leave from ASU visiting the Center for Applied Linguistics in Washington DC. Professor Arias is the principal investigator for several national professional development programs with funding of over $1.8 million to support the professional development of teachers working with English language learners. Her focus is on instructional programs and policies for English language learners. She is a nationally recognized expert in the area of desegregation remedies for english language learners. She has been appointed by federal district judges as a compliance monitor and to various expert panels in San Jose, Denver and Los Angeles.

Steven Z. Athanases (professor, School of Education, University of California, Davis) teaches and studies diversity and equity in teaching and learning English and in teacher education. He has published widely on these issues, receiving distinguished research awards from Association of Teacher Educators and the National Council of Teachers of English.

Erica Bowers, EdD, is an associate professor in the Reading Department at California State University, Fullerton (CSUF). She is the director of the Hazel Miller Croy Reading Center, where she guides graduate students in their work with struggling readers. She has coauthored articles focusing on academic English and reading motivation.

Douglas B. Clark is an associate professor of the learning sciences and science education at Vanderbilt University. His research focuses on students' learning processes, generally in the context of technology-enhanced or game-based environments. In particular, his research focuses on students' conceptual change processes, argumentation, and use of representations in these environments.

Luciana C. de Oliveira is associate professor of literacy and language education and director of the English language learning licensure program in the Department of Curriculum & Instruction at Purdue University. Dr. de Oliveira's research focuses on issues related to teaching English language learners (ELLs) at the K-12 level.

Christian J. Faltis (PhD Stanford University, 1983) is the Dolly and David Fiddyment Chair in teacher education and professor of language, literacy and culture in the School of Education at University of California, Davis. He is author and editor of 18 books, and more than 70 scholarly journal articles and book chapters on bilingual education, Latino immigrant students, and emergent bilingualism. In 2001, Christian was recognized by AERA as a distinguished scholar of the role and status of minorities in education. Prior to coming to UC Davis in 2008, he taught at Arizona State University since 1991. Christian has been a Fulbright scholar and visiting professor at UC Berkeley.

Shanan Fitts is an assistant professor in the Department of Curriculum and Instruction at Appalachian State University. Her research and teaching interests include preparing teachers for multilingual and multicultural contexts, effective instruction for English language learners, and the development of bilingual and bicultural practices in children.

Tomás Galguera directs the single subject humanities credential program in the Mills College School of Education. His publications and research interests include teacher preparation pedagogy for language minority students, teacher research, and documentation of teaching practice. Before Mills College, Professor Galguera was a Spanish bilingual teacher in Oakland.

M. Cecilia Gómez is a doctoral candidate at the School of Education at the University of California, Davis. Her dissertation work focuses on the professional development of exemplary teachers and their perspectives on teaching second-language learners and academic language. Her research interests include teacher education and second language acquisition.

Paula Patricia Guerra-Lombardi was born in Uruguay, where she worked as a mathematics teacher in middle grades and high school for 5 years.

With an Organization of American States scholarship she moved to Arizona to complete master's studies. Not only she graduated with her masters in 2007, but also with her doctorate in 2011. She is currently an Assistant Professor at Kennesaw State University. Her research interests are gender and race equity in mathematics education, as well the mathematics schooling and success of English language learners.

Karen E. Lillie (PhD, applied linguistics) is an assistant professor of TESOL at SUNY Fredonia, where she teaches graduate courses in SLA, sociolinguistics, L2 research, and linguistics. Her research revolves around language/education policy and forensic linguistics (language and law-related matters for ELs). Dr. Lillie's recent publications address policy implementation effects on ELs in school.

Silvia Llamas-Flores is a doctoral student at ASU with an emphasis in mathematics education. Her research focuses on understanding how language policy, teacher beliefs, and practice impact equitable access for ELL students. She is a former high school math teacher of ELLs and has worked extensively with teachers of ELLs to provide effective and equitable practices to ELLs.

Audrey Lucero is an assistant professor of language and literacy education at the University of Oregon. Her research focuses on the development of bilingualism and biliteracy in young language minority children.

Al Mendle has been a lecturer teaching mathematics methods and educational technology at UC Davis since 1993. He has contributed to books for the college preparatory mathematics and activity resources publishing companies. He has also served as director of the University of California at Davis Mathematics Project.

Barbara J. Merino is a professor in the School of Education at UC Davis, where she also served as the director of teacher education from 1990 to 2009. In this capacity she launched a 15 month credential MA targeting teacher inquiry as a path for advocacy for equity in culturally and linguistically diverse settings. She received her PhD in education and linguistics at Stanford University. She has led several major efforts in the study of teacher effectiveness, bilingual program evaluation, performance assessment in teachers and clinicians and language acquisition in bilingual children.

James A. Middleton is professor of engineering education and director of the Center for Research on Education in Science, Mathematics, Engineering, and Technology at Arizona State University. His research focuses on motivation and the design of courses, curriculum and classroom environments that promote productive mathematical disposition, particularly with disenfranchised learners.

J. Richard Pomeroy is a science teacher educator in the University of California, Davis School of Education. He began his career as a science teacher in a culturally and linguistically diverse rural community teaching 17 years in the alternative/continuation high school. For the past 15 years, Pomeroy has worked collaboratively with other teacher educators to prepare teacher leaders who are reflective and collaborative practitioners, investigators of their own practice, and advocates for educational equity. He serves in leadership positions in state and national science education organizations.

Frank Ramírez-Marín is the coordinator of the Language Center at the Universidad Veracruzana at Boca del Rio, Veracruz, Mexico. His research focuses on sociocultural perspectives of learning, specifically language learning. In particular, Frank's reasearch focuses on second and foreign language education in Mexico and the United States.

Juliet Michelsen Wahleithner is a PhD candidate in the School of Education at the University of California, Davis. Her dissertation research examines how high school English teachers use their knowledge of writing instruction to negotiate the diverse writing needs of their students and the pressures of high stakes accountability.